SHETLAND
· PONIES ·

SHETLAND
· PONIES ·

VALERIE RUSSELL

Whittet Books

HALF TITLE *A pony showing good growth of mane and forelock as protection against the wind in Shetland*
FRONTISPIECE *The Berry Stud's Gingi of Berry, 2nd prize winner in the 34" and under class at the 1995 Breed Show*

First published 1996
Reprinted 1998
Text © 1996 by Valerie Russell
Whittet Books Ltd, Hill Farm, Stonham Road, Cotton, Stowmarket, Suffolk IP14 4RQ

British Library Cataloguing in Publication Data. A catalogue record for this book is available from the British Library.

ISBN 1 873580 26 6

The author and publishers are grateful to the following for permission to reproduce illustrations (page numbers of pictures appear in brckets): Beamish, the North of England Open Air Museum (39, 111, 112, 115, 117); David Bird (127); Dennis Coutts (93); Coventry Evening Telegraph (121); Countess De La Warr (50, 52, 55, 57, 58); Gilsons (134, 210); Leslie Lane (9, 89); Northern Institute of Mining Engineers (108); Paard & foto (186); Photo Bureau Sport (185); Anthony Reynolds (136); Mr John Scott (41); Scottish Farmer (82); Shetland Museum (19, 22, 29, 31, 37, 38, 102, 105); Eva Smith (frontispiece, 21); Trustees of National Museums of Scotland (18)

The author and publishers gratefully acknowledge the permission of A. and C. Black to reproduce the passage on p. 202 from Maurice Cox's *The Shetland Pony*.

Printed and bound by WBC

CONTENTS

Author's note

Although all possible care has been taken to avoid factual mistakes in this book, it emerged during research that there are a number of errors in the Stud Books. For example, some ponies have been entered twice, and others have been entered with two numbers. I hope readers will be forgiving if they encounter such mistakes in the text. For any other errors that may be found, I accept responsibility.

Acknowledgments

This book could not have been written without the help of a great many people who have given generously of their time and knowledge. They have made researching the book a real pleasure, not least because I have made many new friends among them. My sincere thanks to: Miss Diana Ashby, Dr Sue Baker, Mrs Marie Brooker, Mrs Lorna Burgess and daughter Leona, Mr Copelaw, Dr Gus Cothran, Miss Grace Cook, Countess De La Warr, Mr Dougal Dick, Mrs Else Enemark, Mrs Sonya Evart, Mrs Myrna Flaws, Mrs Lucy Giles, Mrs Angela Gosling, Mr John W. Halcrow, Mrs Nina Häkonson, Mrs Eleanor Hall, Mrs Vivien Hampton, Mr and Mrs John Hill, Mr John Holmes, Mrs I. Hoveklint, Mrs Margaret Hunter, Mrs Marit Jonsson, Mrs Teri Kovacs, Mrs Lesley Lewis, Mr Lionel Hamilton Renwick, Miss Vicki Maclean, Mrs Marjorie Martin, Mr Bertie Nicolson, Mrs Felicity Painton, Mrs Lucy Poett, Mrs Pat Pope, Mr Tony Priest, Mrs Roweena Provan, Miss Jackie Rawlings, Mrs Pat Renwick, Mrs Heather Ronald (on whose knowledge of and writings on the breed and its history in Australia I have drawn extensively), Mr John Scott, Mr and Mrs Harry Sleigh, Miss Eva and Mr Jim Smith, Mr Willie Spence, Mrs Dianna Staveley, Mrs Jill Stevenson, Mrs Helen Thomson, Dr Alma Swan, Mr George Vyner, Mrs van Tienan-Engelsman, Mrs Rosemarie Webb and Miss Barbara Wilson.

My thanks also to the following societies and institutions: The Shetland Pony Stud Book Society, The Shetland Islands Museum, Library and Archives, Lerwick, the Beamish Open Air Museum, Co. Durham, the RSPCA, the Institute of Mining Engineers, Northern Institute of Mining Engineers, the (former) Coal Board and the Dutch Shetland Pony Stud Book Society.

Last, but not least, my grateful thanks to my publisher Annabel Whittet, for her unfailing helpfulness and patience.

1
INTRODUCTION

In the first book devoted to the Shetland pony, *The Shetland Pony*, published in 1913, Charles and Anne Douglas wrote ' ... in the end it is idle to deny that it is not his indisputable economic validity that binds the Sheltie's lovers to him: rather it is himself – his wisdom and his courage, his companionable ways, his gay and willing service ... he provides ... the dual charm of a creature at once wild and tame – wild in his strong instincts, his hardihood, and his independence – domestic in his wisdom and sweet temper, his friendly confidence in mankind, and his subtle powers of ingratiation.'

More than three-quarters of a century later, although their 'economic validity' has largely passed into history, it comes as no surprise that Shetland ponies continue to endear themselves to their admirers for the qualities so eloquently described by the Douglases. In addition, their diminutive size and abundance of hair in mane, tail and forelock make them the most immediately recognisable of all the equine breeds, and, with their enthusiastic participation in everything they are asked to do, ensure that they have become the object of widespread affection and admiration, even among the least 'horsey' of people.

It may be more of a surprise to know that admiration for Shetland ponies was recorded at least as early as 1568, when Ubaldini wrote in *Description deal Redo di Scotia*, 'Their horses are very small and tiny in stature, not bigger than asses, nevertheless they are very strong in endurance'. In *Historical Description of Zetland* in 1773, Gifford recorded, 'Here are horfes, but of extraordinary fmall fize, fome whereof are very pretty and of excellent mettle, and will carry a man over thefe mountains and moffess, where a large horfe could be of no ufe, and they are otherways very ferviceable to the country people, and would be more numerous if any way cared for; but they lie out in the open fields fummer and winter, and get no food but what they can find for themfelves ... ' In 1809, Edmondstone, in *A View of the Ancient and Present State of the Zetland Isles*, commented that, 'The native Zetland horse is very small, seldom exceeding ten hands high, but well proportioned,

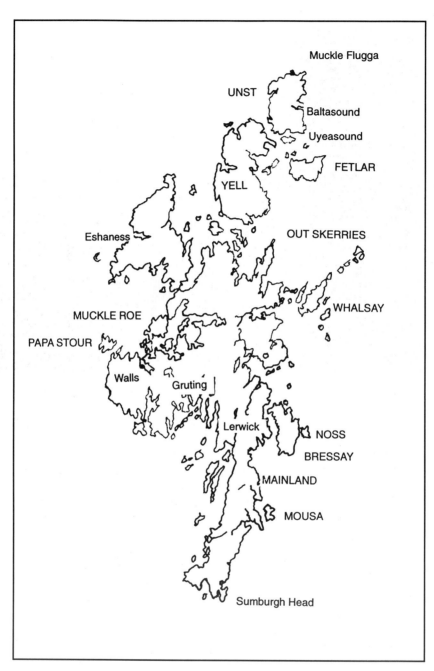

The Shetland Islands in 1809.

Ponies on Mousa Island, with a Pictish broch (round tower) in the background.

strong, and capable of enduring great degrees of fatigue ... Although never regularly broken in, they soon become docile and tractable, and exhibit proofs of great sagacity'. The manner in which Shetlands win over even some of the more sceptical is recorded in 1839 by Christian Ployer, the Danish Governor of the Faroe Isles, who said, 'I had despised the Shetland pony before I mounted him, but I soon got to respect him. Little he was, no doubt, even less than most of ours, but he was used to carry a rider ... '

The attributes which have made Shetlands such ideal mounts have long been recognised, and are summarised admirably by Robert Cowie in *Shetland: Descriptive and Historical*, in 1871 – although in a somewhat different context to the modern day. 'These little animals are easily tamed, wonderfully hardy, sagacious and surefooted. The rider whose course lies over trackless moors and quaking bogs and along yawning precipices, even on a pitch dark night, need not fear, if his Shetland steed only knows the country. He has merely to give the animal "his head" and be carried safely through.'

Shetlands were the sole means of transport in the islands. Former Breed Society Secretary, the late Mr Tom Myles, shows that the ponies are still capable of carrying adults.

The physical features that have contributed so much to the popularity of the breed, as well as ensuring its survival into the foreseeable future, are the same features that have enabled it to withstand the rigours of the harsh environment of the Shetland Islands. The pony is very much a product of that environment, and to understand the breed fully, at least some knowledge of the islands is essential. The strength of the Shetland means that, despite its small size, it does not suffer from bearing the weight of an adult.

The Shetlands are a group of islands lying just over 100 miles to the north of Scotland and, of significance when considering the ancestry of the ponies, some 200 miles west of Bergen in Norway. The distance from the most southerly point of the islands to the most northerly is 70 miles. Of the one hundred or so islands, about a dozen are now inhabited.

The three largest islands – Mainland, Yell and Unst – present a picture of rolling hills and moorland, often heavily rock-strewn and with prominent rocky outcrops and cliffs. The hills are clad in heather, rough grasses, mosses, rushes and sedges, often growing on vast peat beds, while brown peaty lochs and pools are scattered throughout the valleys and low-lying areas. Some of the valleys contain good fertile land, and some areas have been reclaimed and re-seeded. That the islands are virtually tree-less and shrub-less often leads to them being described as bleak, but the changing colours of the heather, grasses and mosses at various times of the year frequently offer a scene of breathtaking beauty.

No point on Shetland is further than four miles from the sea, and much of the coastline is spectacularly rugged, with sheer cliffs, and indented with numerous long, narrow inlets or 'voes'.

Considering the islands' situation, it might be thought that the climate would be similar to those of the nearby Scandinavian countries, with very severe winters. However, the warmer north-flowing sea currents around the islands exert a modifying influence, and in terms of actual temperature, the winters approximate to the British mainland, although summers are appreciably cooler. Nonetheless, conditions for the ponies are extremely demanding – arguably more so than for any of the other eight British Mountain and Moorland breeds. During the long months of winter, the islands are frequently lashed by fierce gales, accompanied by driving rain, sleet and snow, during which the wind-chill factor has the effect of making it seem bitterly cold. No-one who has not actually experienced the gales can imagine what they are like, and a description written by Captain John Smith in 1633 is in no way an exaggeration.

> The coldest weather is by reason of great Winds in the Winter; the Wind blowing so violent that no ships dare look on the North coast; so that the people of these islands have little Commerce with the Nations in that Quarter. I can speak by experience, being blown down flat to the ground by the violence of the Wind. I was forced to creep on my hands and knees to the next Wall, and going by the Wall, got into an House.

That the breed as a whole has survived is due to the fact that the Shetland pony is the most wonderful example of adaptation to the environment and of natural selection. To quote an unattributed article in *The Shetland Times* of 1897, 'The Shetland pony has been finished in Nature's workshop, and fitted in the process of time by modifications, wrought chiefly through the law of natural selection, for the sphere he inherits ... the "Sheltie" has been evolved in the distinctive form we now find him, admirably suited to his conditions of life.' The small size, the thick double-layered winter coats, neat ears, and protective tails, manes and forelocks, all combine to produce a pony of incredible hardiness.

The most obvious feature is the size and compactness of the breed. This is probably influenced by a combination of factors. Firstly, the geneticist Bendt Ljungren showed that when a population of horses of mixed origins (and this will be discussed further in Chapter 2) is isolated on islands, they become smaller as one phase of their development. Secondly, there is a scarcity of food during the long, hard winters, a condition exacerbated by the physical limitations of grazing areas available to animals, such as Shetland ponies, that live on the islands. This has ensured that, over the centuries, the smaller ponies which need less food have survived. Thirdly, according to Allen's law, body parts such as legs and ears tend to be shorter/smaller relative to overall body size in animals that live in cold climates, compared to those living under more temperate conditions.

'The Great Winds of Winter'. The ponies survive ferocious gales in Shetland.

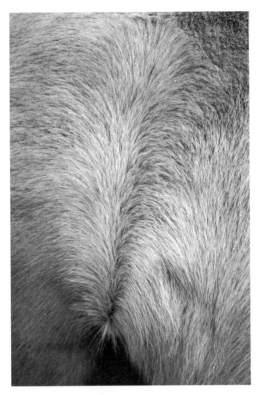

The vortex on the flank which leads rain and snow away from the less well protected belly of the pony.

The lack of trees and shrubs in Shetland means that the ponies must find shelter from the winter storms among the hollows and hummocks of the moors, behind rocks and stony outcrops, and, since the coming of man, in the lee of dry-stone dykes (walls) and croft houses. Obviously, the smaller the pony, the more readily it can find shelter. Similarly, the smaller the animal, the smaller the surface of the body from which heat can be lost – and maintaining body temperature in the icy gales is vital. The physical characteristics of short legs, compact body, and the small, neat ears, which contribute so much to the alert, lively, and essentially native pony appearance of Shetlands, all combine admirably to offer the least possible surface area from which heat may be lost. Heat loss is also minimised by the double coat that the ponies grow in winter. This consists of an inner layer of short, fine hairs, over which is an outer layer of longer, coarser hairs impregnated with greasy particles. (Careful examination also reveals a rudimentary third, rather fluffy layer, which is the beginning of the summer coat.) The inner layer is thought to act as insulation by trapping air, while the outer layer not only prevents heat loss, but acts as a very efficient waterproofing. Waterproofing is essential; a pony can usually survive cold, but if rain penetrates to the skin, the combination of cold and wet can be lethal.

So effective is the insulating property of the double coat that snow will lie, unmelted, on the pony's back for some time – a sure indication that little heat is being lost.

Work done earlier this century by Professor James Speed, a comparative anatomist, of the Royal Dick Veterinary School at Edinburgh University, and his wife, the former Miss Etherington, showed that the part played by the coat in channelling of rain and snow off the ponies' bodies is truly remarkable. The Speed's work was done principally, but not exclusively, on Exmoors, but it applies to all Mountain and Moorland ponies. They demonstrated that the hairs of the coat, far from being arranged as a flat, virtually featureless layer, grow in definite streams, fringes, whorls and vortices.

Furthermore, when the coat is wet, it can be seen that the hairs form themselves into small triangular-shaped groups, with the apex of each triangle pointing downwards. Clearly, water runs down these trian-

The tail, showing the protective 'snow chute'.

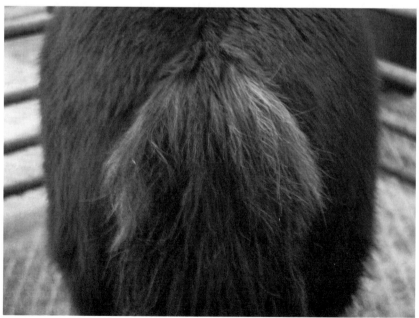

gles towards the apex. But there is more to it than that. The apices of the triangles actually lead the water towards the hair streams (known technically as *flumina pilorum*), most of which end either in fringes, such as the beard on the lower jaw, or the hair tufts on the fetlock and so on. Other streams end in strategically placed whorls or vortices of hair. (See photograph on p.13.) The overall result is to lead water off the surface of the coat, and away from sensitive areas, such as the under-belly and the dock.

Arguably, the most important of the vortices is the large and very obvious one situated at the rear of the flank. The Speeds suggested that if this vortex is incorrectly formed, or is not positioned precisely – i.e. vertically, with its upper limit just in front of the point of the hip bone, and its lower limit in front of the thigh, it becomes ineffective, and the animal thus affected will be less able to survive the winter. As can be seen from the photograph, the triangles of hair in the upper part of the vortex fan upwards and then forwards or backwards. The water from them then joins the hair stream which leads it away from the inside of the thigh and under the belly.

Mention has already been made of the profuse growth of hair in the Shetland's mane, forelock and tail. In the islands and in the north of the Mainland, the growth of hair is often extraordinary. Photographs of a stallion bred in the last quarter of the 19th century, Multum in Parvo, show his curtain-like mane almost trailing on the ground, as did his tail, while forelocks that hide all but the muzzle are not unknown. The protective properties of these are obvious. The tail has an additional feature – a thatch of short hairs, known as the 'snow chute', which fans out over the base. (See opposite.) This snow chute is, in fact, a continuation of the hair stream which runs the length of the back, and, together with the tail, it gives added protection to the dock and to the less well covered body surface between the hind legs.

So, the scarcity of food, the need to conserve heat, and the effects of being an isolated population, have combined to ensure that the smaller, more compact ponies have survived best. These characteristics are now fixed in the genetic make-up of the breed, and are not altered when, for instance, the ponies are bred under more favourable conditions.

2
AN ANCIENT BREED

---◆---

Tracing the early history of the Shetland pony is far from easy, and much of it is speculative. Investigations, using modern techniques, are now being undertaken by scientists at Leicester University, University College, London, the Animal Health Trust at Newmarket, and the Universities of Edingisby, Kentucky, and Uppsala (Sweden). These may show that the speculations are correct; equally, of course, they may show they are wholly or partially wrong! The techniques applied to bone comparison, the study of blood proteins and DNA fingerprinting may reveal much that is at present unknown (or at best, the subject of conjecture) regarding not only the origins of the British native breeds, but more about the evolutionary links between the ancestral equines and modern horses.

The following account of the origins of the Shetland breed is thus based on a combination of facts and of deductions made by respected investigators such as Professor Cossar Ewart and Professor and Mrs James Speed, working with the evidence available to them prior to the introduction of the more modern techniques.

Although it is generally acknowledged that the Shetland is an ancient breed, tracing its history is made more difficult by the absence of pony fossils in the Shetland Islands. The earliest known evidence of the presence of ponies comes from bones found in excavations made at Jarlshof, a late Bronze Age settlement at Sumburgh in the extreme south of the island of Mainland, and occupied from about the 6th to the 1st centuries BC. In 'Excavations at Jarlshof' by Hamilton, a report on 'The Animal Bones' from late Bronze Age layers, the late Miss Margery Platt, M.Sc. of the Royal Scottish Museum, wrote (in the 1940s and early 50s) 'The remains of pony were sparsely scattered throughout the levels. Bone measurements compare favourably with those of the Shetland pony as it is, therefore it is possible that they belong to this type'.

Further bones were found in higher layers of the excavations, which Miss Platt identified as coming from the Viking settlements of the early

9th century AD. She reported that 'the Ponies represented were not of large size, but exceeded the very small breeds in Shetland today. They were generally relics of adult animals.' Additional bone fragments were found in the late Norse Middens of the 11th-13th centuries, similar to those of the Viking era.

Thus there is physical evidence that small ponies have been in Shetland for well over 2,000 years, but how and when they arrived there is still a matter for conjecture. The most generally accepted theory is that they arrived in Shetland before the end of the last Ice Age, about 8000 BC, either by means of land bridges which still connected the islands to Europe and what is now mainland Britain, or across the ice fields.

In a letter written in 1964 to Major Maurice Cox (author of the definitive book on the breed *The Shetland Pony*), Professor James Speed suggested that these ponies might have been one or both of two types known to have been present in Europe and Britain during the upper Paleolithic period. The smaller of these two, which Speed referred to as the 'mountain' type, stood about 12.2 hands, while the larger, described as more of a 'cob' type of animal, was about 13.2 hands. Relics of these ponies, dating from approximately 12,000 years ago, have been found in the Mendip caves in Somerset.

Speed believed that the smaller of the two came to Europe and Britain (from North America) by the 'Oriental' route – via Asia Minor and through the Mediterranean region and possibly the Iberian Peninsula by means of land bridges. Evidence of these smaller ponies is found in the lower, i.e. earlier, layers of excavations – both in the Mendips and, in a smaller form, possibly at Sumburgh. The larger ponies were similar to those whose bones were found in great numbers at Solutré in France, as well as in the Mendips. They are thought to have arrived in Europe in the 'Siberian migration' of ponies, which followed a route between latitudes 45-50°. They could thus have reached Shetland via what is now Scandinavia.

Neither of the 'prototype' ponies – the 12.2 hh and the 13.2 hh – match, in size, the bones of the earliest finds at Jarlshof described by Miss Platt as being of similar dimensions to the modern Shetland, i.e. not exceeding about 42 inches (107 cm or 10.2 hh: it is traditional to measure Shetlands in inches rather than in hands). The discrepancy could be explained by applying a biological law that states that animals developed in isolation (as in the Shetland Isles) become smaller as one stage of their evolution. That would account for the Bronze Age finds. The diminution in size could also be a result of adaptation to the environment, as described in Chapter 1.

Speed also made another suggestion about the origins of the smaller ponies. He wrote that 'small ponies rather like Shetlands were in existence fairly generally in Celtic settlements in Britain, for instance, at Blewburton near Reading in Berkshire, in the Iron Age period there, around 250 BC'. He pointed out that by the first century AD the Celts were trading substantially around the Shetlands and the Western Isles.

Some confusion sometimes exists about the name 'Celt' – as it is now more usually taken in its modern connotation of referring to those peoples of Ireland, Wales, Cornwall and Scotland who spoke a particular group of languages. The Celts who introduced the Celtic pony into Britain originated around the Caspian sea. They spread widely over large areas of Europe – north and south – before eventually coming to Britain and Ireland, and Celtic settlements in Shetland took place from as early as the 2nd and 3rd centuries AD.

The Bressay Stone.

The presence of bones is indisputable evidence of the existence of ponies in the Viking/Celtic/Pictish settlements in Shetland. Further evidence, of a very different kind, emerged in 1864, when a carved stone was found near Culbinsburgh church on the island of Bressay. The carving on what is now known as the 'Bressay Stone' (kept in the National Museum of Scotland in Edinburgh) depicts a pony and rider. In 1943 three further ornamental stones were found beside an old church at Papil on the island of Burra. On one of these stones is a carving of two unmounted monks or priests, and a hooded figure on a pony – the pony being of similar size and shape as that on the Bressay Stone. All four stones are thought to date from about the 9th century, and show elements of Pictish, Celtic and Norse art styles. The ponies shown on all the stones are similar, being light of bone and with a high head carriage.

A method of calculating the approximate size of figures of ponies and riders on Pictish monuments, including those on the Papil stone, was devised by Mr Robert Beck, M.R.C.V.S., and described in his book

The Papil Stone found on the island of Burra.

on the Eriskay pony, *Scotland's Native Horse*. He found the pony to be 110 cm., i.e. 43.3 inches – just over the maximum height permitted in the modern Shetland, but within the height range mentioned in a number of historical records.

So, in the light of knowledge at the time the Speeds were working, the Shetland ponies appeared to be the descendants of at least two very ancient types – the 12.2 hh mountain pony type and the 13.2 hh cob type. At a later date, there was a further infusion of the larger type brought in by Viking and Norse invaders, and, possibly, another infusion of a smaller pony introduced by the Celts. It seems a reasonable assumption that the effects of environment and isolation eventually produced ponies of a size approaching that of the present-day Shetlands, and if the measurements calculated for the ponies on the Bressay and Papil stones are accepted, then ponies of that size have existed at least since the later stages of the Viking settlements. (A possible explanation of the lightness of bone compared with present-day Shetland ponies will become apparent when the breeding of ponies for the coal mines is discussed in Chapter 4.

After the date of the Bressay and Papil stones, no further physical evidence exists of the early ponies in Shetland. It is not until the 16th century that the first written records appear, and in them, comparisons with various Scandinavian ponies/horses emerge. It would be expected, if some of the original ponies reached Shetland from northern Europe/Scandinavia, that horses/ponies in those areas would show some evidence of relationship with the Shetland ponies. This expectation is fulfilled, as Douglas, for instance, mentions that in the 16th century small ponies were regarded as being characteristic of Norway and Sweden, and the descriptions of these could easily have applied to Shetlands. A century later, in the 1658 translation of *A Compendium History of the Goths, Swedes, and Vandals, and other Northern Nations*, Oleus Magnus, Archbishop of Upsala and Metropolitan of Sweden, wrote, 'There are many Heards of small Horses, but they are very strong; for by their strength and agility, they exceed many greater bodied horses', and again, 'The Norway Horses are small of stature, but wonderful strong and swift to pass over mountains and stony ways; but those of Sweden and Gothland will travel incessantly, and very swiftly with more meat ... ' Chapter 3 shows that these descriptions match very closely many of the earliest accounts of Shetlands.

The presence of broken colours (i.e. piebald and skewbald) in the Shetland breed may also have their origins in Scandinavia. References are made in various accounts and from different periods to the presence of both Norwegian and Icelandic ponies in Shetland. (These breeds are called, more correctly, 'horses', as the world 'pony' is of British origin.) Views have been expressed that either one or the other was responsible for the introduction of the broken colours into the Shetland breed. When these colours first appeared in Shetland is not known, but in 1701, John Brand in *A Brief Description of Orkney, Zetland, Pightland-Firth & Caithness* referred to 'pied' ponies, and the fact that they 'often prove not so good' – implying that they had been there for some considerable time.

The question of broken colours is interesting, because Shetlands are the only British Mountain and Moorland breed that allow them, and they are not generally regarded as native colours. There is an assumptian that the 'Norwegian' ponies mentioned are the Norwegian Fjords, but as broken colours do not exist in the breed, that seems unlikely. A clue to their origin lies, perhaps, in a reference made in *Cavalarice or the English Horseman* by Gervase Markham in 1607 to Scandinavian horses, ' ... Next then, I place the Sweathland horse who is a horse of little stature, lesser good shape, but least vertue; they are for the most part *pied* (author's italics), with white legges and wall eyes ... ' Exactly where in Scandinavia the 'Sweathland horses' come from is unclear, but the possibility that some travelled with the Vikings cannot be excluded.

More modern investigations and observations seem to confirm that the ancestors of the Shetlands arrived in the island by means of both the northern or Scandinavian migration, and the southern or Oriental route.

Ponies on Unst.

An Icelandic pony in Shetland.

In the 1960s, a Danish veterinary surgeon, Dr Michael Hesselholt, carried out blood type analyses on Norwegian Fjord and Icelandic horses. (The ancestors of the latter arrived in Iceland over 1,000 years ago, again with the Vikings, and have remained there, supposedly in isolation, ever since. They are of all colours, including piebald and skewbald.) Hesselholt found no connection between the two, but subsequently found similarites between the Icelandic and the Shetland. Work done in Holland in the 1970s on genetic relationships, using blood proteins as genetic markers, also suggests that there is *some* similarity between the Shetlands and the Fjords. The Norwegian Fjord horses are much larger than Shetlands, standing between 13 and 14 hands. They are very stocky, somewhat primitive looking, but attractive animals, with two distinctive features: the first is the mane, which is short, straight and erect; the second is the colour, a range of dun, with a dark eel stripe down the back.

Work still in progress on genetic similarities being undertaken by Dr Gus Cothran at the University of Kentucky College of Agriculture also suggests close similarities between the Shetlands and Icelandics. The Fjord, while in the same cluster, is in a position that suggests it could be ancestral, but this is by no means regarded by Dr Cothran as certain. In view of his work thus far, he believes it is most likely that the Icelandics and the Shetlands share some ancestry, probably with the (now extinct) Celtic pony, and with some type of Norwegian horse – but not necessarily the Fjord. This is particularly interesting in view of the discovery, after World War II, of a small group of about 15-20 horses in the north-west of Norway. These horses, known as 'nordlandhest' or 'Lyndgen-horses', were thought to be extinct. They are said to resemble Icelandics in type, size and colour, although the colour range does not include piebalds and skewbalds. Unfortunately, no scientific work has yet been done on these animals.

The possiblity of a link between Shetlands, Icelandics and perhaps the Fjords, is strengthened by the absence of chestnuts (small horny protruberances on the legs) in some specimens of all three breeds. The Celtic pony is also said to have lacked chestnuts, thus underlining its probable ancestral role as suggested by Speed.

A feature that may further link Shetlands and Icelandics comes as something of a surprise. Icelandics are well known for their distinctive pace, the tölt, which is four-beat and lateral, with the same sequence of footfalls as the walk, but performed faster. This pace has been observed in Shetlands, both in Denmark and in Britain, but it has never been seen in Fjord horses.

When all these factors are gathered together, the conclusions are, in the present state of knowledge, that Shetlands are probably descended from (1) the smaller 'mountain' pony coming up via the Oriental route, (2) the Celtic pony and (3) the larger, more cob-like 'Scandinavian' pony coming to the islands from Scandinavia (including Sweden) with the Viking invaders. More recent work suggests that this latter pony was probably the common ancestor of the Shetland, the Icelandic and one or more of the Norwegian and Swedish breeds.

With regard to the subsequent development of the Shetlands down to modern times, the Douglases, in their 1913 book, commenting about the breed as they saw it in the early 20th century, recorded the existence of two different types of pony. It is remarkable that, without any knowledge of more modern scientific work, and especially of the Speeds' theories, they described the two types in the following terms: one as 'closely resembling the Norwegian pony, and the other as "Oriental" – long shouldered, fine-boned, small in head, and with an unmistakable Arab outlook'.

They also observed that the 'Oriental' type does 'not form pure continuous or separate strains within the breed, but crops out here and there, sometimes the parents and sometimes the progeny, of ponies apparently pure Scandinavian'. They pointed out that such a type does not exist in the Scandinavian breeds, and that its existence proved the presence in the breed of some ancestral element not found in the

Scandinavian horse. They drew the conclusion that as 'the Shetland pony as we have it today is sometimes of a purely Scandinavian type, sometimes of an Oriental type', it 'may perhaps be explained by regarding it as a composite of two distinct races, one having common origin with the Oriental horse and the other being identical with the Scandinavian horse'.

The well known early 20th-century breeder, the late R.W.R. MacKenzie (see later), believed that there were always two types of pony in the islands, 'one a thick dray-horse type, the other more blood-like, which may be called the saddle type. Both have intermingled freely, and one finds, even after careful mating, an occasional reversion from one type to the other.' Mr Ian Sandison added a further type to the above two – the miniature pony.

Cox agreed that there were certainly two types at the beginning of the century – the heavier type being bred for the pits, and the lighter type used by the crofters. He did, however, question whether these two types existed throughout the breed's previous history, as no reference was made to them in any of the earlier records. He rejected the theory that the two types could be a permanent result of out-crosses to other breeds. This he did on the grounds that, although there were undoubtedly other breeds, such as Norwegian and Highland on Mainland and on Unst, and, on the island of Fetlar, an Arab stallion, the chances of these influencing the ponies other than in their immediate vicinity was remote. Each crofting community, and each scattald was virtually self-contained, and too far away from its neighbour, and communications between the islands too difficult for this to have happened. If there were differences, he suggested that these were due to in-breeding on the scattalds (the common grazing lands). A more up-to-date reason could also be that the difference in the overall proportions and conformation of the ponies could be due to the widely varying geology of the islands. Thus one area is comparatively rich in certain minerals, while others are devoid of them. Modern veterinary knowledge has shown the importance of the presence or absence of trace elements and minerals in the formation and growth of bone, and consequently of conformation.

3
THE EARLY WRITTEN RECORD

◆

From the later bones found in the Norse middens at Jarlshof (dating from the 13th century AD) there is no further evidence of the ponies until written references begin with Ubaldini's brief comment on their small size (see Chap. 1) in the mid-16th century. There is then a gap until the beginning of the 17th century, but from that time onwards the ponies feature in various records and accounts, the majority by visitors to the islands who, once again, remarked on their size, and also on their courage, strength and hardiness. Taken together, they give some idea of the importance of the ponies in the economy of the islands and of the vital part they played in the lives of the inhabitants.

The Law Books of Shetland record misdemeanours concerned with the ponies from 1602 onwards – mostly in the form of convictions for failing to pay for animals bought, for theft, and for using another man's pony for carrying peats without permission. Of particular interest is an extract from 'The Lating Court of Zetland', dated August 18th, 1612, which sets out, in some detail and in the delightful language of the time, the 'Act for Ryding uther mens horsis and stowing of thair taillis', and the penalties exacted for these crimes. The Act stated that ' ... quhasoever sall be apprehendit ryding ane uther manis hors without licence and leave of the awner inwith the parochin quhair the awner of the hors duellis sall pay to the Kingis Sirref or deput for merks and to the dartre awner iiij merks. And gif he be fund and apprehendit ryding ane uther mans hors outwith the parochin quhair the awner of the hors duellis he sall pay viij merks to the partie ... ' Further penalties were exacted according to the number of parochin (parishes) through which the thief rode the pony!

'Stowing' (cutting) a pony's tail was regarded as a serious offence. 'And quhasoever sall be tryet or fund to stow or cut ane uther mans hors taill the doer thairof sall be pwnischit as a thief at all rigour in exempill of utheris to commit the lyke'. This was not just because it spoiled the appearance of the animal and deprived it of protection from the weather, but in a community where severe poverty was widespread, the hair from the ponies' manes and tails was a valuable commodity. Fishing was a vital part of the crofters' livelihood, and the hair was woven into fishing lines – a practice that continued well into the present century. Such importance was attached to it that, according to John R. Tudor in his book *The Orkneys and Shetlands* published about 1883, an official actually checked that every householder could account for all lines of horsehair found in their possession. The penalties for 'borrowing' ponies do not appear to have eliminated the practice! Writing more than 200 years later, Sir Walter Scott noted that

> There are numbers of shaggy, long-backed, short-legged ponies running wild upon the extensive moors. There is, indeed, a right of individual property in these animals ... but when any passenger has the occasional use for a pony, he never scruples to lay hold of the first which he can catch, puts on a halter, and, having rode him as far as he finds convenient, turns the animal loose to find his way back again as best he can.

The first detailed comment on the the ponies themselves comes early in the 18th century, when the Rev. John Brand visited the islands, and gave a very full and discerning account of them in *A Brief Description of Orkney, Zetland, Pentland Firth and Caithness*. He wrote:

> They have a sort of little Horses called Sheltie. then which no other are to be had, if not brought hither: from other places, they are of less Size than the Orkney Horses, for some will be but 9 Nives or Handbreadths high, and they will be thought big Horses there if eleven, and although so small yet are they full of vigour and life, and some not so high as others often prove to be the strongest, yea there are some, whom, an able man can lift up in his arms, yet will they carry him and a Woman behind him 8 Miles forward and as many back: Summer or Winter they never come into an House, but run upon the Mountains in some places in flocks, and if at any time in Winter the storm be so great, that they are straitned for food, they will come doun from the Hills, when the Ebb is in the Sea, and eat the Sea-Ware (as likewise do the Sheep) which Winter storme and scarcity of fodder puts them out of Case, and bringeth them so very low, that they recover not their strength till about St. John's Mass-Day, the 24th., of June, when they are at their best: They will live till a Considerable Age as 26, 28, or 30 Years, and they will be good riding Horses in 24 especially they'le be the more vigorous and live the longer, if they be 4 Years old before they be put to Work. These of a black Colour are Judged to be the most durable, and the pyeds often prove not so good; they have been more numerous then now they are the best of them are to be had in Sanston and Eston, also they are good in Waes and Yell, those of the least Size arte ain the Northern Isles of Yell and Unst.

The Coldness of the Air, the Barrenness of the Mountains on which they feed, and their hard usage may occasion them to keep so little, for if bigger Horses be brought into the Countrey, their kind within a little time will degenerate; And indeed in the present case, we may see the Wisdome of Providence, for their way being deep and Mossie in Many places, these lighter Horses come through, when the greater and heavier would sink doun: and they leap over ditches very nimbly, yea up and doun rugged Mossy braes or hillocks with heavy riders upon them, which I could not look upon but with Admiration, yea I have seen them climb up braes upon their knees, when otherwise they could not get the height overcome, so that our Horses would be but little if at all servicable here.

Gifford, in a *A Historical Description of Zetland* in 1733, also commented on the size and strength of the ponies, and on the privations they suffered during the cruel winters. He, however, in a single telling paragraph, offered an explanation for the difficulties faced by both ponies and people – difficulties which, as will be seen, have had a profound influence on the Shetland breed. He wrote:

It will, no doubt, be wondered at by ftrangers, that fo little care is taken about thefe fheep and horfes which are fo ufeful and beneficial; the reafon whereof is, that the poor inhabitants, having ufed their utmoft endeavours, can fcarce find food and fhelter for their oxen and cows, without which they could not live; and in hard winters many of them die for want of fodder, fo they have none to beftow on their fheep and horfes, until they find more time to improve the land.

The majority of the inhabitants of the islands followed the crofting way of life, which, in modern terms, would be described as 'subsistence agriculture'. Some, as mentioned previously, added to their meagre resources by fishing. The crofters were tenants of their houses, which usually stood on a small parcel of land ('in-bye' or 'in-toom' land) amounting to, at most, a few acres. The in-bye land, which was mostly of poor quality, was used for growing crops, and, in winter, for accommodating the oxen used for ploughing, and the cows used for milk, butter, etc. In addition, each little group of crofters had rights over the common grazings or 'scattalds'. These were, for the most part, unfenced hill country, often considerable distances from the crofts, on which the ponies and sheep were turned out to fend for themselves and to feed on whatever rough herbage they could find. Sadly, although some crofters did manage to offer them some food in the form of straw or potatoes, there is no doubt that many starved to death – not from deliberate neglect, but from the sheer inability to find food.

Edmonstone, in his *A View of the Ancient and Present State of the Zetland*

Islands, described the desperate lengths to which some would go in their attempts to survive. 'When the snow remains long on the ground, they approach the houses, and appear to supplicate assistance, having as it were ascertained, that support is nowhere else to be found. Some few more venturous individuals break into the yards during the night time, and destroy the corn.'

The ponies in those days spent most of their lives on the scattalds, and were brought in only when required as transport, or for carrying the peats (the principal fuel) home during the summer. It was a life of grinding poverty for the crofters, as indicated by Gifford, where money was almost non-existent, and bartering for goods was commonplace. (Later, as will be described, conditions for the ponies apparently improved a little, but, until well into the 20th century, the battle for survival was cruel.)

Those crofters living near to the few towns could earn a little money by hiring their ponies to visitors, such as those supplied to a naval surgeon in 1780. He gave a graphic description of his journey: ' ... we were furnished with little horses and set out over hill and moor, rock and stone. We trotted along brinks of dreadful precipices where I would not venture to trust myself on the best hunter in England. The motions of these little Shetland horses are so very quick and short that I made many narrow escapes from falling over their necks.'

Seamen from the Dutch fishing fleet proved another source of income. On arrival in Lerwick, the seamen would hire ponies, as riding was prescribed by Dutch doctors as both remedy and prevention against diseases for those confined in ships for long periods. Low, in *A Tour through the Islands of Orkney and Shetland,* gave an amusing description of how the wily Shetlanders made the most of their opportunities.

> There is no horse-hire demanded here, unless it be in the summer, when the Dutch are upon the coast. During that time some of the country people bring in their horses for the Dutchmen to ride, and I must own that, if they were not better sailors than riders, I would not chuse to venture my life as far as Gravesend on one of their best Bottoms. There is a spot of ground above the town (Lerwick), about a quarter of a mile in length, and pretty even ground, which is very rare in Zetland. Here the countryman comes with his horse, enquiring, in Dutch, who will ride. Immediately comes a clumsy Dutchman, gives him, a dublekee (that is two pence), then up he mounts. The owner of the horse immediately falls abeating the creature, and pricks his tail with the point of his stick. Then, behold! in an instant, down comes the Dutchman. Up he gets again, and mounts afresh, but before he gets on a second time

Ponies peat flitting on Fetlar in 1938. They are wearing the traditional klibbers to which are attached the meshies and kishies for carrying the peats.

there must be a second doublekee, and he is scarce up before he is down again; so that the fellow often makes a shilling off the Dutchman before he comes to the end of the place. This, together with the money they receive from their stockings, is all the cash they have from one year's end to the other, unless when any of the Dutchmen fancy any of their horses; then, they chance to make a good profitt, as they will sell a horse to a Dutchman for a pound that they cannot sell to their neighbours for three half-crown.

Low also recorded that the ponies were bought by strangers as curiosities and for children to ride, at a price of 20 to 30 shillings.

As more and more people visited Shetland, so the reports about the ponies increased – nearly all commenting on their hardiness, and expressing astonishment, amounting almost to disbelief, at their strength, abilities as riding animals, and their native instinct for survival.

A delightful story which illustrates these qualities to the full appears in *A View of the Ancient and Present State of the Zetland Islands* written by Edmonstone in 1809, and describes a ride undertaken by himself and two friends.

The distance we had to ride was five miles; and the course lay over a range of mossy hills, in which there was not a vestige of a foot-print.

A guide attended, to point out to us the best parts of the road; and we were obliged to make many circuitous turnings, to avoid the more wet and boggy parts of the hills. We accomplished the journey tolerably well; but we had scarcely proceeded half a mile on our return, when we missed the guide, and found ourselves enveloped in a very thick fog. I proposed that we should wait until the fog cleared up; but one of the gentlemen thought that it would be better to proceed, and gave the horses leave to choose whatever road they thought proper. This last proposal was agreed to, and they brought us back in a shorter time than we had taken to go. The circuits they made on some occasions were so great, that we were often led to believe that they were wandering in the same uncertainty with ourselves; but our doubts were removed, by finding, that after a considerable time they brought us to a spot, which we recollected had in the former part of the day interrupted our progress, and in which we could distinctly trace the marks of their feet then first made in the moss. As we approached the end of our journey the fog cleared up; and when within a mile and a half of the termination of it, the horses, finding themselves altogether unrestrained, made a considerable deviation from the track prescribed by the guide, and conducted us by a much drier and more equal road than that which we had passed over on the former part of the day.

I was much struck and gratified at this display of memory and sagacity. In the devious tracks of the hills they appeared to be guided either by the scent, or the perception of the traces of their own former footsteps, although in the more heathy parts of the road I thought that to be almost impracticable. When they came, however, on ground with which they had been previously familiar, they preferred the track which experience had shewn to be the best.

Although the word 'road' is used frequently in the above account, probably a more accurate description is 'track', as there were no made roads in Shetland until later in the 19th century – hence the vital importance of the ponies to the inhabitants, as the only means of transport. Wheeled vehicles were not known until the second or third decade of the century – one of the first references being by Christian Ployer, who described how, in 1839, he was driven around Lerwick in a carriage drawn by a pony.

Sir Walter Scott, in his journal of 1814, provides the only suggestion that the ponies could, on rare occasions, stumble. He noted that on returning to Lerwick from Scalloway, 'My pony stumbles coming down hill; saddle sways round, having but one girth and that too long, and lays me on my back.' The crofters' life was undoubtedly hard, with little time to spare for anything but working to feed and clothe themselves and their families. However, many went to the local kirk every Sunday. A delightful, evocative, and, one suspects, slightly romanti-

This 1880 photo, taken in Lerwick, of a woman shopping, shows how the ponies were an essential part of everyday life.

cised account by Hibbert in *A Description of the Shetland Islands* in 1821, describes the scene as crofters on Unst made their way to Baliasta Kirk:

> I arrived there on the Sabbath morning: the natives of the Vale were all in motion on their way to the Kirk of Baliasta. The peasant had returned home from the bleak scatthold where he had ensnared the unshod pony that was destined to convey him to the parish kirk. No currycomb was applied to the animals mane, which, left to Nature's care, 'ruffled at speed, and danc'd in every wind'. The nag was graced with a modern saddle and bridle, while on his neck was hung a hair-cord, several yards in length, well bundled up: from the extremity of which dangled a wooden short pointed stake. The Shetlander then mounted his tiny courser, his suspended heels scarcely spurning the ground. But among the goodly company journeying to the kirk, females and boys graced the back of the shelty with much more effect

than long-legged adults of the male sex, whose toes were often obliged to be suddenly raised for the purpose of escaping contact of an accidental boulder that was strewed by the way. A bevy of fair ladies next made their appearance, seated in like manner on the dwarfish steeds of the country, who swept over the plain with admirable fleetness and 'witch's the world with noble horsemanship'. The parishioners at length arrived near the kirk, when each rider in succession, whether of high or low degree, looked out for as green a site of ground as could be selected, and, after dismounting, carefully unravelled the tether which had been tied to the neck of the animal. The stake at the end of the cord was then fixed into the ground, and the steed appeared to be as satisfactorily provided for during divine service, as in any less aboriginal district of Britain, where it would be necessary to ride up to an inn, and to commit the care of the horse to some saucy lordling of the stables.

It seems strange, reading through the various early writings, that only passing reference is made to the work done by the ponies in carrying home the peats from the hills. This is possibly because the majority of the writers were visitors, who used the ponies as transport, and were not involved in the day-to-day working of the crofts. This is perhaps confirmed by the fact that what references there are come from *Statistical Account of the Shetland Islands by Ministers of the Respective Parishes and of the Superintendent of the Committee of the Society of the Sons and Daughters of the Clergy*, published in 1841. In this, the minister of the Parish of Unst recorded that:

> Peats from the hills of Valleyfield and Saxa Vord are the only article of fuel used by the tenantry, and are procured by many at no small labour and expense, especially on the east side of the island, where peat moss is completely exhausted. Besides the labour of cutting and drying them, the people are obliged to employ from eight to ten horses for the space of five to six weeks every summer to carry them home, and these must be attended by a person to put on the loads, and one or two boys to drive the horses ...

The same minister recorded the range of colours of the ponies – white, black, brown, grey, dun, cream, chestnut and piebald, with sizes ranging from 28 inches (71 cm) to 44 inches (112 cm). He also observed, in contrast to Hibbert, that it was a rare occurrence to see an individual riding to church.

One of the most perceptive observations made in this Statistical Account was in the report for North Mavine, as it gives the first indication of a practice that was obviously already having a disastrous effect on the breed – that of selling off the best ponies when the opportunity arose. Who, in view of the dire poverty of the crofters, could altogther blame them for thinking of the day rather than the morrow? The minister, however, took a longer view.

> The breed of horses, it is said, has fallen off very much for some years past, and the reason is that the best of the horses are always sold, and only those of inferior description kept for breeding, and things will never improve till the proprietors interfere and enact a law, which they can very easily do, that the best horses shall always be kept, and this could ultimately be greatly for the interest of both landlord and tenant.

At the end of the account, Laurence Edmonston, a medical practitioner on Unst, having commented on the 'pernicious practice' of crossing the ponies with large and incongruous breeds from Scotland, the progeny, as might be expected, displaying 'all the bad points, with few of the good of the parent', endorsed the sentiments of the Mavine minister. He went further, and suggested: 'One very evident and easy mode of improvement would be for proprietors to keep males of good race and mature age, in different districts, for general use, and insist on all inferior ones being removed, and it could easily be arranged that no party would suffer loss.' In so doing, he anticipated, by some 30 years or more, steps that were taken to improve the overall standard, when large numbers of good, strong ponies were required for the pits, and by more than 50 years, the stallion schemes which were introduced in this century, and which continue to improve the breed in the islands to this day.

It is noticeable that, in the accounts quoted, the ponies are nearly always referred to as 'horsis' or 'horses', except by some of the writers who were visitors to the islands. A paragraph in *The Scotsman* of 1898 offers an explanation. It states that the name 'pony' is such a recent introduction to Shetland that it is doubtful if it was known to the grandparents of the present generation. The name is never, it continued, used by the people among themselves, and it is only heard in conversations with strangers. 'Were a man to talk to his neighbour about his ponies, he would be considered as amusing, as if he attempted to talk in Cockney English.' The name 'Sheltie' is an even later introduction. The pony has borne other names, according to *The Scotsman*. Throughout the Udal period (the period during which Danish laws of tenantry prevailed) it was known by the name of 'heste'. Heste was the name in common use, and has been incorported into various place names in the islands, such as Hestataing, Hestenfiord, Hestensetter, Hestingott and Hestamires.

4

THE DEVELOPMENT OF THE BREED
IN THE 19TH CENTURY

For the Shetland breed, the 19th century is of immense importance. As travel and communications between Shetland and mainland Britain, and Shetland and Europe increased, word of the ponies' qualities spread far and wide, and, as has been mentioned, a number were sold 'as curiosities and for children to ride'. At least some of those were bought by visitors to the islands, even as early as the 17th century, when there are records of ponies being sold to 'foreigners' – probably to the Dutch, as described in the previous chapter.

There is no indication, however, that large numbers of ponies were leaving the islands at that time. It was not until the early 19th century that Edmonstone reported exports on a much increased scale. In 1809 he recorded that 150 ponies were exported, to be followed, in 1824 and 1825, by a further 92 and 140 respectively. That some went to mainland Britain is certain, as Maurice Cox mentions that in 1815 there was a herd of Shetlands running at Ickworth, Suffolk, the seat of the Marquis of Bristol. Shetland herds became a popular feature of a number of 'stately homes' – a variation on the more usual herds of deer. The ponies had the added attraction of providing mounts for the children of the family, and were often broken to harness to pull miniature and small vehicles driven by the ladies. The demand for Shetlands for the latter two uses increased rapidly through the 19th and into the early 20th centuries.

Exports to more distant and sometimes more exotic destinations soon followed. In 1850, *The Illustrated London News* published details of 8 ponies (3 brown and 5 black) from various breeders in Shetland that had been sold to the agent for the Pacha of Egypt by a Mr Orton of Wapping. They ranged in height from 35 to 37 inches (89 - 94 cm), and were valued at about £15 each.

The ponies were being broken to harness by Mr Orton, who drove them in fours every day. They were intended for the Pacha's children to drive – six in a small carriage being built by King's of Long-acre, while the harness, which was described as superb, was made by the famous saddlers and harness makers, Gibson's of New Coventry Street. The report concludes by observing that 'the ponies are rough at present, but they will be got into better condition before they are shipped. The Pacha's agent is, we understand, a German veterinary surgeon, and Master of the Horse to His Highness'. Among the earliest consignments of ponies to travel outside Europe was a group of 24, including 2 stallions, which sailed for Australia in the *General Nowell* (or the *Norfolk*, according to which account is correct) arriving at Melbourne in December 1857. Unfortunately, only 20 ponies disembarked, 4 of the mares having died during the voyage.

In 1885, the first recorded export to the United States consisted of 75 ponies, to be followed in 1887 by a further 129 – all imported by Eli Elliot, to be used as children's riding ponies and in harness.

Without question, the most significant exports from the islands came as the result of an Act of Parliament passed in 1842. The Mines Act prohibited the employment underground in the coal mines of children under the age of ten, and of women. Prior to that, women and children had been employed in transporting the coal from the coal face, initially in baskets on their backs, then on sledges, and finally in wheeled tubs, which they pulled or pushed along the narrow, low-roofed galleries – often on their hands and knees. The passing of this Act was to have a lasting effect on the Shetland breed.

Horses and ponies had been used for a variety of tasks in coal mining for centuries, since the days when mines were little more than holes in the ground. In general, however, they were not used underground. By the mid-19th century, the mines had developed greatly, with long galleries extending horizontally from deep vertical shafts, and, when the use of women and children became illegal, the mine owners looked around for substitutes. They found them in the shape of ponies – ponies that were small enough to work in the very cramped conditions.

The demand for these smaller ponies increased dramatically: the prime requirements were, in addition to being small, that they should be strong, and of equable temperament. It comes as no surprise to learn that the Shetland was generally acknowledged as the very best for working underground.

In Shetland, export of ponies (always males, mares were never used) to the coal mines in the north-east of England began almost as soon as the Mines Act was passed. It could not have come at a better time for the crofters, who, chronically poor, were in an even worse state due to the potato famine. They welcomed a new, and initially, a much steadier demand for their ponies. Predictably, prices increased, and animals that had fetched as little as £1.10s in 1841 shot up to £4 almost immediately (although this often included delivery to the colliery), soon reached £5.10s for a 2-year-old colt, and £8.10 for a mature pony, before rising to £12 in 1861.

While this trade was manna from heaven for the crofters, it had an appalling effect on the Shetland breed. Mention has already been made of the crofters' habit of selling off their best ponies, and paying little, if any, attention to proper breeding policies. This short-sighted practice continued, but on a hugely increased scale – and it was made even worse by the fact that only colts and stallions were required to work in the pits. Whereas previously there were too many males involved in indiscriminate breeding, there were now too few, and nearly all of them were of poor quality. This not only had the effect of producing increasingly poor stock, but ensured that more mares foaled bi-annually. This had always happened to some extent, due to the practice of leaving foals on the mares through the winter. Whatever the arguments for and against this practice, the net result was indisputable – a drastic decrease in quality stallions, and, in the longer term, of good breeding stock. Some idea of the effect on the breed in terms of numbers may be gained from the estimate that there were some 10,000 ponies in Shetland in 1822, but by 1870 the number of ponies *and* horses had decreased to just under 5,000.

Fortunately, from the mid-19th century onwards, a number of landowners in Shetland began to take pony breeding seriously, and established studs. They, together with some of the merchants and the better dealers, took a longer view of the situation, and had the future of the breed and the long-term prosperity of Shetland at heart. Some of the dealers, to keep the number of ponies up, would give a mare to a crofter who could not afford to buy it, provided he had first refusal of any subsequent foal; these were called 'halvers' ponies.

The landowners appreciated the dangers of the breed deteriorating beyond recall, and in an effort to retrieve the situation to some extent, they kept some good stallions on their land, and encouraged the crofters to send mares to them for a very small fee. Prominent among those stud owners were Alexander Sandison of Uyeasound, Unst, John Anderson & Sons of Hillswick, and Mr John Bruce of Sumburgh. Mr Sandison established a sizeable stud and produced some excellent ponies, a number of which were exported to mainland Britain as foundation stock for newer breeders (see Chapter 6).

The dealers, in whose interest it was to have better ponies to sell on, having bought up most of the stallions and colts for the pits, then be-

Ponies from the islands of Noss and Bressay arriving at Lerwick.

gan turning some of the best ones out on the scattalds to improve the breed.

Thus it was landowners and dealers within the islands who first strove to improve the ponies, although on a relatively small scale. In 1873, however, the man who, with his son, was to have the greatest long-term influence on the Shetland breed arrived on the scene. He was an English aristocrat, the 5th Marquis of Londonderry, who owned a number of coal mines around Seaham, Co. Durham, in north-east England. He had been using Shetlands as pit ponies from about 1850, and had a stud in Durham, managed by Mr Robert Brydon, to which he imported ponies from the islands. Over the years, Lord Londonderry had become increasingly concerned about the declining standard and suitability of the ponies arriving from Shetland, and decided to do something about it. He acquired the grazing on the islands of Bressay and Noss, just off Lerwick, and established a stud, managed by Mr J.J.R. Meiklejohn.

The aim of the stud was specifically to breed ponies for the pits – ponies which were strong, and 'with as much weight as possible and

A Shetland class at the Lerwick Agricultural Show (about 1900).

as near the ground as can be got'. To this end, Messrs Brydon and Meiklejohn toured the islands extensively, and bought the very best mares they could, and about two hundred colts and stallions. Not surprisingly, Brydon described the ponies as 'an uneven lot', but six stallions were carefully selected to be used as the foundation of the stud in the spring of 1874. Two of those stallions, **Jack 16** and **Prince of Thule 36**, were to have an enormous and lasting influence on the breed, as will be described in a later chapter. Robert Brydon, writing in *Horses of the British Empire*, noted that the first foals of these matings showed a considerable improvement on the average foals in the islands.

From the earliest photographs available, it appears that many of the crofters' ponies were far from being the low, strong animals required for the pits. It is a little difficult to generalise, because, as already described, the type varied considerably throughout the islands. Many of the groups of crofts were isolated from each other, as were the scattalds, and the type depended heavily on the stallions available. In the photographs, many, although not all, of the ponies are seen to be lighter, more on the leg, and lacking in bone, compared to what was required for the pits. This was no doubt due, in part, to the lack of breeding policy, but it must always be remembered that Shetlands were used primarily for pack and saddle and not, with a few exceptions, as draught ponies.

The aim of the Londonderry Stud, however, *was* to produce stronger, though smaller, draught animals, with a low head carriage, and by careful selection, a considerable amount of deliberate in-breeding and sheer skill, they managed to achieve this. Brydon was a veterinary surgeon, and doubtless brought a certain scientific skill to the breeding policy, but above all, he and Meiklejohn must have been brilliant stockmen. To have practised such close in-breeding (to be described more fully in the next chapter) with indisputable success and, apparently, avoiding the troubles that can occur, argues ability of a very high order.

What came to be known as the 'Londonderry type' was a pony with improved bone and substance, good joints and limbs, and, in the main, lacking the more obvious faults in conformation, such as poor hind legs, short, drooping quarters, and lack of good second thighs so prevalent in the island ponies at the time. On the other hand, Dr and Mrs Douglas criticised a tendency towards straightness of the shoulder and

The Marquis of Londonderry.

lack of withers – features that would not be unexpected in a pony bred for draught purposes. Beyond dispute is that the Londonderry Stud produced a string of stallions and mares that exerted a far-reaching influence on the breed, an influence lasting to the present day.

It is interesting at this stage to compare the management of the Londonderry ponies on Bressay and Noss with that commonly practised by the crofters. When it could be afforded, the crofters' ponies were given straw or potatoes to supplement the rough grazing that was their normal diet. They grazed (as they do to this day), on the coarse grasses, reeds, rushes and some heather. (Most native ponies will eat *some* heather, according to the season, and in Shetland it also provided the ponies with good dry bedding on which to lie when on the hill.) Those ponies with access to the shore ate seaweed, and have also been observed to turn over with their feet the great mounds of weed that are banked high on the upper shore following storms, and eat the fresh shoots of grass that begin to grow underneath it.

It goes almost without saying that the Londonderry ponies' management was vastly superior to anything that could be afforded by the crofters. The Londonderry foals were weaned in November, put on good pasture, and given hay when necessary. They had a large shed in which they could shelter, but were never 'kept in' in the modern sense of the word – and thus their hardiness was preserved. During the summer, the young ponies were turned out on the hills, while the mares were kept on old pasture near the shore, where they ate quantities of seaweed. In winter they, too, were fed hay. Colts and fillies ran together as yearlings, but were separated at two. Sometimes a good, strong, two-year-old mare might be put to the stallion, but more usually, the mares of three years and over were divided into groups of 12 to 15, and put into special enclosures with a carefully selected stallion. This method, as Mr Meiklejohn pointed out, was very successful, both in improving the quality of the foals, and ensuring that most mares foaled every year.

The founding of the Londonderry Stud was the first of two momentous events for the Shetland breed in the last quarter of the 19th century. The second was the establishment, in 1890, of the Shetland Pony Stud Book Society – the first such society for any of the Mountain and Moorland breeds.

There had been a previous attempt, in 1868, at forming 'an association for the improvement of the breed of horses and ponies in Shetland'. The committee included such well known names as Mr John Bruce of Sumburgh, and Mr Robert Bruce of Symbister. The association concerned itself with all breeds, and proposed that

Londonderry ponies on Bressay.

(interestingly) a Norwegian stallion should be imported for the use by crofters and farmers on their mares – and from that the conclusion must be drawn that the aim was to improve what are known in the islands as the 'work horses' (mostly cross-bred), used for ploughing, harrowing, etc., rather than the Shetland ponies. There were plans to acquire the use of land adjacent to Lerwick for the breaking and training of ponies, and for pony racing. Records of the association are incomplete, but it was finally wound up in 1878, apparently due to lack of support.

No such fate was to befall the society formed in 1890, of which the first President was the 6th Marquis of Londonderry, who had succeeded to the title on the death of his father in 1884; Mr George Bruce of Aberdeen was Secretary, and the Committee consisted of John Bruce (Sumburgh), Gilbert Anderson (Hillswick), Anderson Manson (Laxfirth), Alexander Sandison (Uyeasound) and J.J.R. Meiklejohn (Bressay), the latter five all from Shetland, and Gavin Haddie

(Dalmuinzie), R. McDonald (Cluny Estate), James Duncan (Inverness) and Robert Brydon (Seaham Harbour, County Durham).

The first Stud Book was published in the 1891, and contained a list of 111 members (mostly crofters), and entries of 48 stallions foaled before January 1st, 1886, and 408 mares that had produced foals before September 1st, 1890. All the ponies were inspected by the Committee for correctness of type and conformation. The book is also notable for three very interesting articles about various aspects of the ponies at that time. The Stud Book has been published annually since 1891, except for a few years during wars and the Depression.

Despite the interest aroused by the formation of the society and the publication of the Stud Book, many breeders in the islands failed to register their ponies. The Stud Book was closed in 1905, but right up to that date, mares could be entered without a previous generation being registered. At the request of the Zetland County Council, who estimated that there were still many pure-bred ponies unregistered (including, it was thought, some 1,000 mares) the Stud Book was opened again in 1908. Maurice Cox suggested that the real reason for the request was pressure applied by a group of breeders and dealers in the islands who were exporting to America and Canada. Those countries imposed a heavy import duty on ponies that were not registered, and the exporters in Shetland could not find enough registered animals for their trade.

Whatever the reason, five members of the Council were appointed to inspect the mares, but in the event, just over 400 were passed, and entered in Volume 21. It was not until some thirty years later, in Volume 44, that the 1,000th mare was approved for inclusion. In 1971, the book was closed once more, by which time 2,145 mares had been inspected.

Shortly after the Stud Book was opened, a rival society, called the Shetland Islands Pony Stud Book Society, was formed, and it published Volume One of its Stud Book in 1909. The following excerpt from the Introduction to that Stud Book made it clear that there was some ill-feeling between the two societies.

> It may only be natural for those who are ignorant of the state of the Shetland pony trade in the Shetland Islands to ask – Why should there be another Stud-Book for Shetlands ponies; is not one Stud Book sufficient? In the circumstances, it is not. Had the original Shetland Pony Stud-Book been open to the registration of all Shetland Ponies of good stock, the matter would have been different; but when not only Ponies of good stock, but ponies of pedigrees equally as good as those already registered are refused admission, and without any sufficient cause, it is only reasonable that the owners of animals excluded should look after

their own interests. A Stud-Book which refuses to register the very animal whose name it bears is not a Stud-Book in any sense. It can only be regarded as a list of animals of the kind belonging to certain individuals who are willing, as at a certain date, to pay for having their animals advertised.

The writer goes on to say that the Stud Book is open for the registration of all Shetland ponies, owned and kept within the county of Shetland, measuring no more than 43 inches (109 cm) for stallions and mares at 4 years, while mares of 3 years old having produce were eligible for entry provided they did not exceed 41 inches (104 cm). A glance through the entries in Volume One shows a far greater proportion of ponies measuring over 40 inches (101 cm) than in the 1891 original stud book.

Although most of the 336 members were pony owners, it is perhaps significant that of the 20 office bearers, only 4 were owners, and 10 were county councillors. It has been suggested that the society was formed for the sole purpose of supplying export certificates for ponies that had not been accepted by the original society. The fact that so many local councillors were office bearers does intimate, to the cynical, that the revenue to be gained for the county coffers from exports were more important to them than the improvement of the breed. Unfortunately for the society, the American government refused to recognise its registrations, although the Canadian government did so. This provoked a bitter attack on the original society (referred to as the Aberdeen Society) in Volume Two of the Stud Book. The committee no doubt realised that, with the loss of the American market, the raison d'être for the Island Society had, to all intents and purposes, ceased to exist. A further two volumes of the Stud Book were published, but the loss of markets, together with the advent of World War I, spelled the end of the society's short life.

5

FOUNDATIONS OF THE MODERN BREED

◆

There is little doubt that the last quarter of the 19th century saw the foundation of the modern era in the history of Shetland ponies. Although the traditional roles of the ponies as the essential means of transport and as pack animals were retained for some time – the latter until as recently as the mid-20th century, when peat 'flitting' by ponies finally ceased – great changes were taking place. With the coming of the demand for pit ponies, exports on a large scale began. From this, and as the use of the ponies by the crofters declined, followed the inevitable decrease in the numbers of ponies bred within the islands. Although the founding of the most influential of all Shetland pony studs – the Londonderry – was, as has been explained, a purely commercial venture, it was followed by the establishment of other studs, in Shetland, in mainland Britain, and, in due course, overseas. These latter reflected the ever-widening popularity of the breed, not for commercial purposes, but for pleasure.

THE LONDONDERRY STUD

The importance of the Londonderry Stud in the development of the modern breed can scarcely be underestimated. Dr and Mrs Douglas, writing in 1913, were in no doubt about that. 'The Shetland pony, as now produced on the British mainland', they wrote, 'is chiefly derived from the stud established by the Marquis of Londonderry ... It was in this stud that the standard was set by which showyard judging has proceeded during the last twenty years; and it was here also that the type of the modern pony was created by selection and close inbreeding.' Commenting on the skill and enthusiasm of Messrs Meiklejohn and Brydon in eliminating the defects of the island ponies, they continued, 'The consequence was a degree of breed improvement which is perhaps without parallel as the result of less than thirty years of breeding and management.'

The Marquis of Londonderry's great stallion Jack 16.

Not only was this improvement due to a single stud, it is traceable, in the main, to a single stallion – **Jack**. Jack, foaled in 1871, was registered as No. 16 in Volume 1 of the Stud Book(of the Shetland Pony Stud Book Society). Neither his breeder or his breeding is known, although it is fairly safe to assume that he had been a crofter's pony before he was purchased by the stud. He was black, stood 40 inches (101 cm), and was described as being close-coupled, with remarkable bone and substance, finely proportioned, and with a bold and upright carriage. The Douglases and Maurice Cox agree that his prepotency suggests he was closely in-bred – a common occurrence in Shetland at that time, whether by design or accident, as has been mentioned.

The statistics extracted by the Douglases from the first nine volumes of the Stud Book are really remarkable. Nineteen stallions, including Jack, were used. Of these, three were his sons (Laird of Noss 20, Lord of the Isles 26, and Odin 32); eight were his grandsons (Thor 83, Sigurd 137, Emeer 131, Runolf 62, Najal 75, Lava 121, and Otkell). (Numbers appearing after ponies' names are their registration numbers in the Stud

Book.) His great grandson on the dam's side, **Oman** 33, was also used. These sires were used more than any others, and of the 490 foals entered, 248 were by Jack and his three sons, 160 by his eight grandsons, and 36 by Oman 33, his great grandson. A mere 46 were by unrelated stallions. The record of dams used is no less impressive. Of 125 in the Stud Book, 76 were by Jack and his three sons, and 10 by his grandsons.

These days, in-breeding on such a scale would be greeted with undiluted horror! But just look what Meiklejohn and Brydon did – and with what success. Of the 125 mares, 50 were sired either by Jack, his sons, or grandson, out of dams also sired by Jack, his sons or grandsons, while 40 were sired by Jack and his three sons, out of mares sired by them. From 490 foals foals, 282 are by Jack, his sons and grandsons, out of mares by the same selection of sires.

Other stallions were used, but obviously to a lesser extent. Principal of these were **Prince of Thule**, another pony of unknown breeding foaled in 1872, and his son Oman. Oman was out of Norna 198, who was by Lord of the Isles – thus returning to Jack's blood again. This was a recurrent theme, as, of Prince of Thule's progeny, 7 mares were out of Jack's daughters, and overall, of 34 foals, 24 were by Jack and his three sons.

Jack was renowned as a sire of great stallions, but he also produced influential mares. Three of the five tail females (mares to which most or all of the subsequent ponies bred in the stud trace back) of the stud were by him – **Darling** 174 (out of Dandy), her full sister Dumple 179, and Spencie 209 (out of Seivwright), a fourth, Thora 212, was by his son **Odin** and out of Thordisa (by Lord of the Isles out of Thorgerda by Jack), and one, Fra 185, was by Prince of Thule, out of Hethe by Jack. Another renowned daughter of Jack was Peggy, the dam of Pride 202 and Princess 203, both by Prince of Thule, while Jack's son Odin sired Swertha 211, the dam of Silver Queen 1197.

The in-breeding was, of course, meticulously planned. In general, Jack's daughters were put back to their sire, or to their full or half brothers. The same system was used with Jack's sons. Prince of Thule was used as the principal out-cross, but in this case the mares were nearly always put back to Jack's line. Only rarely did a Londonderry mare go back to the same stallion in successive years.

For decades after the dispersal of the Londonderry Stud, many ponies were described as being of 'Londonderry type', or 'Londonderry blood' – and the majority of the historically great Shetland studs were indeed founded largely on Londonderry ponies or their immediate descendants. As the stallions on Bressay and Noss were made available to the local crofters' mares, they must also have influenced, at

Oman 33, bred by the Marquis of Londonderry.

least to some extent, the quality of those ponies. That the Londonderry ponies to a considerable extent standardised the breed is generally accepted. It might even be said that it saved the breed. Had the increasing demand for pit ponies and the consequent sale of the best from the islands without thought for the future continued unchecked, who can say what might have been the outcome? It is at least arguable that the breed would have continued to degenerate into a collection of light-boned, weedy animals lacking in substance, strength and hardiness. Having lost the very qualities that so endeared them to visitors to the islands, could they ever have attained the worldwide popularity they now enjoy?

To say that any modern Shetlands are of the Londonderry type or blood is something of an exaggeration; the blood has been heavily diluted over the intervening years. Also, as Maurice Cox remarked, 'do we want the modern Shetland pony ... to be like the pony which was striven for by the managers of the Londonderry stud? This would be a pony low to the ground, with low head carriage and straight shoulder, not a pony to carry a child, or even a pack, nor to trot smartly in a light gig.'

Odin 33, another influential Londonderry stallion.

While that criticism is undoubtedly deserved in some instances, photographs of some of the most influential Londonderry ponies suggest that, while that may be what they aimed for, they did not completely achieve it – which, with hindsight, is doubtless a good thing! They used, and produced, many much better ponies, so far as can be judged by the photographs of individual animals, and of groups of ponies on Noss and Bressay. Because of the Londonderry ponies' importance to the subsequent development of the breed, it is perhaps useful to look at some of them more closely, as well as mentioning some of their better-known progeny.

Jack 16 (see picture on p.45) has already been described. His son **Odin** was said by the Douglases to be a horse of immense power and robustness, and great masculinity. His bone and substance were his outstanding features, and he was a vigorous and active mover, with strong hock action, but not quite straight. The Douglases described his head as heavy and out of proportion, although, as the photo shows, it is far better than some of the 'coffin-heads' of recent years! He was black and stood 38 inches (96 cm). His dam was Nugget 200, by Tom Thumb 44 – who reversed the trend for ponies being sent from Shetland to mainland Britain, as he was brought back from the pits to produce smaller ponies. He stood just 34 inches (86 cm).

Odin was used extensively, siring 119 foals, of which the males were infinitely better than the females. His sons included Thor 83 (out of Fra, and thus related to Prince of Thule), who was also used a great deal. Thor was said to be a pony of great substance, and an active mover, but with a rather large head, reminiscent, perhaps, of his sire's. He was brown, standing 38 inches (96 cm), and sired some fine and influential mares in addition to Pride and Princess, such as Beatrice 1533, Bracelet 1604, Perfection 1489 and Stella 1692.

Lord of the Isles was a smaller, but solid and compact animal of 36 inches (91 cm), who sired 63 foals. He was best known as a getter of mares, before being exported to the USA. His special place in the breed's history is that, through his dam, Dandy, he introduced into the blood of the Londonderry sires the outcross to Prince of Thule 36 (see below). Among the famous mares he sired were Beauty 167 (out of Darling 174), to whom so many ponies trace back, and also Boadicea 998 (out of Bergthora 523). The Douglases cite Boadicea as an example of the 'Scandinavian' type of pony, and, while acknowledging her relative lack of bone, described her as standing 'almost alone among Shetland ponies as an example approaching closely to perfection, of what a riding-pony should be, with a small and exquisitely shaped head carried high on a clean-cut and well arched neck, shoulders that would not disgrace a good thoroughbred, fine withers and short strong back, and the safe and easy action that properly belongs to an animal of her type'.

Although notable for so many good mares such as Beauty 167, Die 524, Thordisa, Norna 198 and Steinvor 534, Lord of the Isles sired at least one outstanding stallion – Multum in Parvo 28, out of Dandy – a classic example of Londonderry in-breeding, as Dandy was Lord of the Isles' own dam. Multum in Parvo was thus another of Jack's grandson's. Foaled in 1884, he stood 37 inches (94 cm), and was said to be very like his sire – and he too was described by the Douglases as an 'Oriental' type. They wrote that, while he lacked power and weight and strength of action, he was full of quality, and notable for the abundance of his mane and forelock. He died in 1912 at the age of 28.

Laird of Noss 20, by Jack 16 out of Seivwright, was lighter than Odin, and is remembered principally as the sire of Harold 117, Duncan 147 and Hector 183.

One of the few Londonderry stallions said to be totally unconnected with the great Jack was **Prince of Thule** 36. Although his breeding was unknown, his distinctive appearance certainly indicates that any relationship to Jack was unlikely. To him the Douglases ascribed the

Lord of the Isles (left) *and Prince of Thule* (right).

introduction into Londonderry lines of the 'Oriental' type, whereas Jack was definitely 'Scandinavian'. Prince of Thule must have been a striking pony, being 'seal brown with a very bright tan muzzle and flanks', and he also had prominent wide-set reddish hazel eyes. His mane hung to his knees, and his forelock below his nose. He stood only 36 inches (91 cm), and was said to be of exquisite quality, with a small thoroughbred head, and an exceedingly fine muzzle. He was short-backed, with strong, if somewhat drooped quarters, but with a well carried tail. In common with many island ponies of the time, he was said to be cow-hocked, but he had big, wide feet, strong bone and large joints. He also had a good length of rein, high withers, but not the best of shoulders, and moved rather close.

Prince of Thule's most important son was Oman 33, who stood 34 inches (86 cm), and had, in effect, a double dose of his sire's blood. He was out of Norna, by Lord of the Isles, who was himself out of a mare by Prince of Thule. Oman's progeny, both male and female, are of great importance. His sons included Frederick 223 and Seaweed 333, while his best-known daughters were Silver Queen 1197, Sea Serpent 1535, Harriet 1194 and Belle of Bressay 1192.

The Londonderry ponies were a familiar sight in the show rings in Shetland, where they were exhibited with great success, especially at Lerwick. They were also exhibited with outstanding results at the Royal Highland Show, where they won no fewer than 45 firsts and 30 seconds in the years 1884-98. There is no doubt they did much to increase the popularity of the breed. A delightful, if possibly apocryphal story, concerning the expected dominance of Londonderry ponies in the show ring, appeared in *Vanity Fair* in 1897. The Londonderry show handler was so accustomed to winning that at one show in Lerwick he appeared in the ring carrying a halter, and explained to the judges that the pony it fitted had not yet arrived, but, as he had business elsewhere, he would take its prize and go!

It came as a very great shock to the Shetland world when, in 1899, it was announced that the Londonderry Stud was to be dispersed, the reason apparently being that the Londonderry estate had failed to negotiate a new lease for Noss and Bressay.

Rather than sell the ponies in Shetland, with its limited market, and relative difficulty of access, they were shipped down to Seaham in Durham. A grand dispersal sale was held on September 7th, 1899, at Dawdon Dene Farm, the Londonderry stud. And 'grand' it most certainly was, in the manner of the day. Buyers arrived by train from all over Britain. After inspecting the 15 stallions, 70 mares, 30 fillies and 43 foals, the buyers lunched in a large marquee, where toasts were drunk to the Queen and to the Marquis of Londonderry. His Lordship was unable to be present, but Lady Londonderry attended, together with the Countess of Hopetoun and her sisters-in-law, the Ladies Estella and Dorothea Hope – of whom more later.

The *Durham Advertiser* of the day enthused about the success of the stud and the quality of the ponies on offer.

> The stud was founded 25 years ago on the Island of Bressay in Shetland, and it has always occupied an unique place amongst studs. Unlimited expenditure to maintain its efficiency enabled the noble owner to keep a high quality. Careful mating and selection of the breed has contributed to the steady improvement, as evidenced by the slope of the shoulders and the action of the ponies, as well as the size of the head. During the last 12 years the great majority of the prize-winning Shetland ponies have been bred by Lord Londonderry on Bressay, and the stallions used have all been winners at the H. and A.S. *[Highland and Agricultural Society]* Shows ... Thirty of the animals offered belong to the tribe which trace through 'Darling' by 'Jack' to 'Dandy'. This tribe has produced more prize-winners than all the other tribes put together, and every animal of the blood was to be counted a good breeder. Another valuable strain was that traced through 'Spencie' to 'Sievewright' and 'Saucy'. There were 13 representatives of this tribe in the catalogue, most of which were prize-winners. Other valuable strains were those going back to 'Eva', 'Mitchell', and 'Thorgarde', all of which have produced animals of the highest excellence; indeed, it might be stated that every brood mare over six years had some special merit.

Odin, when over twenty years old, with his three best daughters.
(Left to right) *Sigfus, Odin, Thora, Bretta.*

Within three quarters of an hour of the sale commencing, stock to the value of £1,000 had been sold, and at the end of the day, 151 ponies were sold, with the top price of 125 guineas paid for the 3-year-old filly, Fancy Fair, out of Freya. Many well bred ponies went for bargain prices of less than 10 guineas. However, the average was about 20 guineas, and the total raised was just over 3,000 guineas, a considerable sum in those days.

6

INTO THE 20TH CENTURY

◆

THE SOUTH PARK STUD

The dispersal of the Londonderry Stud was the end of one chapter in the story of the Shetland breed, but it was, in a sense, also the opening of another. By its very nature it ensured that Londonderry blood was dispersed far and wide. More importantly, ponies were bought there by breeders whose studs were, in turn, to have a very considerable impact on the subsequent development of the breed.

Prominent among those breeders were the Ladies Estella and Dorothea Hope, daughters of the sixth Earl of Hopetoun, whose seat was at Hopetoun House, Linlithgow, East Lothian. According to their great-niece, the late Lady Joan Gore-Langton, the sisters had a great affinity with all animals 'be it Jersey Cows, Brahmin Bulls, Zebras, Otters, Donkeys, and last but not least a hare called Juggins'. Some time during a winter in the 1870s, they acquired two Shetland ponies, which they named Jack and Jill. It was not until the following summer that, when the ponies had shed their winter woollies, it was observed that Jill was male! Both ponies had been entered in the Stud Book, so the names stood – and Jill is registered as a stallion as number 19 in Volume 1. They were the foundation of what was to become the very famous South Park Stud. In 1886 the sisters and their animals, including the now enlarged herd of Shetland ponies, left Hopetoun House, and moved to England. They lived first at Great Hollanden Farm, near Sevenoaks in Kent, and later at South Park, near Robertsbridge, in Sussex, where they entered enthusiastically and successfully into breeding and showing their Shetlands.

They retained only the best ponies for breeding purposes, and, when satisfied that they had obtained typey, sound animals, they practised close breeding with great success. They had already embarked on the introduction of Londonderry ponies in 1892, when they bought the great Prince of Thule 36 at a Londonderry sale for the bargain price of

30 guineas, and in 1895, Prince of Thule was followed south by his 12-year-old son, Oman 33. The sisters' use of Oman demonstrated their policy of close breeding. One of his best known sons was **Seaweed 333**, who was out of Sea Serpent 1535, who was herself by Oman. In the year of the Londonderry dispersal, the 27-year-old Prince of Thule was killed in a fight with Oman.

The Ladies Estella and Dorothea bought a number of ponies at the Londonderry dispersal, including Odin, who was used extensively and with great success. Outstanding among his sons was Thoreau 392, a particularly handsome pony with fine action, who enjoyed a remarkable show career, both in hand and in harness. Ponies were shown less often in those days, but in a show career lasting only a few years he won the gold medal for the best Shetland at the Highland Show in 1907, another gold medal, six silver medals and eighteen firsts. Thoreau's breeding, too, was typical of South Park. His dam, Thora 212, was also by Odin and out of Thordisa by Lord of the Isles out of Thorgerda. Both Lord of the Isles and Odin were by Jack, as was Thorgerda.

Continuing their use of Londonderry blood, the Ladies Hope bought, in 1903, the 4-year-old 32½ inch (83 cm) stallion Haldor 270, bred by Mr H. F. Anderton. Haldor, too, was in-bred to Jack, being by Duncan 147 who was by Jack's son, Laird of Noss, and out of Dinah 525 who was by Lord of the Isles, and out of Dainty 172. Dainty was by Lion 22 (bred by Mr John Bruce at his Sumburgh stud) and out of Jack's daughter, Dumple. Haldor was an excellent choice and proved a very successful sire. Among his sons was Helium 452 (out of Helga 5288 by Lord of the Isles).

On the female side of the stud, the Ladies Estella and Dorothea bought, among their 12 purchases at the Londonderry dispersal sale, the brood mare, Beauty, winner at the Royal Highland Show, and the daughter of Darling, another Highland winner, and dam of yet another great mare, Bretta 811 (by Odin). They also bought Sea Serpent 1535 (Oman/Sybil 1114 by Thor) as a 3-year-old filly, at Mr R.W.R. Mackenzie's Earlshall stud in 1904, and two mares – the Londonderry-bred Helga (by Lord of the Isles out of Fra by Prince of Thule), and Freesia 1601, by Bonaparte 168 out of Fuschia 1285, bred by the Marchioness of Linlithgow. Bonaparte was by Odin out of Beauty, and Fuschia was a grandson of Odin.

The female side was thus steeped in Londonderry blood, but their legendary foundation mare, the roan **Hoplemuroma** 130, was of unknown breeding. A 35½ inch (90 cm) red roan foaled in 1883, she was the dam of Corona 2015 (by Odin), to whom many South Park ponies

Lady Estella Hope with her 'dining companion'! The pony is the South Park Stud's foundation mare, Hoplemuroma.

trace. Hoplemuroma was equally famous in harness and under saddle. The Ladies Estella and Dorothea were keen whips (the former drove, according to her great-niece, Lady Joan Gore-Langton, 'with tremendous confidence, one could even say nonchalance'!), but it is not recorded who was driving Hoplemuroma when the mare is said to have trotted 4 miles in 16 minutes, 7 miles in 29 minutes, and 9 miles in 43 minutes. With a 4-stone lad in the saddle, and given a 300-yard start, she won a trotting handicap race for ponies 14 hands and under.

Among the most successful of the South Park show ponies were the full brothers, the 33-inch (84 cm) stallion Fairy Light 1259 and 36-inch (91 cm) Fairy Lamp 985 (by Thoreau's son Electric Light 650 and out of Haldor's grand daughter Fairy Tale 3086). Two cream dun stallions, Cuckoo 1536 (a grandson of Thoreau, out of Corona's Climax 4505 by Cafe Cloche 1046) and Ferdinand 1307 (a grandson of Electric Light 650 and out of Felice 3532, a grand-daughter of Oman) were great winners in harness, being successful at Royal Richmond, Olympia and at Aachen in 1938). Among the mares, Belle of the Ball 2333(Oman/Bretta) and Corona's Climax 4505 were very useful.

All the foals were christened with names starting with the first letter of their dams' names. Thus the 'B' family came from Bretta, and were mostly bay or black; the 'C' family were duns, creams and broken colours; the 'R' family were creams with flaxen manes and tails, and the 'Fs' and 'Vs' were nearly all miniatures of various colours, including roan.

The sisters were totally involved with the ponies, their breeding, driving and showing. They sold some of their foals, including Champion, who went to the Empress of Russia in 1901, and Cara, who went to Queen Victoria. Perhaps the most significant sale was that of the stallion, Halcyon of Bodiam 600 (by Thoreau), who was exported to Mrs Maclellan of the famous and influential Shetland Heights Stud in Victoria, Australia (see page 160 ff).

Lady Dorothea Hope died in 1927, but Lady Estella continued to breed and show the ponies, apart from the interruption of World War II. What a great and much-loved character she was! She was devoted to the ponies, and customarily dined in the formal manner of the day, but with one of them standing by her side, as the photograph on the previous page shows. She also drove herself to and from the local railway station. Her devoted stud groom always had the pony and trap waiting for her on her return, and off she would drive to South Park, leaving the groom to find his own way home in time to greet her when she arrived!

The smaller-sized ponies, with which South Park is associated, always took pride of place; the smallest bred there was the 26½ inch (67 cm) stallion Fairy Fly 1537 (by the 33 inch/84 cm Fairy Light 1259 and out of Fairy Friend 5106, who was 29½ inches [75 cm], and by Cherubino 1363, a 30 inch [76 cm] pony also by Fairy Light). It is often forgotten that the sisters also bred excellent standard-sized ponies, the largest being 41 inches (104 cm). Whatever height they bred, their aim was to produce 'a miniature hunter, not a miniature carthorse!'.

Lady Estella died at the great age of 92, but even in her late eighties she was still making plans for the stud, and experimenting with breeding. Sadly, she was a little lax in registering some of her lovely ponies in her later years, in spite of much urging by Mrs Betty Cox (of whom more later).

On Lady Estella's death, the ponies and the South Park estate passed to her great-niece, Lady Joan Gore-Langton. Lady Joan saw the need to introduce a new stallion to continue the various lines, and found the 39½ inch (100 cm) Avening Davy Crocket 1736, a cream dun by Avening Jupiter 1410 out of Avening Carola 4854, and a grandson of the South Park bred Ferdinand 1307. He was full of South Park blood, and proved a great success. Davy Crocket was followed by Baron of Belmont, bred in Shetland, by the South Park stallion, Robin 1607. For the miniature side of the stud, Lady Joan bought Ron of North Wells 1989, a 31 inch (79 cm) black with Marshwood blood.

Painting of the Lady Estella and Dorothea Hope's stallion Fairy Light.

Although Lady Estella had a small family of ponies with the 'Fairy' prefix, she did not use a prefix for all her ponies. Lady Joan decided to continue the Fairy prefix for the miniatures. A chestnut colt, Fairy Bacchus (2545) was bred, and he became a fine stallion to use on Ron of North Wells' daughters.

At the time of her death in 1989, Lady Joan had carried on the famous name of South Park with great success for nearly thirty years. The stud passed to Lady Joan's daughter, but she lives in America, and it is now owned by her niece by marriage, Countess De La Warr, of Buckhurst Park in Sussex. Lady De La Warr's aim is, if possible, to re-introduce some of the old South Park lines. She has recently been given the 21-year-old stallion, Fairy Crumb (out of Fairy Coquette), from the 'C' line; Fairy Rosamund is a young mare representing the 'R' line, and the stallion Fairy Viking from the 'V' line, going back to the stallion Vero 1746 (by Fairy Fly 1537). Viking is now 29 years old, but, according to his owner, 'in cracking form'. The one line that is missing, and being sought, is the 'B' line – apart from one elderly mare, Baroness, who is a grand-daughter of the great Thoreau.

Lady Joan Gore-Langton, who inherited the South Park stud from her great aunt, Lady Estella Hope.

Lady De La Warr has also inherited a wonderful collection of photographs of the South Park ponies and their owners, going back to the very early days – and some of these are reproduced, with her permission, on pages 50, 52, 55, 57 and 58.

Mr Francis Gourlay from Dumfries-shire was yet another patron of the Londonderry dispersal, buying four ponies, including Darling II 175 (Laird of Noss/Darling), to whom a number of Harviestoun ponies trace. Darling II's daughter Delia 2327 (by Thor) was the dam of Drumlanrig 699 (a great-grandson of Thor) and Dunsmuir 1155 (by May King of Penniwells 769, who traced back to Helium 452). Delia's grand-daughter, Delilah 2708 (sired by Delia's own half-brother, Dvorak 375), was the dam of Dollar Boy 1242. This was a relatively small stud, but important, as the stallions were used by several other studs prior to its dispersal in 1931.

EARLSHALL

A prominent stud founded at the end of the last century which used much Londonderry blood was that of Mr R.W.R. 'Bob' MacKenzie of Earlshall, Leuchars, in Fife. His foundation mares, registered in 1894, were bred by Mr Alexander Sandison of Uyeasound, in Unst. These he put to the Londonderry stallion, Pineapple 135, a 34 inch (86 cm) brown pony by Lord of the Isles out of Pride 202 by Prince of Thule. At the time, Pineapple was considered to be the smallest pony in existence – something which seems scarcely credible in view of the current fashion for ponies measuring *under* 30 inches (76 cm).

Robert Brydon, writing in *Horses of the British Empire* compiled by Sir Humphrey de Trafford, described how, when he first acquired Earlshall, Mr Mackenzie turned his ponies out on an area of moorland consisting of sandy bunkers with patches of rough grass, ling and gorse, which he considered ideal. He believed that any extra food was injurious to the ponies, and they existed on the scant herbage of the moor. On visiting the Londonderry Stud on Bressay in 1895 (one of the very few mainland breeders of that era to visit the islands and to buy stock there), Mr Mackenzie was impressed by the more generous feeding programme, which he subsequently put into practice with his own ponies. The result, he reported, was 'a marked improvement in the quality of his stock, which, without increasing in height, acquired more bone and substance, as well as better symmetry and action'. Mr Mackenzie bought 9 filly foals and 6 mares at the Londonderry dispersal, and in due course his stud increased to some 140 ponies, the majority of them full of Londonderry blood, descended from Jack 16 and Prince of Thule, via Lord of the Isles and Odin. He later introduced some mares that had less Londonderry blood, such as Bandrol 635, bred by Mrs Huband. Bandrol was by Charles Langley 403 (by Norseman 31 by Blackie), bred by Alexander Sandison of Uyeasound, and out of the Mackenzie-bred Brighteye 2459. Here the only Londonderry blood comes in, as Brighteye was by Odin's grandson, Monkshood 274.

The most influential stallions at Earlshall were, however, principally Londonderry. These included the Gavin Hadden-bred Rattler 210, who was by the great **Multum in Parvo** 28 (by Lord of the Isles) and out of Moonlight 469. Moonlight was by Giant 10, a son of Jack 16, and out of Mouse 975, who was also by Multum in Parvo – a classic piece of Londonderry-like close breeding. Rattler's son, Helmet of Earlshall 408, was out of Helen 1228 by Oman, and he was used extensively, as was his son, Brass Hat 1212 (a grandson of Darling) bred by Mr Francis Gourlay, and bought in by Mr Mackenzie. Another stallion bought from Mr Gourlay was the 39½ inch (100 cm) black Dollar Boy (Bravo of Earlshall/Delilah). The two Earlshall lines came together in Bandrol's son, Bravo of Earlshall 1081 & 1115, who was out of Brend of Earlshall 3391, who was by Helmet of Earlshall.

In addition to the blacks, bays and browns, Mr Mackenzie strove to introduce greys and chestnuts. He bought Express of Annistoun 1089, who although black himself, was by the grey Gluss Norseman 759, a stallion introduced to Earlshall for the purpose of siring ponies of his own colour. Express's dam was Emblem of Earlshall 3974, also a grey. Other greys at Earlshall included Empire Day 539 (Dreyfus 311/Emily II 1940) and his son Why Not of Earlshall 898 (out of Hillswick White Wings 389 I.S.). Doyen of the chestnuts was the stallion Emillius of Earlshall 1121 (by the brown Sammy of Liberton 947 and out of the grey Emily II 1940), to whom many present-day chestnuts trace.

In time, Mackenzie developed what came to be known as the 'Earlshall' type, described by Cox as being full of quality, with excellent heads, a good top line, and well laid shoulders, and although some were inclined to be light of bone, many of his black stallions were not lacking in this respect.

'Bob' Mackenzie was, by all accounts, yet another great character in the Shetland pony world. Extremely kind and helpful to those who sought his advice on pony matters, he nonetheless had his violent dislikes. One particular breeder inspired his wrath – possibly because the said breeder was rather too often successful with ponies he had not bred, which were produced in what could have been described, in those days, as a 'flashy' manner. They were handled by a stud groom wearing light canvas shoes so as to run the ponies out in a manner similar to the present day Welsh cobs. He also took an inordinate dislike to the

Dollar Boy, bred by F.N.M. Gourlay.

breeder's customary large button-hole, describing it as more suitable for a flower show than a pony show!

Mackenzie himself habitually wore a distinctive top-hat shaped bowler, which, even in those days, was an unusual form of headgear, and a cloth or tweed suit with a coat rather similar to a morning coat, but cut shorter and more square. From the pocket of this coat he would produce a large coloured handkerchief to deal with the effects of the snuff which he frequently took.

At Earlshall, as on many Scottish arable estates of that period, there was one of the old circular buildings in which horses were formerly used to provide the power for a threshing mill. The horses were harnessed to beams projecting horizontally from a single vertical shaft, which in turn worked a mill by means of a bevel wheel as the horses walked round the circular trackway. Mackenzie removed the heavy beams from this building, replacing them with light ones, to which his Shetland stallions were attached, enabling them to be exercised – surely a forerunner of the 'horse walkers' of the present day!

Regular sales were held at Earlshall between 1903 and 1909, to which

Helmet of Earlshall, bred by R.W.R. Mackenzie.

breeders could bring their ponies. Finally, in 1932, the stud was dispersed. Unfortunately, this was during the great Depression, and there was no market for the ponies. Ninety six were offered, and they averaged just over £6.50 – the top prices being 33 guineas for Dollar Boy and the 4-year-old mare, Elderflower II of Earlshall 4604. It was a muted end to a distinguished stud – whose influence on the breed was, and still is, considerable.

TRANSY

A stud founded about the same time as Earlshall, but which is still well and truly in existence, is Transy, now situated at Devonshaw, near Dollar, in Clackmannanshire. This distinguished stud celebrates its centenary in 1996, having been founded by Mr William Mungall, the grandfather of the present owner, Mr D.W.H. (Dougal) Dick. It is undoubtedly one of the great studs in the breed. A significant number of successful present-day ponies in Britain trace back to it, as do many ponies in countries overseas, including Australia, New Zealand and Europe. (See Chapter 10.)

The stud started in a small and slightly unorthodox way. Mr Mungall accompanied a friend who was travelling to Edinburgh to look at two Shetlands he wanted as driving ponies. It was quickly discovered that the ponies, Derby and Joan, were broken to saddle, and not to harness – but Mr Mungall clearly found them irresistible, bought them, and brought them back to his home at Transy, which was then at Dunfermline. There they *were* broken to harness, and put to a newly acquired 4-wheeled dog-cart, still in the family's possession. Mr Mungall's grandson explains: 'They were the "Minis" of the day – to be used to give the carriage horses a day off, and for going into town to do the shopping.'

Not surprisingly, having acquired two Shetlands, Mr Mungall decided he must have more, and in 1899 he attended the Londonderry dispersal sale, where he bought 6 ponies, including 3 mares. The most signficant of these was Silver Queen 1197 (Oman 33/Swertha 211), who was bought with her filly foal Stella 1692 (by Thor 83) at foot. Silver Queen, already a winner at shows in Shetland, was a 39 inch (99 cm) black mare, and is regarded as the principal foundation mare of the stud. Her daughter Stella went on to found the famous Transy 'S' line. (The initials of the Transy lines are taken from the mares' names.)

The first foals bred by Mr Mungall were by Hector 183 (by Laird of Noss out of Hilda 190 by Odin). Hector had already been successful in the show ring for his previous owner, and continued to be so for Transy. He was followed by Eiric 446, who was out of the Londonderry-bred mare, Gudrunna 1716 (a grand-daughter of Laird of Noss). Eiric's sire was Beseiger 235, who was by Odin out of Beauty 167 (Lord of the Isles/Darling 174) and thus traces back to Jack 16, who appears no fewer than five times in the pedigree. Eiric was shown with great success from 1907, when he won his class at the Royal Highland.

Neither Hector nor Eiric had a lasting effect on the stud, and Dougal Dick considers there was no true foundation stallion until 1906, when the 5-year-old **Seaweed** 333 (by Oman) was bought from the Ladies Hope with his dam, Sea Serpent 1535 (Oman/Sybil). Seaweed was registered as a stallion, and produced a succession of extremely good sons, and, says Dougal Dick, 'he really put the stamp on the stud'. It is an interesting fact that every one of his foals has a distinct star – and any of today's ponies with a star will trace back to him. Some of Seaweed's best sons were Silverdale of Transy 620 and Selwood of Transy 619, both out of Silver Queen, and Sonyad of Transy 115, out of Sonya of Transy 2657 by Glencairn 314 by Frederick 223, who was by Oman.

The stud's 'H' line began about the same time as the 'S', with Helen II 1480, foaled in 1895, and bought at Earlshall in 1907. Helen II's breeding is of interest, as she was the last foal got by Jack 16. She was out of

Helga 5228, who was by Lord of the Isles out of Fra 185, who was by Prince of Thule out of Hethe, who was also by Jack 16 and out of Hester, who was bred by John Bruce of Sumburgh.

In 1921, Mr Mungall bought Pole Star 884 from Mr Anderson Manson. Pole Star was a 37 inch (94 cm) black, and his Londonderry blood was a little more dilute than some of the other Transy ponies. He was by Diamond Star 697 out of the unusually named Othello 2051. Diamond Star was by Erling 448, whose sire, Beseiger 235 was by Odin out of Beauty. Othello was by Captive by Odin 219, and out of Bronte 1277 by Laird of Noss.

The stud showed with very great success, winning regularly at the Royal Highland and the Royal of England right up until the years between the two world wars. As Mr Mungall's daughter, the late Mrs William Dick (who inherited the stud on her father's death in 1936), described in *A Century of Shetlands*, the ponies were prepared for the show ring with great care and attention to detail by her father, with the help of a stud groom, an under-groom and two stable boys. They were trained to stride out well by using a 30-yard line of railway sleepers set in an ash bed, the sleepers being the length of a good pony stride apart. The ponies then stepped from sleeper to sleeper. They were also lunged daily for at least half an hour.

Showing and breeding came to an abrupt, if temporary, halt during the years of World War II, when most of the land at Transy was requisitioned for war purposes. Mr Kerr of the Harviestoun stud agreed to take some mares and the stallion, Bergastor of Transy 1360 (by Pole Star out of Bergia of Transy 4608, by Sonyad of Transy), on loan, and continue breeding with them. A similar arrangement was made with Mrs Cox. Bergaster proved a very successful sire, being used on both Transy and Harviestoun mares.

It was not until 1953 that the remaining ponies returned to Transy from Harviestoun. Only 6 mares remained, but, fortunately, they represented most of the original Transy bloodlines. Dougal Dick became actively involved in the stud, and he bought the stallion, Joseph of Marshwood 1561 (Supreme of Marshwood 1467/Roseblossom of Maryfield 4703), from Mrs Cox. Joseph sired, among others, the stallion Stelmor of Transy 1701 & 1775 (ex Stelfrenda of Transy 4932) , who was used in the stud before being exported to Holland. A well known daughter was Wells Vasha 5480 (out of Bonnyton Beauty II 5219) who became a legend as a brood mare for the Sleigh's Wells stud in Aberdeenshire.

Two further stallions, both from Miss Ritchie's Netherley Stud, have had a major influence in the stud. These were Auditor of Netherley

Seaweed 333, regarded as the Transy Stud's foundation stallion.

The Transy Stud's Bergastor of Transy 1360.

1510 (Harviestoun Beau 1369/Audrey of Netherley 4827) and Pericles of Netherley 1987 (Gay Gordon of Netherley 1653/Pandora 5609). Auditor's best known son was Rosethorn of Transy 1750, out of Rosepetal of Transy 4930. Rosethorn has produced good, if not outstanding stallions; his daughters are, however, excellent, the most notable being Rosequeen of Transy 14352. Two of Rosethorn's sons have been kept to cross back to Pericles mares.

Pericles, on the other hand, sired both colts and fillies of the highest quality. All his daughters, which include Rosallyn of Transy and Heltern of Transy (the latter was champion at the Great Yorkshire Show in 1995), were put to Rosethorn – and thus combined Netherley and Harviestoun blood.

The Transy 'R' line, of which Rosethorn is an example, was founded by a mare called Rachel 664 (Odin 32/Ruth 108), foaled in 1889. This line was not so much to the fore in the years between the two world wars, which were dominated by the 'S' line. In the present day, the reverse is true, with the 'R' line doing extremely well. The stud recently had the misfortune to lose three 'S' mares to hyperlipaemia, but the stallions are still there, and Mr Dick has managed to buy back a representative of the female line from Ireland.

The stud has also, for many years, been known for its breeding of performance ponies, both in harness and under saddle, and for the exploits of these, including such outstanding ponies as Boffin of Transy (Rosethorn of Transy/Belinda of Transy) and Bard of Transy (Pericles of Netherley/Babette of Transy)(see Chapter 8). The 'B' line, to which these ponies belong, has had a slightly chequered existence. It was founded by Bergthora 523, who was foaled in 1886, by Holmside 14 out of Mattie 195 – both of unknown breeding. Bergthora was bought from the Seaham Harbour Stud (from among the few remaining ponies of the Londonderry stud) in 1909. During World War II, the 'B' line ponies were among those that went to Harviestoun, where the direct descendants all died out. However, after the war, Dougal Dick managed to bring the line back to Transy by buying Harviestoun

Carolyn Dick and Boffin of Transy.

Bedelea 5425, who was by Harviestoun Beau 1369 out of Harviestoun Beda 4938. Harvistoun Beda's dam was Bergia of Transy 4608, who was by Sonyad of Transy and out of Berga, who in turn, was out of Bergthora. Thus the current Transy 'B' line was started by Bedelea, and is now represented by the stallion Barba of Transy 3722, by Ross of Transy 2020, who goes back to Joseph of Marshwood.

Mr Dougal Dick has been joined in partnership by his two daughters, Carolyn (now Mrs Pleness), and Sarah (now Mrs Ross.) The family have a remarkable record of service to the breed and the Stud Book Society, as Mr Mungall, his daughter, Mrs Dick, and his grandson, Dougal, have served on the Council (apart from the recently introduced statutory year off) continuously since 1904 when Mr William Mungall was elected. Three members of the family have been President – Mr Mungall in 1906-7, Mr William Dick in 1959-61 and Mr Dougal Dick in 1969-71.

AUCHLOCHAN STUD

Dr and Mrs Douglas, to whom reference has already been made as the authors of the first book on the breed, founded their Auchlochan Stud in Lanarkshire in 1904. Londonderry blood featured prominently in most of the mares, and their stallion, Crown Prince 342, was a grandson of Oman on his sire's side, and of Odin on his dam's. The Auchlochan prefix appears in the pedigrees of ponies in some other studs, notably through Crown Prince's son, Phoebus of Auchlochan 777, who was out of Primula of Auchlochan 1826, a grandson of Pineapple.

HARVIESTOUN

A name already mentioned in connection with Transy, and which appears in the pedigrees of many ponies both in this country and abroad, is Harviestoun. The Harviestoun Stud – another of the outstanding studs in the breed – was founded just prior to World War I by Mr J.E. Kerr of Harviestoun, near Dollar in Clackmannanshire, and Castle Campbell. He had his first registration in the 1914 Stud Book. Mr Kerr was a supreme stockman, successfully breeding and showing an enormous range of animals from white mice, through guinea pigs, birds, dogs, Hackneys, Clydesdales and, of course, Shetland ponies.

Some of his first purchases were the mares, Snowdon Second 2947, a 35 inch (89 cm) black bred by Mrs Wilson, by Huntly Baron 550, who traced back to Odin, and out of Shah 2415 by Rattler 210. His foundation mares, however, came principally from Earlshall and Transy, while his stallions, apart from home-bred animals, came from Mr Francis Gourlay, and included Drumlanrig, Dollar Boy and Dunsmuir, who

Harviestoun Beau, bred by J.E. Kerr.

was Drumlanrig's half-brother (by Mayking of Penniwells 769, a grand-son of Hector). Dougal Dick describes how Mr Kerr visited Transy to buy two ponies, but went away with eight! These included Perfecta of Transy 3272 (Seaweed 333/Perfection 1489) and Silvera of Transy 3273, another daughter of Seaweed and out of Silver Queen.

Although he had been President of the Society in 1923-4, Mr Kerr really focussed most of his efforts on the ponies from the early 1930s, and he served a second, very long term as President from 1938-55. His showing successes were legion. His first of 13 Royal Highland Show championships was won in 1935 with Harviestoun Pixie 4727 (by Dunsmuir); and he won both the Royal Highland and the Royal in the same year eight times, and twice won the Royal Highland, the Royal, and the Royal Northern show in the same year – surely a feat unsur-passed by any other breeder. Mr Kerr's meticulously kept records reveal an outstanding run of show successes from the 1930s, with a series of ponies whose names appear in the pedigrees of many top class ponies of the present day, both in Britain and overseas.

Among the successful ponies were Harviestoun Pearl 4726 (Fickle

Mr J.E. Kerr of the Harviestoun Stud with Tearlach.

of Transy 1260/Harviestoun Pryde 4544), the stallion Balgair 1403 (Dollar Boy 1242/Harviestoun Bess 4595), and his son Beachdair of Harviestoun 1427 (out of Harviestoun Pixie 4727), both of whom were Royal Highland champions. Harviestoun Pat 5296 (Bergastor of Transy 1360/Harviestoun Princess 4920) and Harviestoun Rene 4964 (Dollar Boy 1242/Rosa of Transy 4554) were two of his last great champions, winning the Royal and the Royal Highland championships for him shortly before his death in 1962. Rene was the dam of Harviestoun Roma 5683, champion at the Royal Highland in 1968, and the Royal in 1970, who was an outstanding example of the superb action for which the stud is noted.

Cox considers that J.E. Kerr was probably the instigator of the fashion for the larger ponies – from 39 inches (99 cm) upwards – and indeed Mr Kerr exported Balgair to Australia, deciding that he was too small at 38½ inches (98 cm).

Following Mr Kerr's death, the stud was put up for sale by the estate factor, and Miss Ritchie, of the Netherley Stud, bought a number of ponies, including Harviestoun Polly 5468, who proved to be a major influence on the Netherley ponies. In 1985, when illness forced Miss Ritchie to give up her ponies, she invited Mr Kerr's grand-daughter,

Mrs Lucy Poett, who had continued the Harviestoun name, to choose any of her mares for Harviestoun. Mrs Poett chose 8 mares and 3 foals – her choice being influenced largely by the quality of the foals. The ponies included the yearling, Merry Rose of Netherley 14277 (a grand-daughter of Harviestoun Beau), who went on to win the Scottish NPS championship in 1989. During the last 20 years, Harviestoun ponies have won many more prizes, including reserve champion at the Royal Highland on seven occasions.

KIRKBRIDGE

Just prior to the formation of Harviestoun, Mrs W.T.R. Houldsworth founded her Kirkbridge Stud in Ayrshire, with the 39 inch (99 cm) Scrabster of Auchlochan 518 (Frederick 223/Steingerda 1733) as foundation stallion. The stud was passed on to Mrs Houldsworth's son, Colonel Sir Reginald Houldsworth, Bart., who was President of the Stud Book Society in 1963-5.

PENNIWELLS

An English stud that had many show ring successes was Penniwells, founded in 1910 by Mrs Etta Duffus in Hertfordshire. It was in the post-war years that Mrs Duffus' ponies really made their mark at shows, and in 1922, when the Royal Highland was at Dumfries, she virtually swept the board, taking the championship and reserve, a silver medal for an extra stock champion, and a first in every other class except the fillies, in which she was second. There is a suggestion that some of her ponies, although good, were perhaps lacking a little in quality, and it was felt that some of their success was due to the brilliant showmanship of her stud groom – a situation that has its parallels today!

Probably her best home-bred pony was the stallion, **Dibblitz of Penniwells** 1087, as 39 inch (99 cm) black, by Blitz 848 (who traced back to Oman), and out of Diddy 2193, a grand-daughter of Odin's bred by Francis Gourlay. Dibblitz's progeny in this country were not, on the whole, outstanding, and he was exported to Australia in 1932, where he did extremely well as a sire. The Penniwells Stud was sold in 1932.

MARSHWOOD

A stud that has been influential in mainland Britain, in Europe, Australia, and not least, in Shetland, is the Marshwood, founded by Mrs Betty Cox (wife of Major Maurice Cox) in Dorset in 1922. The immense contribution made to the breed in other ways by Major and Mrs Cox is described elsewhere.

The Marshwood stud was founded with the purchase of three fillies bought at the (then) annual Perth sale of Shetlands. These were the 3-year-old in-foal mare, Empire Maid 4055, bred by Perth business man, Mr Buchanan Dusmore, and by Boaventure of Earlshall 641, a grandson of Rattler 210, out of Hallgerda of Mondynes 3664, bred by Miss L.J. Irvine Fortescue; the yearling Syra of Earlshall 4197 (Dragon of Earlshall 5951/Silvertail 545) described by Maurice Cox as being rather too light of bone and lacking substance; and Amethyst of Woodlea 4196, by Everlasting of Auchlochan 703 out of Apricot 2636.

For the foundation stallion, Mrs Cox went to R.W.R. Mackenzie at Earlshall, and asked his advice. They bought from him a grey 3-year-old, unhandled and straight off the hill. This was Bohemian of Earlshall 1079 (by Gluss Norseman 759 out of Bohea of Earlshall 3923 by Helmet of Earlshall 408). Bohemian was full of quality, with a lovely head, and was a good mover, but a little light of bone. Only a short time later, Bob Mackenzie advised them to buy another mare he heard was on the market in Aberdeenshire. This was the 35½ inch (90 cm) black, Verona of Maryfield, bred by Peter Manson in Shetland, and which carried some of the best bloodlines, being by Erling 448 (a grandson of Odin) and out of Othello 2051 (a grand-daughter of Odin). Verona had won every time shown at the Lexica show and proved proved to be a great brood mare. She was the dam of the first stallion to be registered by Marshwood, Venture of Marshwood 1236, by Bohemian of Earlshall.

Venture inherited his sire's good movement, and he was a success in the show ring, and was later broken to harness. His talents by no means ended there. In 1932, Betty Cox and Anne Bullen (mother of Olympic dressage rider Jennie Loriston-Clarke) staged a circus in aid of the Veterinary College and the local hunt. All the performers were Shetlands, apart from Mrs Bullen's 11 hand riding pony, and Mrs Cox trained them all, including the two stud stallions, Venture, and his grey full brother, Seidlitz of Marshwood 1268, to do a series of tricks. These included lying down, jumping over each other whilst prone, and jumping through a burning hoop. During training, Venture and Betty Cox's terrier, Jumbo, established a great friendship. Jumbo decided he would like to ride a pony, so he was put on Venture, who was turned out in a blue and gold saddle cloth. The terrier stood happily on Venture's back while the pony trotted round, or lay quietly on it when waiting to go into the ring.

In the late 1920s, Mrs Cox bought a number of ponies from Graham Clark, a Crieff (Scotland) dealer. Among these was a particularly nice black mare, Jessie, without papers. She was put to Venture, and produced a lovely black filly, who was inspected, and registered as Jessie II of Marshwood, and became the foundation of the famous

Mrs Betty Cox with Venture of Marshwood 'ridden' by Jumbo.

Marshwood 'J' line. In time, she was the grand-dam of a quite remarkable series of outstanding stallions that have contributed much to the breed – Supreme of Marshwood 1467 (Sprinter of Marshwood1423/ Jessamine of Marshwood 4845) and his full brothers, Supremacy of Marshwood 1612, Superior of Marshwood 1633, and Supervision of Marshwood 1724.

With full brothers Venture and Seidlitz established as the stud stallions, Betty Cox decided that an unrelated stallion was needed. After the careful consideration and observation typical of this great breeder, she decided to visit Lady Hobart's Standen stud on the Isle of Wight. She bought the black Rustic Sprite of Standen 1343, from among a group of 2- and 3-year-olds. He was by the South Park sire, Fairy Lamp 9885, and out of Rose Noble 4280 by Ivanhoe 658, who traced back to Oman. Maurice Cox described him as 'the most kindly and gentlemanly stallion all his life, a sure breeder, who went superbly in harness and had considerable success in the show ring'. He was only shown 9 times, but was first in his debut at the National Pony Society show, champion at the Royal twice, reserve twice, and champion at the Bath and West.

Sprite was a great influence on the stud. His grandson, Supremacy of Marshwood (by Sprinter of Marshwood 1423) was the stud's senior stallion for many years, and a son, Spook of Marshwood 1632, was also a successful sire at the stud, as well as going to Shetland under the Premium stallion scheme.

In 1936 the Coxes paid what was to be the first of countless visits to Shetland. This was prompted by the news that Peter Manson of the Maryfield Stud on Bressay was disposing of his remaining ponies. The Coxes were very impressed with the ponies, which were of special interest as they were from impeccable Londonderry and Maryfield lines. Moreover, as Maurice Cox recorded, 'let it be quite clear that they did not have excessive bone or short legs and neck, with straight shoulders as one had heard so often was what the pit trade required. These ponies showed lots of quality, good shoulders, and limbs with sufficient flat bone, and definite joints, and masses of hair.'

The upshot was that they bought five black 4- and 5-year-old mares that had not been bred from, and a fine 39 inch (99 cm) 5-year-old then unregistered and unused black stallion, Alert of Maryfield 1351. His sire (and that of the mares) was Bright Star of Maryfield 1045, who was by Pole Star, a descendant of Odin. One of the mares, Hiker of Maryfield 4701 (out of Thora of Maryfield) produced, to Rustic Sprite of Standen, the top class colt, Sprinter of Marshwood 1423, who had superb action, and became an outstanding sire.

Tragically, within a short time, the country was at war, Marshwood was requisitioned, and Mrs Cox ordered to dispose of her ponies. Although homes were found for some, nearly all the mares and fillies were permanently lost to the breed. Rustic Sprite of Standen and Sprinter of Marshwood were retained, as was Jessamine of Marshwood, who produced two war-time foals, but the stallion, Alert of Maryfield was badly kicked by a cart horse and had to be put down.

In 1945, the Coxes, plus 2 stallions and 5 mares, and assorted farm animals, moved from Marshwood to Barncrosh, Castle Douglas, in Scotland, and began the task of re-building the stud. Although some mares and fillies were bought in, most of the re-building was done using the pre-war lines. In the 1950s, the demand for coloured ponies increased, and Betty Cox decided to find a suitable stallion to breed to the coloured mares she already owned. She found a 34 inch (86 cm) blue roan, Firebird 1440, bred at South Park, by Silver Fox 1269 by Helium 452, and out of Fire-Crest 4674 by Fairy Light 1259. The 8-year-old arrived at Barncrosh, was licensed and registered, and bred some good ponies, although rather too small for the stud's purposes. Probably his best-known son was Fireball of Marshwood 1650 & 1688, out of the island-bred Nun of Houlland 5227.

The Marshwood Stud moved to Barstobrick, Castle Douglas, where, eventually, they had some 130 ponies. A succession of great stallions graced the stud – Supremacy 1612, Spook 1632, Robber 2621, Rodney 4162 and Rason – the latter two reflecting the gradual introduction of Transy lines, being by Rosetaupe of Transy 2017.

In 1960, the Coxes bought a property at Gletness in Shetland, where they spent several months every year. There they founded the **Gletness** stud (while retaining Marshwood), from crofter-bred filly foals sired by the Premium stallions bought at the annual sales. They continued their Marshwood policy of fairly close breeding until 1980, when they

Supremacy of Marshwood 1612.

Major Maurice Cox.

sold the property, and moved all the ponies down to Barstobrick. Maurice Cox died in 1983, and the stud was dispersed. However, the bloodlines live on, not just in Britain, but in ponies exported from Marshwood to many countries, all over the world, as will be seen in Chapter 10. With the death of Betty Cox in 1993, at the age of 92, a remarkable era ended. Betty and Maurice Cox were perhaps the most important influences on the Shetland breed for the greater part of sixty years. Without them it is unlikely that the Premium stallion scheme (see page 140 ff) would have been devised and implemented. They gave freely of their knowledge and experience of the breed in judging and giving talks, both in Britain and in many places around the world. Maurice Cox was, as has been said, the author of the definitive book *The Shetland Pony* published in 1965, and in an abridged edition, re-published in 1976. They were a truly remarkable couple to whom the breed owes much.

WELLS

The Wells Stud was started as the St John's Wells Stud in Aberdeenshire by Mr John Sleigh, grandfather of the present owner, in 1901, but the first ponies were not registered in the Stud Cook until 1915. The foundation ponies were the stallion Eldorado of Auchlochan 860 (Thor 83/Empress Eugenie 1523), and the filly Beeswing of Auchlochan 3619 (Thor 83/Belinda of Auchlochan 1823).

This stud was dispersed in 1929, and re-established in 1947 by Mr H.P. Sleigh, father of the present owner, Mr Harry P. Sleigh. He bought four ponies – one each for his son and three daughters. The stallion was Wells Monarch 1469 (Harviestoun Beau 1369/Agnes of Earlshall 4548), bred by Miss Ritchie, and the three mares were Beauty, Fairy and Fenella. The real foundations of the stud were, however, from Harviestoun and from Mr Wyllie of Longhaugh. The first stallion from Harviestoun was Wells Trueform 1488 (Bergastor of Transy 1360/ Harviestoun Troya 4860).

The most influential mare was Wells Saidee 5115 (Balgair 1403/ Saidee of Transy 4448), the dam of Wells Superb 1721 (by Wells Satisfaction 1551), who was unbeaten in the show ring. The story of Superb shows that luck as well as skill can play an important part in running a successful stud. When Superb was born, he showed no sign of being anything special, and Mr Sleigh sold him as a foal at Aberdeen Mart for 12 guineas, and lost track of him. Five years later, Mr Sleigh, his daughter, Marjorie (now Mrs Martin of the West Park Stud) and Mr John Smith of Berry were driving to a Stud-Book Society council meeting in Perth, when they saw a stallion standing on a hillock in a field by the road. 'That's some stallion,' remarked Mr Sleigh. He found the name of the owner, and, to his astonishment, discovered that the stallion was his home-bred Wells Superb that he had sold five years

Mr H.P. Sleigh of the Wells Stud, with some of his ponies.

Wells Final Command 3150 – a son of Wells Vasha.

previously. He bought Superb and the piebald mare he was running with, for 100 guineas. That was in March, 1960, and in June of the same year, Superb won the Royal Highland – and was the only stallion ever to beat another top class Wells stallion, Trademark 1639 (Wells Satisfaction 1551/Harviestoun Troya 4860).

The famous Wells mare, Wells Vasha 5480, was also acquired in a slightly unusual manner. She had been bought, after the war, by Mr Sleigh's brother, with a couple of other mares. Mr Harry Sleigh happened to see her, realised her potential, and bought her. She was bred by Mr Simpson, and is by Joseph of Marshwood 1561 out of Bonnyton Beauty 2nd 5219. Bonnyton Beauty 2nd's dam, Bonnyton Beauty, was an inspected mare, so the rest of her grand-dam's line is unknown. Vasha was the start of the remarkable Wells 'V' line, and the dam of a series of outstanding stallions. She has the distinction of producing more Highland and Royal Show champions than any other animal (i.e. including cattle, sheep, etc.). Her daughter, Wells Vanity 5935, won the

Highland mare championship once; her son, Wells Supreme 1882, was Highland champion, and her sons, Wells Vijay 2067 and Wells Final Command 3150, were both champions at the Highland and the Royal 4 times – a record that is unlikely to be broken. Wells Final Command then established the record price of £12,000 when sold to France.

Another good Harviestoun mare was H. Promise 5053 (Balgair 1403/Harviestoun Pearl 4726), the founder of the Wells 'P' line. Promise's daughter, Wells Puzzle 5729 (by Merry Boy of Berry 1626) was the grand-dam of the stallion, Wells Rising Tide 3574 (Wells Final Commmand/Wells Princess), who also won the Highland four times and the Royal once, and went on to be the reserve in the 1993 Creber championship – the over-all championship of the show. Mrs Martin, who worked with the ponies for 28 years, explained that her father chose the Harviestoun/Transy ponies as his foundation stock because of their great presence, their good bone and their excellent heads. Looking back at old photos, she commented that Wells Trueform seemed so small, and with such narrow quarters, compared to what her father eventually bred. He was also a great breeder of Clydesdales, and Mrs Martin said he concentrated on breeding more of the Clydesdale type, with strength and power, and the stronger hindquarters.

In addition to the 'V', and 'P' lines, Wells also has an 'E' line, from Wells Elaine 4988 (Berlad of Transy 1335/Wells Eileen 5440), and a 'T' line from Wells Tiara 5204 (Bergastor of Transy 1360/Harviestoun Troya 4860). No outside stallion has ever been bought.

These days, Wells is recognised as a stud of black ponies, but at one time, Mr Sleigh bred many coloured ponies, all for the export market to America. When that trade was at its height, hundreds of ponies could be seen grazing in fields near Bridge of Don in Aberdeenshire, waiting to be shipped across the Atlantic. Other Wells ponies have been exported to many other countries, and in Australia, in particular, and thence to New Zealand, they figure prominently in the pedigrees of ponies in many of the leading studs.

The founder of the Stud, Mr J. P. Sleigh, was President of the Stud Book Society in 1924/25, and his son, Mr H. P. Sleigh from 1961/63 and 1977/79.

WEST PARK

Mr Sleigh's daughter, Mrs Marjorie Martin, began her own stud with ponies bought from her father, and registered her West Park prefix in 1947. Her foundation mare was Wells Edissa 6466, and she used her father's stallions until his death in 1987. At present she has her home-bred stallion, West Park Gay Rising Star 3935. She also has the old mare, Wells Victoria 9254 from the Vasha line, and is relying on Victoria's 3-year-old daughter to provide her with a colt for the future.

Other studs based upon, or containing an appreciable proportion of Wells blood include Hose (see pages 88-9), Mr and Mrs Howell's Dewlands, Mr and Mrs Sellars' Dryknowl and Mrs O'Brien's Annwood.

NETHERLEY

In 1928, Miss Aileen Ritchie founded the Netherley Stud, which was to become one the best-known of its time. Her foundation mare was Winnie the Pooh 4491, bred by Mr Francis Gourlay, by May King of Penniwells 769 out of Discovery of Tynron 4060, a daughter of Drumlanrig 699. Winnie began a female line at Netherley which lasted until 1973, when the mare, Perseverance of Netherley 6244 (Gay Gordon of Netherley 1653/Patience of Netherley 5611) was sold. Perseverance's colt, Perception 2460, by Harviestoun Sceptre 1584, was used as a stallion for six years.

Four year later, Miss Ritchie bought three Earlshall mares, Agnes of Earlshall 4548 (Gluss Norseman 759/Angelina 3383), Emita of Earlshall 4073 (also by Gluss Norseman, and out of Emily II 1940) and Millie of Earlshall 4517(Roseberry of Earlshall 1175/Nettie of Earlshall 4297). Millie was the foundation of the well known Netherley 'M' line, Agnes

Miss Aileen Ritchie's prolific stallion, Gay Gordon of Netherley, who has been influential in the breed world-wide.

the 'A' line and Emily the 'E' line. A descendant of Millie's, Peerie of Netherley 5543, was champion at Ponies of Britain in 1959, while other successful 'M' line ponies were Madcap 4898, Merrylegs 5199, Meridian 6984 and Merry Marion 10102. The 'A' Line produced Ava 5434 and Avalanche 6332, and the stallion, Arrogance 3517, who did exceptionally well in Australia until his recent death.

The first stallion at Netherley was Phoebus of Auchlochan 777 (by Crown Prince 342, a grandson of Oman, and out of Primula of Auchlochan 1826, a grand-daughter of Pineapple 135). Miss Ritchie then bought Dunsmuir 1155 from Mrs Dick, and he was part-exhanged for Harviestoun Beau 1369 (Drumlanrig 699/Harviestoun Bess 4595) in 1939. Beau did very well in the show ring, and was also a great influence in the stud, as he nicked well (produced good stock) with the Earlshall mares. He died in 1955.

The next stallion was the home-bred Gay Gordon of Netherley 1653 (Golden Glory 1514 of Netherley/Merrylegs of Netherley 5199). He was used at the stud for a remarkable 26 years, and was put down when he was 30. He bred 29 registered stallions, including Arrogance of Netherley, which have been exported all over the world.

Miss Ritchie was a familiar figure in the show rings, travelling extensively both north and south of the border.

WAULKMILL

Mrs Roweena Provan's Waulkmill Stud is based on fillies given to her by her mother, Mrs Eileen Lewis, of the Normandykes Stud, in 1960. Mrs Lewis founded her stud in 1944, with the foal of a mare she saw grazing on Aboyne golf course, not far from Aberdeen. The mare was Marvel of Netherley 4840 (Dunsmuir 1155/Mischief of Netherley 4734) and the foal was Princess of Normandykes 4977 (by Harviestoun Beau), bred by Mr J.J. Beattie. Mrs Lewis then bought a piebald stallion, Airborne 1426, who was by Berlad of Transy 1335 and out of Daphne of Dunira 4834. Airborne sired a number of piebald and skewbald foals, many of whom were sold to England. Despite this, the Normandykes ponies were principally black.

Princess was a great Lewis family favourite, and used to pull the children on sledges, they rode her, and she was also shown, doing well at the Royal Highland. Years later, when Princess and Airborne were both in their twenties, they produced the colt, Normandykes Aith 2142, which Mrs Provan bought from her mother. Princess was closely related to Mighty Fine of Netherley 1459 (Harviestoun Beau 1369/Mischief of Netherley 4734), whom Mrs Lewis bought from Miss Ritchie. Mighty Fine was also a family favourite, and was used at Normandykes

Mrs Roweena Provan's Waulkmill Fetlar, the first pony to bear the Waulkmill prefix.

to pull sledges and lawn-mowers, and he too, was successful in the show ring, winning at the Royal Highland.

The first foal produced with the Waulkmill prefix was Waulkmill Fetlar, by Normandykes Feochan 1822 (Slacks Mighty Fine1631/Foula of Normandykes 5300) and out of Eilean of Normandykes 5805, who was one of the original Normandykes fillies. Eilean of Normandykes was then put to Normandykes Aith, to produce Waulkmill MacDuff 2540, who was to become a very handsome stallion. MacDuff sired Leo of Wilverley 3480 (out of Berrystead Saturn 1213B), who was the sire of the outstanding stallion, Waulkmill Maclaren 3982. Maclaren was the Supreme Champion at the Shetland Breed Show in 1995 – the first Scottish-based winner of the top award since 1982. Maclaren's dam was Tanira of Waulkmill, whose dam, Eilean Tigh of Waulkmill, was out of Eileen of Normandykes and by Normandykes Aith.

Maclaren (seen on the front cover), although shown lightly, has an impressive list of championships. He won the 3-year-old class at the Centenary Show, and was reserve junior champion; he was supreme champion of all breeds at the Angus show in the same year, first and reserve champion at Glasgow, also at Ayr, and at Fife was reserve cham-

pion Mountain and Moorland, and came second at the Royal Highland. He was only shown twice in 1991, and won the stallion class at
Glasgow and the Great Yorkshire. He was not shown in 1992, but in
1993 was champion at Ayr, won at the Great Yorkshire, and was first
and reserve champion at the National Pony Society Centenary Show
at Malvern. In 1995, in addition to being Supreme at the breed show,
Maclaren was champion at the Shetland Central Scotland Group show.

In the early days of the Waulkmill stud, in the 1960s, the vogue was
for the heavier type of pony. But Mrs Provan, as her young family
began to ride her ponies, wanted to breed an animal that moved more
freely and had a higher head carriage. To do this, she bought a stallion,
Blackhall Andy 2057 (by Rustler of Markinch 1717 out of Blackhall
Beauty 5601), who was a little light of bone, but had a lovely head
carriage, good hair, and a good, small head. He produced the type of
pony that was needed – slightly lighter, but with the good action and
the higher head carriage that enabled them to carry themselves well.

Mrs Provan has used other outside blood from stallions such as
Rosethorn of Transy 1750, who sired Fern of Waulkmill 12259 (ex Fastnet
of Normandykes 10858 by Normandykes Aith), who won a great deal
under saddle, including the Ridden Shetland class at the Royal Highland. The only mare that had been brought into the stud was Jolly of
Marshwood 9402, who was a bay of great quality. She was used by
Mrs Provan to prove that quality coloured ponies (against whom there
was prejudice at that time) could win against the dominant blacks.

A number of ponies from Waulkmill have been exported to Europe.
One of the first colts to go to Poland for a very long time was Waulkmill
McPhee 4302, by Leo of Wilverley, while Waulkmill MacKay (by
Maclaren) went to Finland. Waulkmill Macallan, also by Maclaren, is in
Denmark, as is Waulkmill Fyn (Leo of Wilverley/Waulkmill Fern) and
the colt, Waulkmill MacFeochan (Waulkmill Maclaren /Waulkmill Fern).

BIRLING

One of the studs founded in the post-war years was the Birling, in
Suffolk, owned by the artist, Lionel Hamilton Renwick. He and his
sisters had, before World War II, owned a little South Park mare. She
stood 34 inches (86 cm), was a great character, and liked to lie down in
puddles and in nettle beds. After her demise, as a result of severe laminitis, another South Park pony arrived, and just before the war, the
Hamilton Renwicks were given a pair of blue roans, also from South
Park. They were Firebrand 1579, who was by Cherubino 1363 (by Fairy
Light 1259 out of Chocolate Cream 4589) and out of Faery Firefly 4720
(by Silver Fox 1269 out of Fleurette 4650) and Fireaway 1921 (Cherubino

Mr Lionel Hamilton Renwick's stallion, Fandango of Wetherden 2424.

1363/Fly Away 4785). When war broke out, the pair went back to South Park, and were subsequently sold to a Mr Cavill from Bristol, who provided ponies for pantomimes, and they duly appeared on the stage.

After the war, Mr Hamilton Renwick started to build up one of the first of the post-war studs to specialise in small ponies of 34 inches (86 cm) and under. He went to visit Mr and Mrs Gosling at Wetherden, in Suffolk, and although the Goslings primarily bred standard blacks, they had a few small coloured ones. Among them was the yearling colt, Fandango of Wetherden 2424 (Spinner of Marshwood 1998/Fallacy of Wetherden 5866), who had a significant amount of South Park breeding. He was bought, and his new owner was so impressed that he decided to find a mare of the same breeding as Firebrand and Fireaway, to run with him. For this, he returned to South Park, now owned by Lady Joan Gore-Langton, and bought Becky Sharpe 7210 (Fireproof of Marshwood 1792/Ballare 6354).

Becky Sharpe was joined by the palomino yearling filly, Longmead Glamour Girl 8073 (Ardmair Lightening 2005/Longmead Golden Glamour 6394), bought at Reading Sale, and, following a trip to Devon, Longmead Golden Glamour herself, a 31 inch (79 cm) chestnut, with a light mane and tail. The foundation stock of the stud was completed with the purchase from the Wetherden stud of Fandango's dam, Fallacy of Wetherden 5866, by the 28 inch (71 cm) South Park stallion, Vero 1746 (by Fairy Fly 1537).

That Mr Hamilton Renwick's choice was astute is confirmed by the fact that five of Fallacy's sons have become good stallions, and that the 31 inch (79 cm) Fandango had a great show record, winning in classes for standard ponies, as well as those for the 34 inches (86 cm) and under. At Essex County, he took the breed championship and went on to be reserve Mountain and Moorland champion, beaten by a Dartmoor 'under which', as his owner remarked, 'he could easily have walked.'

In recent years, the stud has introduced a stallion unrelated to Fandango – the grey Birling Grey Mirage, 4211 by Hippominimus Peter Pan 3304/Kington Parsley 1510B. Grey Mirage's half-brother, Birling Snow Knight, is doing very well in Holland. A son of Fandango, Birling Snow Knight (out of Longmead Glamour Girl), is also being used to produce palominos. Sadly, Fandango has just died at the age of 25, and is much missed.

Birling ponies have been exported all over the world – to the Sheik of Abu Dhabi, to Holland, Barbados, the USA, France, Holland and to the King of Morocco, as well as being the basis of a number of studs in this country that breed small ponies.

BINCOMBE

One of the most successful studs in the south of England over recent years is Caroline and Edward House's Bincombe stud near Nether Stowey in Somerset. This was founded in 1967, with Ickworth Countess 81st 5418 (Border Chief 1474/Ickworth Countess 51st 4964), bought from Major Hambro. A daughter of hers is still in the stud. The mare was sent to stud, but this proved unsatisfactory, so the Houses decided to have a stallion of their own. They answered an advertisement by Miss Ritchie of the Netherley Stud in *Horse & Hound*, and this resulted in the purchase of the foal, Philistine of Netherley 2427, for just £50. He has proved the most wonderful bargain.

Following the death, foaling, of Ickworth Countess, the 2-year-old filly, Braes of Greenock Vanessa (Braes of Greenock Bonny Boy 1531/Braes of Greenock Vimiera 5109) was bought for 100 guineas at the 1970 Reading Sales. In due course, Vanessa was put to Philistine, and these two bargain buys have produced one of the most impressive series of ponies to be shown in England and Wales in the last twenty years. The stallions Vanguard 2743 and Venture 2839, and the mares Velvet 11472 and Victoria have all made their names. Bincombe Venture is the only Shetland to have qualified for the Lloyds (the Supreme

Mr and Mrs House's champion stallion Bincombe Venture.

in-hand championship at London's Horse of the Year show, for which finalists qualify from a range of prestigious shows), and he did it twice, in 1980 and 1982. He also won the Mountain and Moorland championship at Royal Windsor in 1980, the Royal Welsh on a number of occasions, the Supreme Mountain and Moorland stallion championship at the National Pony Society's annual show, and the New Forest Show Mountain and Moorland supreme championship. Bincombe Velvet and Bincombe Victoria qualified for the National Pony Society's Ridden Mountain and Moorland championship at Olympia, although, sadly, Victoria died before she was able to compete. Philistine sired a third Olympia qualifier, Bincombe Pearl.

Philistine, at 26, although retired from stud duties, can and does gallop around the field like a 2-year-old. Venture is still doing well, and Vanguard (who is now in France) left his son Pebble 3191 (out of Donnachaidh Penelope 6391). Pebble's son Peat AA0975, won at the Royal Welsh in 1994.

HOSE

A stud based principally on Wells blood is the Hose, founded in 1970 by Mr and Mrs Jack Stevenson, and their daughter-in-law, Mrs Jill Stevenson. The late Mr Stevenson was President of the Stud Book Society in 1983-84. This Leicestershire-based stud concentrates on black ponies (although they did have coloureds at one time) in the height range 38-41 inches (96-104 cm).

The stud began with a with a chestnut colt, belonging to Mrs Jack Stevenson, Sysonby Thunder 2601 (Slacks Thunderflash 1674/Slacks Shelagh 5695), who was joined by three mares bought at Reading – Merit of Netherley 5542 (Harviestoun Pippin 1417/Madcap of Netherley 4898), Wells Vanity 5935 (Wells Superb 1721/Wells Vasha 5480) and Wells Elsa 7383 (Wells Supreme 1882/Wells Esta 5817). One of the most important subsequent purchases was Wells Vanda 9732 (Wells Three Star 1598/Wells Vanity 5935), who was in foal to Wells Manifesto 2356 (Wells Superb 1721/Wells Esta 5817). The foal, born in 1976, was Hose Vanesto 3095, and he has proved to be one of the most influential stallions, with a significant percentage of the Hose ponies tracing back to him, including the stallions Hose Personality 3376 (out of Hose Pandora 10907), Hose Elevator 3738 (out of Wells Elsa) and Hose Marshall 3492 (out of Hose Millie 11637).

A particularly successful Hose line is the 'E', by Hose Vanesto out of Hose Elation 13588, who was Wells Elsa's first foal (by Wells Super Star 3093). The 'E' line ponies were the mares Ella AB1494, Elan AA1941, Element 16572 and the colt Hose Ebony AC2648, now three and just licensed as a stallion. The stud has recently introduced a Transy stallion, Rosdon of Transy AA2057 (Rosemalin of Transy 3243/Rosdart of Transy 12094), and his first foal, the filly Hose Elaine, out of Hose Eline (Hose Vanesto/Hose Elsa), looks very promising. Rosdon was bought because he is from the famous Transy 'R' line, and because the Stevensons did not want their ponies to get any bigger or stronger.

The Hose stud has had many show successes over the years. The highlight has been winning the Supreme Championship at the Breed show in successive years with Hose Element as a 2- and 3-three-year old. The Royal Highland has proved a successful venue for the stud, while in 1994, Hose Elan AA1941 (Hose Vanesto/Hose Elation) was champion filly at the Royal of England, and Hose Peonie 13925 (Hose Vanesto 3095/Hose Pandora 10907) also won in the brood mare class.

Hose ponies are doing well for other exhibitors, with Mr and Mrs Robert Irwin's stallion, Hose Reynard 4146, yet another son of Hose Vanesto, and out of Wells Virol, winning extensively.

ULVERSCROFT

Mrs Pat Renwick's Ulverscroft Stud in Leicestershire is noted for its production of performance ponies, although as she says, 'I don't think there should be a difference between the ridden and the in-hand ponies, but there is, and if we're not careful we'll end up having a "sports Shetland" (as in some European countries), and another Shetland.' The stud was founded over twenty years ago, with ponies from Mrs Grasby's Ashorne Stud, from Mrs Knight's Lockinge stud, and some mares and the stallion, Ebony Rhu 2200 (Rosewall of Transy 1852/ Harviestoun Runach 5298), from Mrs Greaves' stud in Scotland. From the start, Mrs Renwick looked for ponies that could move, and with this in mind, she used Mrs Shearer's Newtown Cloud 2123 (Pegasus 1420/Newtown Coral 4983), who was a little more 'on the leg' than some of the others, on the Ebony mares.

In the early seventies, when her daughter, Emma Leivers, had been riding the ponies for some time, Mrs Renwick went to Shetland for the first time, and what she saw was a revelation. 'I saw that most of the ponies moved well, but the larger ponies – up to 42 inches (107 cm) – they *really* could move; they covered the ground, and they went across ditches so easily. I also realised that it was possible to lengthen the stride, which would give better performance ponies. Also, I was becoming interested in Working Hunter classes, and if you're going to jump a Shetland, you need a larger pony with a good pair of hind legs and a good second thigh – because at that time they were expected to jump 2 ft 9 inches.'

So a number of the larger ponies from the islands were brought down to Ulverscroft with the aim of increasing the length of stride of her stock, but also to help preserve some of the rarer bloodlines. Among more recent island-bred stallions are two sons of Hope of Housabister 2364 (Fireball of Marshwood 1686/Helen of Housabister 316B), one of whom is the 42 inch (107 cm), Terrick of Waterloo 3968, out of Twinkle of Waterloo 12136, and others with Mousa blood. Most of the stock, however, trace back to Transy and Harviestoun.

There are, in the 1995 edition of the Shetland Pony Stud Book Society's magazine, in excess of 150 advertisements for studs. Clearly, it is possible to mention only a few. Some that have played a role in the history of the breed, and have not been mentioned elsewhere include Mrs Caroline Berry's **Firth** stud of small ponies; the Duchess of Devonshire's **Chatsworth** stud; Mrs Hester Knight's **Lockinge** Stud; Mr and Mrs Gosling's **Wetherden** Stud, which not only did well in Britain, but has played an important part in the breed in Australia and New Zealand; Mrs Edwards' **Knock** Stud in Cumbria, founded on Marshwood lines, and which has produced some top class ponies, including Knock Jessamine, Supreme Champion at the Breed Show in 1986, and Knock Good Luck (Surety of Marshwood/Knock Good Fortune), Supreme champion at the Breed Show in 1989; Mr and Mrs Tindale's **Abbeyfield** stud, founded on Mrs Knight's Lockinge bloodlines; Mr Ian Thomson's **Drum** Stud in Aberdeenshire and Mrs Lory's **Southley** and **Trevassack** studs.

THE ISLAND STUDS

As mentioned briefly in Chapter 4, a number of important studs had been founded in Shetland prior to those of Lord Londonderry. One of the most influential was that of the Mr Alexander **Sandison**, one of the original Stud Book Society Council members. Mr Sandison, whose stud was at Uyeasound on Unst, registered more than fifty ponies in Volume 1 of the Stud Book. From this is may be inferred that his stock had some considerable influence on breeding in Unst, and, as a number of ponies were exported to mainland Britain as foundation stock for the newer breeders (including Mr R.W.R MacKenzie), the stud was significant in the breed as a whole. As Mr Sandison used home-bred and island-bred stallions almost exclusively, they would have been a useful variation from Londonderry blood, little, if any, of which was used by him. The most important stallion was Blackie, a 42 inch (107 cm) pony foaled in

Ponies on Mousa Island.

1882, and subsequently registered in the Stud Book as Number 87, and described as being sired by a 'pure 39 inch (99 cm) Shetland stallion'. Blackie sired several good stallions, including Nestor 29, Norseman 31, and Triptolemus 45. The 39 inch (99 cm) St John and the skewbald Cardinal also stood at Uyeasound. The latter followed the trend of colours other than black at the stud, with a number of creams, whites and duns being registered. The stud was dispersed in the 1920s, but was re-started at Houlland in Unst by Mr Sandison's son, Ian.

A stud which came to be more closely associated with the Londonderry ponies was that of Mr Anderson **Manson**, a member of the original Stud Book Society council. The stud started life at Laxfirth on Mainland – but, following the departure of the Londonderry ponies, it moved to Maryfield Farm on Bressay, remaining there until 1936, when it was dispersed by Peter Manson, son of the founder, who previously had ponies at Lunna on Mainland.

Alexander Manson's ponies figured prominently in Volume 1 of the Stud Book, with 2 stallions (both bred by Alexander Sandison), and 46 mares being registered. Most of his ponies prior to 1899 were home-bred, but he attended the Londonderry dispersal sale, where he bought 5 ponies; these, together with the home-bred 35 inch (89 cm) black stallion Chacma 290 (by Thor 83 out of Bronte 1277 by Laird of Noss 20), foaled in 1900, ensured that the stud, from that time onwards, contained a large amount of Londonderry blood. Among the ponies bought at the dispersal was the stallion Sigurd 137 (by Lord of the Isles 26 out of Swertha 211 by Odin 32); a filly foal by Sigurd, and out of a Laird of Noss mare); the black mare Dollie II (by Lord of the Isles out of Dixie 664 by Odin) and the mare, Bronte 1277 (by Laird of Noss out of Beauty 167). Other successful sires were the home-bred Diamond Star 697 (a great-grandson of Odin on his sire's side and a grandson on his dam's), his son, Pole Star 884, and his grandson, Bright Star of Maryfield 1045 (out of Wallflower 3573). The Londonderry bloodlines were reinforced in 1912, by the purchase of the stallion Transy Superior 577, from Mr Mungall. Superior was by Hector 183 (by Laird of Noss out of Hilda 190, a daughter of Odin) and out of Sovereign 1730, also by Odin. Superior appears many times in Maryfield pedigrees, especially through his son, Coram 810, who was out of a Chacma mare, Rosealie 2498.

Mr John **Bruce** of Sumburgh established three separate studs during the middle years of the 19th century – on Mousa, a small island off the east of Mainland north of Sumburgh, at Sumburgh, and on Fair Isle. One of the Sumburgh-bred stallions, the 36 inch (91 cm) Lion 22, has already been mentioned. Most of the Sumburgh and Mousa ponies were, as far back as 1880, of the smaller size, around 32 and 33 inches. Exceptions were the 37 inch (94 cm) stallions, Corporal 112 and Captain 70, with Londonderry blood on the side of their sire, Vane Tempest 47, who was by Prince of Thule. The studs were, according to Cox, primarily commercial concerns, with ponies being exported to America. By 1927 most of the ponies had been sold, but the stud on Mousa was re-established by Mr Robert H. W. Bruce of Sand Lodge after World War II, only to be dispersed again in 1983.

Some of the Mousa ponies figure prominently in the present day very successful **Grutness** Stud belonging to Mrs Myrna Flaws of Grutness House, Virkie, Sumburgh, and some went out to 'Shetland Heights' in Australia.

One of the studs established in Shetland during the last century after the founding of the Londonderry stud was that of Mr H. F. Anderton of Vaila, a small island lying off Walls on Mainland. Mr Anderton bought three in-foal mares from the Londonderry stud in 1897, and bought three more mares from the dispersal sale. The latter included Empress II 1417, a 36 inch (91 cm) black mare by Odin out of Edith 1110 (by Prince of Thule), and Highland Mary 1359, a 4-year-old by Thor out of Hilda 190 by Odin, who was a first prize winner at Lerwick in 1897 and 2nd at the Highland Shetland classes in 1897. His best known stallion was Duncan 147, sire of Haldor 270. The stud was sold up in about 1926.

BERRY

The Berry Stud, owned by sister and brother Eva and Jim Smith, is in two parts. The coloured section of small ponies is managed by Jim Smith at the family farm near Scalloway in Shetland, while the bigger ones, which were originally all black, belonging to Eva Smith, are now at Pitmedden near Aberdeen in Scotland.

The Smiths grew up with ponies. Their father, John 'Sheepie' Smith, was a well known and influential livestock dealer, who, at one time, it is said, dealt with nearly half the livestock sales in the islands. There were often 100 or more ponies at Berry. Jim Smith has a fund of stories about catching up the ponies for sale when he was a young man. He recalled one day spent trying to catch about a dozen ponies that were out on a hill. 'We got there early in the morning,' he said, 'and we tried to drive these ponies. They'd never been handled, and they were leaping over the fences like greyhounds. We went round and round after them – and we could run in those days! One of us would run with them for, say, half a mile, then another would take over.

'On another occasion, two of us went to catch a four-year-old stallion – and he'd never been handled either. We took a long rope, and thought all we'd need to do was to get him in a corner. The old man that owned him – he was in the field there, with his coat and hat on, and a stick – and we told him to get out of the field in case he got caught with the rope, but he wouldn't. And right enough, we'd almost got the horse in the corner, when he took off, and went right through the rope. The rope took the old man at the back of the knees, and he did a complete back somersault, and landed on his feet. He went home after that – and we caught the horse!'

The basis of the Berry stud, just after World War II, was three top quality piebald Shetland-bred mares, which were eventually inspected and registered as Berry Countess, Berry Queen and Berry Duchess. All were about 36 inches (91 cm), but from time to time, they would produce a foal that developed into a much smaller pony. To add to this, Jim had a mare that abandoned its filly foal, and that foal, Poppet of Berry 5730, was the real basis of the small ponies in which Jim Smith now specialises. Poppet, by Vane of Berry 1766 out of Rose of Berry 5154, although 36 inches (91 cm), produced the stallion, Patch of Berry 1933, who was just 32½ inches (83 cm). Patch's sire was the 37 inch (94 cm) Nord of Houlland 1834, whose dam, Nutkin 5947, was 34 inches (86 cm). Patch was kept, together with the grey mare, Yo Yo of Berry 6076 (Terry of Berry 1767/Coreen of Berry 95B) and together they have produced many small foals of excellent quality which were retained, so they have been of great importance to the stud.

The Berry stud began producing small ponies long before the present fashion. Jim Smith explained that he had a deliberate policy of breeding down, gradually, and only if the ponies were good enough. They had to be the best and the smallest. So successful has he been that the Berry name appears in the pedigrees of many of the small ponies in the south of Britain. Among those sold on were Speckle of Berry (Bon Bon of Berry 2692/Coreen of Berry) and Recovery of Berry. Other stallions used on the stud have included the 39 inch (99 cm) piebald, Airborne 1426, the piebald Norseman 1448 (Berlad of Transy 1335/ Ireta of Longhaugh 4837), the 33 inch (84 cm) skewbald, Wells Rainbow 1550 (bred by Mrs Atkinson, by Flamenco of Felbridge 1404/Ruby of Felbridge 4839), the 40 inch (101 cm) grey Polydor of Holne 1421 (Knave of Holne 1313) and the 38 inch (96 cm) skewbald, Terry of Berry 1767(Wells Rainbow 1550/Twinkle of Berry 5209).

The black section of the stud began when the brother and sister were given a Maryfield stallion by Mr Alex. 'Bankie' Davidson of Mundurno in Aberdeenshire. Mr Davidson sold many ponies for the coal mines, and when the Maryfield ponies were dispersed, he bought a large number. The stallion was Mundurno Banker 1430, by Birk of Manar 1301 a son of Rambler of Maryfield 1279, who traced back to Pole Star, and out of Thora of Maryfield 4228 (by Coram 810, a grandson of Hector 183, out of Savona 3112, who was by Erling), and out of Erling's daughter, Savona 3112. At the same time, the brother and sister were given four Mundurno mares by their father, who at one time rented the Maryfield farm on Bressay. These were Valetta of Mundurno 4916 (Birk of Manar 1301/Valetta of Maryfield 4482); Thora of Mundurno 4770 (Birk of Manar 1301/Thora of Maryfield); Lucky Girl of Mundurno 4914 (by Silver Prince of Mundurno 1402, a son of Birk of Manar, and out of Lucky Lass of Mundurno 4765, whose parents were Birk of Manar/ Pandora of Maryfield 4445); and Golden Girl of Mundurno 4913, also by Silver Prince of Mundurno, and out of Golden Wing of Mundurno 4763, who was by Bright Star of Maryfield 1045. The Aber-

The Burgess family's Robin's Brae Jess 2042 I.S., with her twin foals, Robin's Brae Pride 2124 and Robin's Brae Joy 2125.

deenshire ponies remained exclusively black until the introduction of the piebald Airborne, who was in Shetland for a number of years, before going to Mrs Lewis of the Normandykes stud in exchange for Mighty Fine of Netherley.

Other well known studs in the islands include that of Mr Tom Burgess of **Quendale**, Dunrossness, which was dispersed in 1994, and Mr Brian Hunter's stud at Uyeasound in Unst. The Nicolson brothers' stud at **Brindister**, founded in 1966, has bred some very good smaller ponies using the 32 inch (81 cm) Sonny Boy of Tangwick 2453 (Fireball of Marshwood 1686/Baby Toddles 66B), and his 31 inch (79 cm) son, Swarthoull Virna, and the 32 inch (81 cm) So Bo of Berry 3559 (Patch of Berry/Yo Yo of Berry).

Mrs Lorna Burgess's grandfather, Mr Alex. Irvine, had ponies registered in the Stud Book in 1910 under the prefix 'Vatchley'. Mrs Burgess has bred some good performance ponies bearing her prefix **Robin's Brae**. The stud had the distinction, in 1968, of producing one of the only three known sets of twin foals in the breed (the others being twin colts bred by the Coxes of Marshwood, and unregistered twins from a Mousa mare). Robin's Brae Jess 2043 I.S. was due to foal, and Mrs Burgess described what happened. 'My father and I had been watching her, I can remember my father looking out of the window and calling, "I think we'd better go out. It looks as if she's had a foal, and there are more legs than there should be." When we went out, we found there were *two* foals; we checked to see if another mare had foaled at the same time – but no, they were twin fillies, and we called them Robin's Brae Pride 2124 and Robin's Brae Joy 2125.'

Clothie

Mrs Marie Brooker had always been interested in Shetlands, but did not have the opportunity of owning any until she and her doctor husband moved to the islands. Before founding her stud on her Clothie croft at Levenwick, she visited a number of leading studs such as Lockinge, Transy, Normandykes and Marshwood. Her first two ponies were bought at the islands sales. They were the Mousa stallion, Pan of Mousa 2092 (by Eschonshan Bacchus), and the Marshwood filly, Penny of Dandies 6797 (by Sparkler of Marshwood 1434), and a Marshwood line has been maintained in the stud down to the present day. The first foal by Pan out of Dandy was Clothie Aster, who is still going strong at the age of 27. Mrs Brooker then bought the grey Fetlarbred stallion, Star of North Dale 2390, who was out of a grey mare, and goes back to Thunder of Marshwood 1525 through his sire, Noggin of Luckdon 1698 (out of Mystic of Netherley 5028).

Mrs Brooker decided in the 70s to breed blue roans, of which there were very few at that time. She bought, as an old mare, the blue roan, Bluebell of Bothen (1234 IS), and the blue roan stallion, Lockinge Macaroon 2064 (by the blue roan Firedust of Marshwood 1769 out of the grey Lockinge Eclair 5902). Macaroon was the sire of most of the stud's blue roans, out of the red roan mare, Clothie Flobell 1517B.

At about the same time she made the conscious decision not to breed small ponies, but to go for animals between 37 and 41 inches (94 - 104 cm), that could be used. That policy has been oustandingly successful, for not only have Clothie ponies done well in-hand, they have done exceptionally well in all kinds of performance classes. For example, Clothie Eswick, a son of Bluebell of Bothen, and by Beburu of Kirkholm, has represented the breed in the National Pony Society Ridden Mountain and Moorland Championship at Olympia, as well as competing in the famous Shetland Grand National. Mrs Brooker, a very keen and skilful whip, has driven her well known home-bred pair, Clothie Gluss 333G and Clothie Gloup 334G, to many successes, including the best driven pair award in the Performance Scheme, and winning in open driving classes against horses. Star of North Dale has won the best driven stallion in the Performance Awards. Her enthusiasm is unbounded, and she and her ponies have been closely involved in teaching a number of youngsters to drive, both in Shetland and in Aberdeenshire. Two of her students, Philippa Dobson and Elinor Bosenquet, have gone on to win major scholarships. An account of a marvellous drive through Shetland in 1989 led by Mrs Brooker is told elsewhere (see page 126).

The present stallions now based at Cothal, in Aberdeenshire, are Star of North Dale, Leo of Wilverley 3480 and Clothie Orchard 3791 (the later two both tracing back to the Bluebell of Bothen line and thus to Marshwood), and Clothie Inchture 4402, who is out of a Waulkmill mare and by a Transy stallion.

GRUTNESS

One of the most successful present-day studs in the islands is Grutness, belonging to Mrs Myrna Flaws of Sumburgh. Ponies from Grutness do very well in the local shows, and a number have been exported to Europe. The stud, which is close to Sumburgh Airport, was founded by Mrs Flaws' father, Mr Jim Black, in 1969, when he bought a bay and white Fetlar-bred pony, Nell of Aith 333B (Nero of Houlland 1590/ Rosa, an inspected mare) bred by John Laurenson. She was followed by the Unst-bred piebald, Nancy of Crosbister 575B (Nero of Houlland 1590/Nellie of Crosbister 1395 IS) and Violet of Burragarth (Trigger of Bardister 1703/Vesta of Burragarth 2203B). He then bought the chest-

Ponies at the Grutness and Laaward studs at Sumburgh, owned by Mrs Myrna Flaws and her daughter, Sonya: Rena of Knowle and Laaward Twyla.

nut colt, Craigie Sixpence 2503 (Thor of Berry 1832/Craigie Trudy 299B) and the filly, Donside Mina 1082B (Coolhurst Gary 1868/Donside Myrtle 2064 IS), an inspected mare.

Mr Black's most important purchase was, however, the Mousa filly, Wilful of Mousa 7485 (by Harold of Mousa 1687 out of Peerie Yin of Mousa 6113). Harold was bred by Mr R.H.W. Bruce, and is by the Cox-bred Sparkler of Marshwood 1434 out of Frolic of Mousa 5224. Sparkler traces back to Fairy Lamp 985, bred at South Park, by Electric Light 650, who was by Thoreau 392. Foaled in 1969, Wilful is regarded as the real foundation mare of the Grutness ponies, and the founder of its principal Mousa line. The present black ponies are nearly all from her. There are a number of features of the Mousa ponies that Mrs Flaws likes – they move well, they have plenty of bone and substance, good proportions and lots of spirit. For a number of years, the senior stallion on Mousa was Eschonchan Bacchus 1730, bred by Miss S.E. Ferguson. Bacchus, a 39 inch (99 cm) black, combined Harviestoun, Transy and Marshwood lines, being by Harviestoun Rusko 1560, who traced back through Harviestoun Pat 1416 to Dollar Boy 1242, and out of Boadicea of Marshwood 5074, who was by Sophimore of Transy 1323 by Sonyad of Transy 1105 by Seaweed 333. Mrs Flaws bought his son, Majestic of Quendale 3619 (ex Lyra of Haybrake 8425), and after some years in the stud, he is being exported to Denmark. When the Bruces sold up on Mousa, Bacchus went to the Quendale Stud, and Mrs Flaws was able to send Wilful to him, and she produced a number of his foals over the years.

Bacchus, by this time, was getting old, and Mrs Flaws decided she would like another stallion to carry on when he was no longer available. For some time she had had her eye on another of Bacchus' sons, Noggin of Quendale 3685 (ex Borage of Mousa 9380). She liked the way he moved, and although he was a bit bigger than her normal height range of 36-37½ inches (91-95 cm), she bought him, and he has proved an outstanding sire.

In 1987, Mrs Flaws bought a number of colt foals for a buyer in Scotland. After the sales, when she had a closer look at them she decided to keep one – a grey colt, Zeal of Houlland 3979. Zeal is by Sprite of Berry 3271 out of Gillian of Houlland 8271, so an out-cross from the Mousa lines, and he is now running with the Mousa mares, and throwing some really fine stock.

There is a second Mousa line at Grutness, represented by the 13-year-old mare, Lena of Quendale 12791, who is by Bacchus, but out of Alison of Mousa 9848. Lena's 2-year-old black and white son, Viscount of Grutness, by Zeal of Houlland, is also on the stud, and has passed his stallion assessment. Lena has done exceptionally well in the show ring, winning at the prestigious Cunningsborough show for 6 or 7 years, and Viscount has won each time he has been shown, including taking the Junior Championship at Cunningsborough.

Also at Grutness is Gletness Jenny Wren 7872, a dun with an eel stripe. She was Mrs Betty Cox's breeding, by Superstition of Marshwood 1850 out of Gletness Winkle 6556. Her daughter, Toffee of Grutness 16632, by Majestic, is also dun with an eel stripe. The dun is believed to have come from the stallion, Robin 1607, who was on the scattald (see page 145). Toffee's chestnut foal, Xcalibur of Grutness, by Starfire of Berry (Veister of Berry 1932/Liz of Berry 5936), won at Lerwick Sale in 1994, and was bought by a Norwegian breeder. An interesting sidelight concerning Gletness Jenny Wren is that she was the foal being born in one of the delightful and interesting films made by Mrs Jenny Gilbertson (mother of Mrs Helen Thomson) about many aspects of the Shetland Islands, including, of course, the ponies. 'The Shetland Pony' was produced in 1960, and 'The Peerie Horses of Shetland' in 1980. Mrs Flaws is thinking about increasing the height of her ponies, and in view of the preponderance of very small animals in Shetland, this would be an excellent move for the breed as a whole.

7

FROM PEAT-FLITTING TO STEEPLE-CHASING - *uses down the years*

◆

'Useless little things – no good to anybody'. How often, over the years, have Shetland enthusiasts fumed at the staggering ignorance of such comments! Ask a descendant of the Shetland crofters whose livelihoods depended on the usefulness of the ponies; ask the pit owners and miners who relied on the strength and willingness of pit ponies; ask the Dutch small farmers who turned to Shetlands when the use of dogs for pulling small carts and agricultural implements was banned! None would have dismissed Shetland ponies in so cavalier a fashion. Now that the ponies are no longer used in a commercial capacity, just look at the pleasure they have given and continue to give to innumerable children and adults all over the world in an astonishing range of roles.

The importance of the ponies as the sole means travelling from place to place in their native islands before the building of roads has already been described. Of no less importance to the crofters was the work done by countless thousands of ponies down the ages in transporting peat – the traditional and, until modern times, the sole source of fuel for cooking and heating in Shetland.

Much of Shetland is covered, under the moorland vegetation, by thick layers of peat. The crofters had rights to dig this peat from certain areas, known as the peat banks, which were sometimes 2 to 2 ½ miles from their crofts.

The peats, each measuring about 10 inches by 6 inches by 4 inches, were dug with special tools, and left to dry. By the beginning of the July, weather permitting, the peats were ready to be carried by the ponies from the banks down to the crofts – the process known as 'flitting (or flittin') the peats'. Only mares were used, and they were brought down from the scattald for the duration of flitting, and tethered 'in-by', close to the croft. Those that had foals were tethered by the foot, just above the fetlock, so that the foal did not get caught up in the rope. The tether was usually about 20-30 feet long.

Flitting usually involved the whole family, including the children, who were on holiday from school. Although it was very hard work for crofters and ponies alike, there was often something of a holiday atmosphere, especially if the weather was good. To quote a well known Fetlar crofter, the late James (Jamesie) L. Laurenson, in a series of interviews in the local dialect given to Robert L. Johnson in 1982, 'It wis a kind of a jolly life, it wis, not altagidder, but they lookit upon it as a kind of a herty business … Lightsome, lightsome'.

Flitting started very early in the morning, any time between 2 and 4 or 4.30. The 'simmer dim' – the nights that never really get dark in these northern isles – enabled work to start early, so as to finish early before the heat of the early afternoon affected the ponies.

The first task in the morning was to put the 'bend' on the pony. This was the special tack used for carrying the peats, and it was all hand-made by the men during the long, dark, winter evenings. It consisted of a 'flakkie' or pad, traditionally made of woven Shetland oat straw, but in the later days it might be a folded jute feedstuff sack. This was placed on the back, and on it was placed a pack saddle called the 'klibber', made of two flat wooden boards (da klibberbrods), to which were attached two projecting horns or 'nugs', the top of which were shaped into inverted hooks. One nug was thicker, and had a slot through which the smaller one was passed, and the two nugs were secured, where the one passed through the other, by a wooden pin called a 'varnagl'. This allowed a certain amount of pivoting movement so that the klibberbrods could be adjusted to fit the pony's back comfortably. The klibbers were also hand-made, using drift wood, as the only timber on the treeless islands was imported and expensive. The flat boards were usually of soft wood, but the horns needed to be hard wood, as they bore the strain of the load. Although the klibbers were not always made to fit an individual pony, when one was found that fitted well, the pony's name was written in pencil on the klibberbrod. It is quite touching, almost fifty years after flitting with ponies ceased, to see the name of a pony long gone, pencilled on klibbers that people have kept. From the lower edge of each klibberbrod was attached a rope loop or quintek, to which the jute girth (winegirt or warnegirt) was tied. This was fastened by a special locking knot, and, needless to say, the ponies often blew themselves out as this was being

The late James (Jamesie) Laurenson of Fetlar, with pony and cart.

Present-day pony showing peat-flitting tack of flakkie and klibber.

tightened, and it had to be checked for slackness after they had gone some distance. To prevent the klibber slipping forward, a special crupper or 'tailgirt', also made of jute, led from the klibber under the tail.

The next items to be attached were the meshies or maishies – large mesh nets made from bent (tough grasses) or floss (rushes). These were hooked on to the horns of the klibber, one on each side, and initially left hanging down. Next came the 'rivakeshies' or 'kishies' (the names vary slightly from district to district). The rivakeshies were flexible baskets into which the peats were packed. They were made of the same material as the maishies, and had handles top and bottom to help with emptying out the peats. The rivakeshies were hooked on, one each side, and, finally, the bottom of the maishie that had been left loose was picked up, brought up over the rivakeshie and tied to the horns of the klibber by an attached 'fettle' or rope.

Flitting with ponies finally stopped in the 1950s, so there are people in Shetland who not only remember it, but actually worked as peat

Peat ponies coming down from the peat banks at Lambhoga on Fetlar (note the fineness of the limbs).

boys or girls – leading the ponies up and down to the peat banks. Two of the former peat boys, Tony Priest and Willie Spence, both living on Unst, emphasised the care taken with the ponies. They explained that it was necessary to pack underneath the front of the klibber with moss or heather to stop it rubbing the withers and shoulders, and how the tailgirt was wrapped in cotton sheeting or sacking to prevent rubbing, and, if this did occur, how they treated the rub with vaseline. 'Everyone was extremely careful with the ponies,' explained Tony Priest. 'The ponies had to work, and they were your strength, and you looked after them very, very carefully.'

When all the ponies were ready, they set off for the peat banks, often involving a walk of an hour or more. They followed the well worn tracks ('gaets') that wound up the hill. If a new track was used, the ponies would walk with their noses to the ground, sniffing carefully to avoid the soft and boggy areas. Many of these tracks can be seen to this day, gouged deep into the hillside by the passage of hundreds of thousands of hooves over the centuries. I followed one of the best known of the paths to the peat banks of the Lambhoga Peninsula on

Fetlar, and in the gathering dusk of a misty autumn day, such was the atmosphere of that remote place that I half expected to meet strings of ponies wending their way down with their loads.

But on a lovely summer's day, what a delightful sight it must have been, as the mares, with their foals running loose by their sides, made their way up the well worn tracks. On a long walk, foals often tired, and lay down among the heather for a sleep, re-joining their dams as they made their return journey. But, of course, the weather was not always good. Sometimes the tracks became so slippery that work had to be abandoned. Even if that was not necessary, the rain tended to shrink the woven gear. The girths then had to be let out, and when they began to dry they had to be tightened again, as did the 'fettles' securing the maishies and rivaskeshies – because if they became too slack, the peats would fall out, and the equipment would hang down so low it would catch on the rocks and vegetation.

The young boys, and sometimes the girls, were in charge of leading or driving the ponies up the tracks to the peat banks and down again to where the peats were being stacked. Normally about 6 ponies made up a string, led by the 'boss' mare (and woe betide any other mare who tried to usurp the lead position!), but sometimes it might be 8 or 9. Over 9 was considered too many, and they would have to be split into two sets, with one set up on the hill being loaded, and the other down at the peat stack near the croft unloading. This could cause difficulties because, as a former peat boy explained, when the two sets met on the track it was a job to keep them apart, especially when the foals were playing around as well! Not only that, too long a string, say of 12 ponies, resulted in the lead pony having to stand around waiting at the bottom of the hill, with its heavy load, for the last ones to arrive. Sometimes, if this happened, some of the crafty old mares wouldn't wait, but continued on home to the croft before the peat boys could stop them! So, one string of ponies was the most practical. On the other hand, two sets of rivakeshies made for efficiency; as one set was going down the hill on the ponies to the peat stack, the other remained at the top, being filled with the next load.

The crofters often worked more than one bank in a season, and the mares only had to be led once to the new bank – after that, they made their way to it without direction. The number of journeys or 'gengs' made each day obviously depended on the distance between the peat banks and the stack, but the number was fixed. This the mares knew, and when it came to the last geng, instead of quietly grazing or standing still, they would become restless, and often set off down the hill before they had a full load. Whatever happened, the last geng was always undertaken at a much brisker pace! Sometimes, at the end of the flitting season, just one extra geng on the last day would finish up all the peats for that year. Predictably, the mares objected strongly, and the crofters had real difficulty in getting them up the hill again – they had to be driven firmly, not led. In spite of the occasional difference of opinion, the crofters clearly respected their ponies, and as one former peat boy said, fondly, 'They're wise, they're very wise.'

The ponies usually started work as 2- or 3-year-olds. Although most had followed their dams up and down to the peat banks, they still had to be 'tamed' and halter broken, before having a light load put on their backs. For the first few trips up to the banks, the youngsters had long trailing ropes attached to their halters, so if they suddenly decided to 'take off' the peat boys could, with luck and a bit of agility, grab the rope as the ponies went past, or at least put a foot on it! Once 'tamed' a pony could work until well into its twenties.

The importance of the ponies to the crofters was perhaps best illustrated by a disaster which befell Fetlar in 1886. A merchant landed a horse with sarcoptic mange on the island. The disease spread like wildfire, and 500 or more ponies had to be destroyed. With no ponies, the crofters had to flit the peats themselves, carrying them down in kishies on their backs, or even pushing them down in wheelbarrows – and one has to *see* the terrain to appreciate the demands those two methods made. Jamesie Laurenson described how one of his aunts lost all the skin off her back with carrying the kishies.

This situation went on on for several years, until help arrived in the shape of Bressay breeder, Peter Manson, and the Sandisons of Unst. Jamesie Laurenson described what happened. 'Peter Manson o Bressay an da Sandisons of Unst, just beginning to breed da ponies, came to da rescue an said, we will not see you helpless, so day give dem ponies. Bit Manson came with da old Earl (the Earl of Zetland inter-island ship), a mare to each house. An he made them draw fur dem, draw fur da mare. So dis wasna so bad. An afer a bit, an he said, dats alright, if dey have stock, give me da half of dem, keep da other half to yourself o whit you sell. So dey blessed Manson fur as da time dey lived.'

This was not the only time that sarcoptic mange hit the ponies in Shetland. In 1891, an order restricting the movement of horses, ponies, asses and mules within specified districts was issued due to an outbreak of sarcoptic mange and of strangles. There is, to this day, near a village in the south of the Mainland, a depression in the ground which is all that remains of a pit in which large numbers of ponies were buried following their destruction.

Flitting the peats occupied just a few weeks in the summer, but the

A scene from the 1930s – a pony and cart with stooks.

ponies were used for other tasks on the crofts. Wearing the same tack or 'bend', they brought in the hay and the straw from the fields, And, especially when bringing in the hay, the mares had a vital extra piece of equipment called a 'kebber' – a small wooden board that was placed in the mouth, which was fixed by ropes round the back of the ears, to prevent the pony from eating the hay.

Although it was not general throughout the islands, some of the ponies were used for ploughing and, more commonly, for harrowing. Special small implements were made, the harrow usually having a wooden frame and metal teeth. In some areas, they drew small carts – and indeed, peat-flitting was done by cart on parts of the Mainland. In Walls (on the west side of Mainland) peats were often brought down in sledges, and the hay and straw was transported on pieces of net pulled by the ponies. Most of the general farm work was, however, done by 'work ponies', chiefly cross-breds – Shetland/Highland, Shetland/Norwegian or even Shetland/Faroese being the most common, with a few pure-bred Highlands. These animals were nearly all larger than the Shetlands, standing anything from 12 hands upwards.

The days of the working pony are largely a thing of the past, but there are still a few that make their contribution. In *The Shetland Pony Magazine* of 1985 (published by the Stud Book Society), there is a description by Mrs Angela Gifford, of Shetlands doing work which 'can be economically carried out by horse-power'. The writer describes how two ponies, Lockinge Caesar and Tan, did all the carting work on the 260 acre Easton Court Farm in the summer. Wood was carted for the winter fires, tea taken to men in the fields, bales of hay and straw moved, and fencing materials transported. Supplementary food was taken to the cattle, and in the winter of 1981/82 the ponies carted all the feed for 10 days when the diesel in the tractors froze. The haulage was usually done by a team of heavy horses, but they could not stand on the ice, whereas the Shetlands used short, fast steps, and managed to stay upright. When a building programme was undertaken, the ponies helped in hauling the hardcore for foundations – the pair of them pulling a ton of stone in their wagon over even ground. In the autumn, they ploughed the vegetable garden and harrowed it in the spring, as well as competing in ploughing matches with a pony plough. So, when the world finally runs out of oil, look who is ready to take back from the internal combustion engine the work which they did for centuries!

Nothing could be much further removed from the life of the ponies in the islands, harsh though it frequently was, than that with which they came to be most closely associated in the minds of the general public of that era – life in the coal mines.

The idea of Shetland (or any other) ponies spending virtually their whole lives underground is totally abhorrent, and would certainly not be tolerated in the present climate of concern for animal welfare. It is almost impossible to approach this period of the ponies' history objectively. It is easy to record the many evils that occurred; it is less easy to record the measures that were taken for the ponies' welfare without appearing to justify the unjustifiable.

As mentioned in Chapter 4, the use of ponies underground was the direct result of the Mines Act of 1842, which forbade the employment of women and children in the pits. The establishment of the Londonderry studs in Bressay and in County Durham, and the effect that these have had on the breed in the long term have been discussed. When the ponies who were to work underground – be they Shetlands, Dartmoors, Welsh Mountain or cross-breds – arrived at the mine, they had, of course, to be trained. Robert Brydon wrote that the Shetlands' 'docile temperament enables them to be trained for pit work in almost as many days as it takes weeks with Welsh ponies.' As already explained, it was the smaller animals who worked underground, as they were ideal for the narrow, low-roofed galleries along which they had to haul the tubs of coal which ran on rails. The larger ponies and horses were used on the surface. Transporting the coal in tubs was known, according to the district, as 'putting', 'hauling' or 'ganging'. The ponies certainly earned their keep. Robert Brydon estimated that a pony could travel as much as 3,000 miles each year in the course of his work, and move the same number of tons of coal.

Nearly 100 years after the Londonderry Stud began breeding ponies with 'as much weight as possible and as near the ground as it can be got' for the mines, 'Achievement Tests' were carried out in the Netherlands. These showed that not only were Shetlands able to pull a proportionately greater load for their weight than horses, but that the smaller, stockier animals were stronger than the taller ones. In a paper entitled 'Shetland ponies' the German writer, Dr Flade, stated that his observations show that a Shetland can pull between 250% and 500% of its own weight. He also explained that the pony, when pulling away with a load, pushes himself (and thus the load) forward using his hindlegs, instead of, as in the case of draught horses, first lowering the forehand, thus putting excessive strain on the forelegs. Dr Flade states further that, in the Shetland method, a straight line of pull is drawn along the animal's back in the direction of the load, thus overcoming the load's resistance.

As in any industry, 'time was money' in the pits, and some of the training was sketchy in the extreme. At its best, it was similar to present day methods of breaking to harness, starting with haltering, followed by the addition of a full harness, then the introduction to pulling a log or railway sleeper attached to traces. The next stage involved replacing the trace harness by shafts or limbers, followed by the attachment of a coal tub. With the tub attached, the ponies were sometimes led round the streets to accustom them to the weight of the vehicle and the noise that it made. At some pits, the ponies were introduced to more of the considerable noise they would work in down the pit by being taken to the top of the pit shaft, where they could not only hear the sound of the winding gear, but were taught to go in and out of the cage that would eventually transport them underground – if, indeed, that was they way they were taken down.

That first experience of going underground into the noisy darkness must have been appallingly traumatic for even the most placid of ponies. The method varied from colliery to colliery. At one drift mine (i.e. a mine that was entered from the surface, and not by means of a shaft) the ponies, as mentioned above, were led in and out to accustom them to the darkness. In others, however, they were taken down in the cage which usually carried the miners, enclosed in a net or basket. To quote from the translation of the French author Simonin's *Underground Life* of 1869, 'the horses do not make the slightest movement, being paralysed with fear and to all appearance dead, but when they reach the

Although this is a French picture, it shows the method by which some Shetlands were taken down the mine shafts in Britain.

bottom of the pit they gradually recover their senses'. An even more horrifying method was that of immobilising the pony with a network of straps, and lowering it down, as shown in the picture opposite. As a concession to the ponies' instinctive reluctance to go from light into darkness, the first trip down the pit was sometimes undertaken at night, so the difference between the surface light and the gloom of pit shaft bottom would be less disturbing. Some ponies never adapted to the life, but Robert Brydon wrote that the temperament of the Shetland was such that he never knew one that had to be withdrawn.

Once the pony was down, he was led to the underground stables where he would spend almost all the remainder of his life when not actually working. Further training was usually necessary underground to accustom the pony to 'britch' or back the load tubs, and to open the ventilation doors that were sited at intervals along the galleries. The latter was usually done by attaching several tubs to the pony when it was standing on a slope, and then removing the locking blocks from the tub wheels, so that the weight of the tubs would push the pony through the door. The animal soon learnt that the easiest way was to approach the door with his neck turned slightly. A sharp flick of the head was then all that was needed to open the doors.

The conditions for ponies and men underground were, by any standards, demanding, especially in the mines worked by Shetlands. It was dark, dirty and, with ventilation systems that were sometimes less than efficient, often hot and humid. The narrow, low-roofed roads, with uneven surfaces and variable gradients, made manoeuvring for animals and men very difficult. In John Bright's book, *Pit Ponies,* a description is given of the technique adopted by the ever-resourceful ponies when turning to make the journey back from the coal face. 'A pony would tuck his head between his front legs, turn slowly till his neck touched the sides, then bring his back legs in and spin like a top.' Other ponies 'virtually climbed up the side of a restricted roadway to turn round'.

The low roofing was obviously a hazard, and eventually ponies were equipped with protective leather head guards, which were later improved to give protection to the eyes as well as the top of the head. The practicality of the Londonderry breeding of ponies with a low head-carriage is obvious, but so low were some of the seams that animals' backs were skinned as they scraped along the rough, frequently jagged, surface of the roof – an injury known as 'roofing'. The more experienced ponies are said to have crouched when going through a particularly low section.

Danger was never far away in the pits, and mining disasters took the lives of many ponies as well as of miners. There are, however, stories of the ponies' 'sixth sense' in anticipating danger, and saving themselves and their handlers from accidents. Most tell of ponies refusing to go forward along a roadway where there was a subsequent roof fall – an action that can probably be explained by their acute sense of hearing. More difficult to explain are tales of ponies apparently taking deliberate action to save their handlers. Such an incident is described by a miner in *Pit Ponies*. 'I was running down a steep hill to turn a railing in order to allow the full tubs to proceed, and as I bent down to to turn the "point", I slipped on a wet sleeper and fell down with Fido and the tubs almost upon me. Obviously realising the tubs would hit me, Fido shoved his back end into the breach and shot his front legs straight out, thus "throwing" the first tub off the rail inches from where I lay'.

The boot was sometimes on the other foot, and the pony boys had to save or help their four-legged partners. Some mines were liable to flooding, with water and sludge a constant threat. The ponies often had to wade through up to their bellies, and sometimes stumbled and came down on the uneven flooring. Their lad then had to work frantically, kneeling in up to two feet of sludge, to hold the pony's head up to prevent it drowning. Another well chronicled (and photographed) story concerns a very small Shetland pony called Spider, who was not quite strong enough for the work required of him. So attached were the miners to him that they concealed his limitations from the 'bosses' by pushing his the tub for him (see photo opposite).

Some public misconceptions undoubtedly existed about the ponies. It was widely believed at the time that all animals working underground went blind. That some ponies developed cataracts is true, and prior to the 1911 Coal Mines Act forbidding the use of blind animals underground, there were some working that had lost their sight through ill-treatment or accident. But these were, it seems, the exception. The widespread belief appears to have been based on the fact observed by miners and at least one veterinary surgeon that, when the ponies were brought up from the pits into daylight, it took between 24 and 48 hours for their eyes to accommodate fully to the light. They could thus give the appearance of blindness.

It has been mentioned that many of the ponies, once they went down the pit, spent virtually the rest of their lives underground. A number of reasons were put forward for this. The first was that bringing them up to the surface was just as terrifying as their original descent. When they were turned out into fields, not only could they not see very well, but, naturally enough, they raced about, kicking and bucking, and in-

Spider – a great favourite with his 'lads' in the mine.

evitably doing each other considerable damage, even though their hind shoes were removed. The ponies became accustomed to the more or less stable temperature range and atmosphere of the mines, and were prone to respiratory problems and chills in the variable atmosphere above ground. There were no antibiotics in those days, to effect a rapid cure. Also if their stay above ground was prolonged, as in the case of miners' strikes, they lost fitness; it could, according to one vet., take 3 or 4 weeks to get them back to working fitness after going back onto hard feed after a rest at grass. Whether these reasons were sufficient to deny those ponies a regular holiday, is of course, another matter. Towards the end of the pit pony era, however, holidays were much more common, due, presumably, to the availability of antibiotics to deal with possible illnesses and also the increased awareness of welfare issues.

Conditions and behaviour have to be viewed, to some extent, in the context of the age in which they occurred, and many of what we

It was not all work for the ponies and miners: a pit pony class at the 1950 Langley Park Gymkhana and Show.

would now regard as abuses were not the result of deliberate cruelty; it was a harsh era, for people and ponies alike. Coal mining was a business; ponies cost money, and death or injury affected profits – so it was in the interest of the mine owners to keep them in working order. There were, however, many cases of careless and accidental injuries, and punishment of the miner and mine deputy responsible followed. On the other hand, there were, without question, many recorded instances of prosecutions for quite sickening assaults on the ponies by miners. Most underground workers were on piece-work, and a stubborn or unco-operative pony affected their earnings, with predictable results. No legislation covered the welfare of pit ponies until 1887, when under The Coal Mines Regulations Act mines inspectors were given the authority to 'enquire into the treatment of horses and other animals in mines' – and sets of rules and regulations for named mines were published. This was, at best, a start. Various societies, including the RSPCA (founded in 1824), the National Equine Defence League (founded in 1909) and The Pit Ponies' Protection Society, campaigned vigorously for improvements. In 1911, a Royal Commission on Mines was set up to investigate, among other items, 'The Treatment of Pit Horses and Ponies'. The Commission acknowledged the intent of the 1887 Act, and the accompanying rules, but commented that 'It is, however, one thing to have rules and another to secure their observance ... ', and it referred to reports in newspapers of proceeding against miners for cruelty, and representations made by the welfare societies.

A principal witness before the Royal Commission was Mr Francis A. Cox, Honorary Secretary of the National Equine Defence League, and one of the most outspoken critics of the treatment of pit ponies. As he admitted to the Commission, his complaints 'were often couched in very flamboyant language'. He spoke, for instance, of 'the constant moan of dull dispairing agony which is rising from thousands of helpless dumb animals', but he was able to produce much evidence from miners and others who had witnessed cruelty. The members of the Commission accepted that there *was* some deliberate cruelty, and also that conditions for the ponies should be regulated.

As a result, The Coal Mines Act, which contained a Schedule on the Care and Treatment of Animals (Sections 86 and 109), passed into law in 1911, and became known colloquially, as 'The Pit Ponies Charter'.

Under the Act, and for the first time, the law required certain measures to be implemented for the improvement of the conditions under which pit ponies (and horses) lived and worked. The Act is summarised in an RSPCA publication of 1924, thus:

No horse shall be taken underground until it is four years old.

All horses underground shall be housed in properly constructed stables, which shall be lime-washed at least once in three months and shall be continuously ventilated.

Horse-keepers shall be appointed in the proportion of at least one horse-keeper to every fifteen horses.

A sufficient supply of food and water and medicines shall be provided.

Horses shall not be allowed to go out to work unfit or improperly shod, or with ill-fitting harness. No blind horse shall be worked in a mine.

Cases of sickness, injury, or ill-treatment shall be reported to the manager or under-manager.

A daily record shall be kept of the times at which horses are worked.

An annual return shall be made to the Government inspector showing the number of deaths and cases of injury and ill-treatment.

A representation by Keir Hardie MP (himself a former miner) for RSPCA inspectors to be allowed down the mines to ensure that the law was being enforced was rejected as a general principle, although the Society's own publication, *Animal World*, of 1896 stated that several of their inspectors were allowed to visit some pits; there was suspicion, however, that, as notice had to be given, conditions were improved for the occasion. The Mines Department appointed its own inspectors, which was a step in the right direction, but in practice, even by 1924, the RSPCA was complaining that there were only 8 inspectors for some 60,000 horses and ponies.

While the welfare societies wrote of insanitary stables, cruelty, injuries and over-work, it has to be said that most of this was hearsay, at least during the 19th century, as the mines were private property, and, as has been seen, inspections by outsiders were virtually non-existent. Nonetheless, it must be assumed that conditions were, in many instances, unacceptable. But there is some evidence that, even prior to legislation, attention was being paid to the ponies' welfare. That this was largely aimed at gaining maximum efficiency, and thus profits, can hardly have concerned the ponies. For instance, as far back as 1892 the Institute of Mining Engineers discussed the design of 'an improved head-gear for pit horses', which gave more protection to the eyes, which, as was pointed out, are particularly vulnerable to injury in the confined space underground. The special feature of this new head-gear, as shown opposite, was the semi-circular guard of thick leather covering the protuberant bone above the eye, and thus offering greater protection. Of considerable importance was the fact that this new head-gear cost little more than the standard one, which lacked the eye-guard. The inventor of the head-gear, one George J. Binns, concluded his presentation of the idea to the Institute with a delightful comment 'that anyone who had studied the evolution of the unidactyl Equus from its first ancestor the five-toed Eohippus, must have been seized with a desire to breed for pit work a horse with a recessed eye, but he was afraid the time at their disposal would hardly allow of this, and under the circumstances, his suggestion seemed to be one way of getting out of the difficulty'! Apparently the engineers agreed, and the head-gear can be seen on various contemporary photographs.

The Institute of Mining Engineers also considered, in 1894, an automatic horse feeder, designed 'to give feeds to the ponies at early morning and other time, in the absence of the the groom or other attendants'.

The engineers also discussed 'Underground Stables' in some detail in 1902 and 1903, and heard a paper presented by W. C. Blackett. It began with a spirited defence of the treatment of pit-ponies in Durham and Northumberland (almost certainly the Londonderry mines), and remarked that 'Cruelty is an extravagance which even the callous cannot afford.' He offered as typical of many examples of long and trouble-free service by ponies, his possession of a polished hoof, with

A present-day pony at the Beamish Open Air Museum showing tack and tub used in the coal mines. (Note the protective headgear with guard protecting the bone above the eye.)

a silver-mounted inscription, that was on his desk, the inscription reading 'SWALLOW. A 10 hand Shetland pony, was 5 years old when put to work down Kimleworth pit on May 2nd, 1876. He ceased work 20½ years later on October 12th, 1898, aged 27 years. During his whole working life he never had a sick or sorry day, the 6 weeks strike in 1879 and the 13 weeks' strike in 1892 being the only occasion on which he was idle. On August 8th, 1896, when 25 years old, he took third prize amongst 20 other pit ponies shewn in Durham.'

Most accommodation, certainly after the passing of 'The Pit Ponies' Charter', but in some collieries even before then, consisted of lines of stalls, usually with concrete floors, with a fall of 1 in 30. Bedding was of sawdust, moss, or straw, although in some mines a kind of platform of pitch pine was laid over the concrete. This measured 5 feet by 6 feet by 1¼ inches thick with ¾ inch spaces between the boards. It was so constructed that it was level, to avoid the strain on the flexor tendons and quarters caused by standing on the sloping concrete. The boarding was made in two sections for ease of removal and for drying and cleaning when the pony was at work. The ponies could stand or lie on it, and remain dry, but one does wonder about capped hocks and elbows! Most stalls had the pony's name on a board, and on the wall opposite the complete working harness was hung on hooks.

Much thought appears to have gone into the best type of food for working ponies. The ever-innovative Robert Brydon, at Seaham Colliery, experimented with the feeding of grass in place of hay during the summer months of 1869 – a practice that was generally regarded as dangerous. The admirable Mr Brydon reported to Earl Vane in some detail, showing that a saving of nearly £600 was made on the feeding of 400 ponies. No ill-effects were reported, and indeed, Brydon considered the ponies to be in better condition and to work more efficiently than those on hay. Mr Brydon received thanks and congratulations from the Earl and the mine management.

In the late 19th century, a diet of 17-35% maize, 17-25% oats, 35-40% chopped hay, and 9-12% pulse was common, but this varied from pit to pit. A typical ration designed for ponies of about 10 hands, as listed in an Institute of Mining Engineers paper, consisted of: 4½ lb of hay, 2 lb of oats, 1½ lb peas, 4 lb maize – a total of 12 lb. Some pits would not feed maize because of its heating effect, while at others, the amount of maize was increased because oats were considered too expensive. In 1894, a number of horses/ponies died as a result of eating seeds of the poisonous vetch *Lathyrus sativus*, which apparently came in with a consignment of peas from abroad.

All ponies that worked underground were clipped, had their manes hogged and their tails shaved, for obvious reasons of hygiene, safety and ease of cleaning in the dusty, dirty surroundings. As they returned to the stables after work, either their legs and bellies were hosed or they went through a shallow bath. They were then groomed in their stalls.

At the very height of the use of Shetlands in the pits, it is estimated that about 500 were taken from the islands every year. An RSPCA report states that there were in 1878 some 200,000 ponies (not all of them Shetlands, of course) working in pits, falling to half that in 1895, while Coal Board figures show that in the years leading up to World War I, there were some 70,000 horses and ponies in mines throughout Britain. Their contribution to the wealth and prosperity of the country must have been impressive.

While the hard work, privations and instances of cruelty make disturbing reading, there were happier aspects of the pit pony story. There is a report, from the 1930s, of a pit manager in a South Wales mine, who felt so strongly about the welfare of his ponies that he had gramophone records made to be played to every shift of miners before they

Ponies in the bath after working their shift.

went down the pit, reminding them of their duties to the animals. They said, 'Manager calling ... Hauliers, take care of the horses under your charge; don't abuse them; treat them kindly; take your horses to the stables at the end of the shift. Cases of ill-treatment will be severely dealt with.'

Tales of the bond between pony and miner are legion. To quote Robert Brydon once again, 'Ponies have been known to follow their drivers like dogs, and to be as dejected as a forsaken maiden when, from any cause, they were separated from each other. Boys – and big boys, too – have wept for the loss of their ponies, killed in an accident, as though the little Shetland were a human friend.'

In their leisure time, even in the darkest years of the Industrial Revolution, the miners and their ponies took part in special pit pony classes at shows, and there was great inter-colliery rivalry in these contests. In later days, so great was the competition in the turn-out classes that it is said judges had to use a white handkerchief to wipe inside the ponies' ears and sheath in order to decide which was just that little bit better-prepared than the next! Pit pony races were also a popular feature of the summer months – so it was not all work and no play, at least for some ponies.

Happily, pit ponies are now a thing of the past – the last ponies having retired, amid considerable publicity, on February 24th, 1994: the last of the many hundreds of thousands that served industry faithfully for some 300 years.

It might be thought that 1994 saw the end of the employment of ponies in a professional capacity. Not so – but the work that Shetlands still undertake in many countries, including Britain, can hardly be further removed from working in coal mines, or even flitting the peats. From the darkness and dirt of the coal mines to the lights and glamour of the stage and the circus is a mammoth step – but one made by Shetland ponies with their customary adaptability and aplomb!

Dorset-based John Holmes is well known in the film, stage and TV world as a trainer of all kinds of animals for shows, and he has been supplying Shetlands to pull Cinderella's coach in pantomime for over 30 years He has the very highest regard for the breed, and says they are incredibly easy to train for the stage. Nearly all ponies for pantomime must be grey, and Mr Holmes now breeds his own. They are based on the Littlestoke lines bred by Mrs Nancy Ducker, who used to produce a Shetland liberty act for Bertram Mills circus. Mr Holmes acquired some of those, as their temperament is so good.

Initial training for the stage is similar to the early handling of any youngster. Mr Holmes sometimes does not handle them until they are weaned, but he then halters them, teaches them to lead, and goes through the usual stages of breaking to harness, with long-reining, etc. After that, the training changes somewhat! The ponies are put in a loose box with two radios on, each playing a different programme at full volume; sacks are hung for them to walk through, and they are also broken to traffic – all to accustom them to the noise, the curtains and the other strange things they will meet back-stage and on stage. But, as Mr Holmes says, 'They never take any notice of these things anyway. All this rubbish about Shetlands being difficult is just that – a load of rubbish! And what the ponies put up with on stage is unbelievable. They stand there in "Cinderella", with the pumpkin exploding, the curtain going up and own and often touching them – and they don't blink an eyelid.'

The ponies start to work in theatres at the age of about three, and quickly become accustomed to the back-stage arrangements, and go up the many stairs quite easily, although coming down can be more difficult. The ponies never wear blinkers, because there are so many obstacles back-stage that they really need a wide field of vision. As everyone knows, Shetlands are quick learners, and after a couple of rehearsals, they know exactly what to do, and they know the beat of the music on which to move. As Cinderella enters the coach, the band goes 'Boomph' and off the ponies go! They are always led, never driven, but they anticipate the leader after a very short time.

Mr Holmes supplies all their harness and decorative plumes, etc., but the theatrical company provides the coach, and that can cause big problems, as theatrical designers may know about stage requirements, but most do not know about ponies. One coach was so heavy that the ponies couldn't move it at first – and when they finally gave an extra heave, the whole undercarriage came out from under it, and the coach fell on top of them. As Mr Holmes remarked, 'It *did* take some time to get them settled again after that.' It emerged that the linch pin on the carriage turntable consisted of nothing more substantial than a 6 inch wire nail!. On another occasion, the stage had such a rake on it (all professional stages slope up from front to back), and it was very slippery. Two of the ponies slipped and fell, and the coach started to slide towards the orchestra pit. Fortunately it was at rehearsal, and the Good Fairy managed to grab and hang on to the whole outfit, as the stage hands rushed on and got the ponies back on their feet.

Someone always asks the question – what about ponies 'misbehaving' on stage? Mr Holmes explained that careful timing of feeding and watering can usually avoid that; for instance, the evening feed is given after the show, not before – in the best traditions of the acting profession! Even if the occasional accident does happen, the audience love it! There is one priceless, if probably apocryphal story about a team of 4 ponies that had been trained to do their droppings only when it was dark. One night, the predictable happened – the lights failed – and when they came up again, there were four little steaming piles on the stage!

One of the less obvious problems encountered by the owners of stage ponies is where to stable them. In bygone years, stables were commonplace in cities and towns. Not so these days, and the Holmes ponies have found themselves living in police horse stables, brewery stables, and even in stores at the back of the theatre.

For nearly thirty years, Shetlands have moved in the exalted circles of the Royal Ballet. In one ballet, *La Fille Mal Gardée*, a pony appears in two scenes, pulling a small trap with two dancers in it. The first pony to do this was Mrs Kathleen Grasby's home-bred Ashorne Seagull, a 34 inch (86 cm) grey, who was selected at an audition at the Coventry Theatre in 1963. Prior to joining the ballet, Seagull had appeared in pantomime, so she certainly didn't suffer from stage fright. Mrs Grasby's daughter, Diana, appropriately dressed as a groom, led the pony in the early performances. They appeared at Stratford-upon-Avon and in Bristol, and then in the Royal Opera House, Covent Garden. When Sir Frederick Ashton saw Seagull, he was so delighted with her that he insisted she must be used in all performances, and this she did until she retired, well into her twenties, in 1971. She was replaced by her daughter, Ashorne Lisa, who has appeared ever since – and she is now into her thirties. In 1974 Lisa, led by Diana Grasby, represented the Royal Ballet in the Lord Mayor's Show.

As with all things concerned with the theatre, there have been moments of added drama. Once, when Diana and the pony were en route to Covent Garden, the trailer had a puncture in the Bayswater Road. Time was getting on, so Diana unboxed Seagull and led her the considerable distance through the London streets to the theatre, leaving the driver to deal with the puncture. On another occasion, when the touring section of the Royal Ballet became Sadler's Ballet, they did a matinée in Stratford with Sadler's Wells, then dashed down to London for the evening performance with the Royal ballet at Covent Garden. Although the great ballerina Margot Fonteyn did not dance in *La Fille Mal Gardée*, she visited the theatre during a rehearsal, and was so enchanted with Seagull that she insisted a photograph be taken of them together. It is reproduced opposite.

In 1985, the Royal Ballet in London and Sadler's Wells in Birmingham were performing *La Fille Mal Gardée* at the same time! Lisa, with all her experience, was dispatched to London, and another pony, Sundew, who had never been in a cart before, let alone in a theatre, had a crash course pulling a log round a field. That night she was 'put to' the vehicle for the first time, went on, and behaved perfectly, accepting the dancers, the music, and the general confusion that goes on back-stage as if she had been doing it all her life.

Lisa may be in her thirties, but in 1992 she still managed to show true Shetland independence of spirit, and in so doing attracted headlines in London's *Evening Standard*. 'Covent Garden Ballet Star Flees on the Pony Express' topped the story of how Lisa, minus her headcollar, escaped from the theatre, and trotted briskly along the pavements through Covent Garden before being apprehended by a policeman opposite the Waldorf Hotel. The policeman described what happened 'First we harnessed it with a belt – but the bloke who donated it kept losing his trousers, so a cabby produced a rope and we made a head rein ... The funny thing is, I've been applying continually to join the mounted police during my five years in the force. I almost felt as if I

Dame Margot Fonteyn with Ashorne Seagull.

had arrived!' Lisa was returned to the theatre unscathed, but under police escort.

Two of the Grasby ponies, Ashorne Cinders and Twylands Ticketyboo, appeared with the Beatles in a Christmas show at the Hammersmith Odeon in London. The 'Fab Four' were intrigued with the ponies, and Diana Grasby had to teach Paul McCartney how to lead them.

Shetlands have appeared in several films; most famously, perhaps, in the Herbert Wilcox film *Victoria the Great*, just before the war. In this, Anna Neagle, as Queen Victoria, drove a pair of brown Marshwood ponies to a park phaeton (the genuine one from the Royal Mews). Anna Neagle had never driven before, and to make matters even more difficult, the ponies' scenes were not filmed until some three months after they arrived at the Denham studios. During that time they were turned out and not worked at all. But, beautifully schooled by Betty Cox, as would be expected with

Marshwood ponies, when the time came, they behaved faultlessly, and Betty Cox received a letter of appreciation from the studio.

In the 1930s, some of the Berry ponies appeared in the film *The Edge of the World*, which was filmed on the island of Foula.

It is a far cry from the glamour of stage and screen to the horrors of the battle field, and, while acknowledging the extraordinary versatility of the breed, an article headed 'The Shetland Pony as a War Horse' is not what one would expect to see. Nonetheless, it actually appeared in a copy of *The Shetland Times* of 1898, over a quotation from the *Pall Mall Gazette* of the same year! In an article discussing the various British native breeds, the writer concluded that:

> The small horse is the war horse of the future, and it is fortunate that we have in the United Kingdom several native breeds of ponies which may be suitable for such work. The little horses of Dartmoor and Exmoor and the New Forest, of Wales and Western Ireland, the Shetlands of the far North, and the Galloways of Southern Scotland may furnish a large supply for military work; and in each district where the ponies are found, serious attention is now being given to the problem. It may seem absurd to speak of the 'Shelty' as a horse fit for a yeoman or a hussar; but horse breeders know better. He is the hardiest, most sagacious, and most docile of the horse tribe, cunning yet tractable, and free from vice; sturdy and ready for any work; with power of endurance no less remarkable than his intelligence. In his native wastes, he lives in the open air, making a meal of seaweed, or swimming a voe to find fresh patches of herbage, and he knows well how to open a gate if there be provender on the other side of it ... The Shetland is very small and rarely exceeds 9½ hands, but he is all bone and substance, and it is believed that these qualities may be employed to furnish the ideal mount required by the fighting men of the future.

Amusing though the idea appears, the following report from the *The Daily Telegraph* of July 22nd, 1882, suggests that Shetlands *did* actually serve in the Army in some capacity! 'Twenty six horses and a number of Shetland ponies, from Woolwich, arrived yesterday afternoon at the Wellington Barracks. They are intended for the use of the 1st Battalion of the Scots Guards, stationed there'. Extensive enquiries have failed to establish exactly what role the Shetlands played, although an officer (from another service) immediately gave his opinion that the Guards probably ate them!

There are a number of instances of Shetlands serving in the Army as mascots. In 1928, H.R.H. Princess Louise, Colonel-in-Chief of the Argyll and Sutherland Highlanders, presented a Shetland to the 1st Battalion. As far as can be established, this was the first Shetland to be

Anna Neagle as Queen Victoria, with two Marshwood ponies to a park phaeton.

a mascot. He was called Cruachan, and he was succeeded, over the years, by Cruachan II and Cruachan III. The Parachute Regiment has had several Shetlands. There have been three named, appropriately, Pegasus, and also Bruneval, Arnhem and Ringway, marking historic engagements in which the Paras took part.

Away from the military scene, the Shetlands that so often graced the parks surrounding large country houses were sometimes put to good use. They were employed for light draught work, carting lawn-mowings or leaves, and also pulling lawnmowers, their hooves encased in leather boots so as not to spoil the billiard-table surface they were helping to perfect.

In this 'green' age, it seems inevitable that Shetlands would be in-volved sooner or later. In the late 1970s, Shetlands were used by a conservation body in south-west Cornwall to graze 'predator' plants, such as gorse and willow, so as to allow the growth of rarer plants like the Cornish heath. This was a task they undertook with their custom-ary enthusiasm.

8

SHETLANDS AT PLAY

◆

Shetlands, like all our native pony breeds, are great survivors. Their small size, coupled with their great strength, enabled them to survive in their native islands, and it also ensured that, as pit ponies, they not only survived, but played an important role in the Industrial Revolution. But would they survive when their economic uses were overtaken by modern technology? The answer is obvious – of course they would! They now bring great pleasure to hundreds of thousands of children and adults worldwide, their popularity is unquestioned, and they take part in a huge variety of equestrian sports and activities.

The Shetland is, without doubt, the ideal pony with which to introduce young children to the world of horses. Shetlands and small children were surely meant for each other, and the most magical partnerships are so often formed between the two – with pony and child entering into everything they do together with shared enjoyment and enthusiasm. The size of the pony not only gives a child confidence when learning to ride, but enables the youngster to help with grooming and looking after it, saddling, and so on. The innate commonsense and sure-footedness of the Shetland usually make it a safe, sensible ride for youngsters, yet it can be spirited enough to be the greatest fun as the child's ability increases. There are few equestrian sports in which Shetlands will not 'have a go' – be it showing (a small child can learn the art of showing in-hand with a pony of a suitable size), jumping, cross-country, long distance, hunting, racing and, of course, driving.

Driving is a pastime enjoyed by adults and children alike. Shetlands excel in harness, a fact that was appreciated by Queen Victoria, who drove a pair of Shetlands to a park phaeton. In the present day, it is not unusual for parents or older siblings to take over outgrown ridden Shetlands for this purpose. While the elegant days of horse-drawn transport are now past, the skills required have been translated and adapted into a variety of competitive driving events.

Scurry driving could have been designed for Shetlands, as speed, accuracy, manoeuvrability, and, above all, enthusiasm, is what it is all about! It is a sport in which Shetlands compete and win against larger, less agile breeds. In this exciting event, vehicles are driven against the clock round a twisting course of cones, with penalties for dislodging balls placed on top of the cones. If ever a pair of ponies can be said to have 'put Shetlands on the map' for the general TV viewing public in Britain, it was Mrs Christine Dick's fabulous pair of scurry ponies, Pavlov and Peanuts, performing at the Horse of the Year Show in London. No-one who saw them will every forget this pair scampering round the complicated course of cones, the vehicle often on two wheels round the corners, with the ponies responding to Mrs Dick's blandishments, and to Raymond Brookes-Ward's commentary, which increased in decibels as the ponies increased in speed. It was spectacular, it was unbelievably skilful, it was fun, and there was no doubt the ponies enjoyed it every bit as much as the audience.

For the best part of a quarter of a century, Shetlands have taken part in combined driving events – the driven equivalent of a ridden one- or three-day event. Mr David Morgan-Davies was one of the first in the field, with both pairs and teams, winning Lowther Driving trials in 1974 with his team of four stallions – Ickworth Avenger, Ickworth Bismarck, Norge of Belmont and Treasure of Belmont. Another gifted young whip, who tragically died as the result of a road accident, was Bianca Sergeant, from the New Forest, in Hampshire.

The Staveley family – Dianna, a former President of the Stud Book Society, her husband John and daughter Anna – thoroughly enjoyed themselves driving, as is related in Chapter 12.

It has to be said, however, that Shetlands are at something of a disadvantage in combined driving under FEI rules, particularly for the single pony owner. There is a mandatory minimum weight for the vehicle, there must be two people in it, and while pairs and teams can manage, it is asking rather much of a single pony over a long, demanding course.

In the more formal Private Driving, Shetlands have always done well, with Betty and Maurice Cox competing with great success before and after World War II Immediately after World War II, however, the discipline went into something of a decline in the breed, but was revived in the 1960s, due largely to Miss Nan French, Mrs Swannack and Lady Joan Gore-Langton. Since those days, Shetlands have scored notable successes in open classes. These included the Staveley family's win in the pairs at the Royal Show in 1977, while the slightly less formal under 13.2 Ride and Drive was won by Mrs Beryl Rae's stallion Hannibal of Hinton at the British Driving Society's show in 1976. More recently, Mrs Vivien Hampton's Lockinge Edward, driven by her daughter, Abigail, has done outstandingly well. At the British Driving Society's show at Windsor in 1994 he was reserve champion against all breeds in his height section, and he is almost always placed in all-breed classes. His greatest triumph so far was winning the Supreme Harness championship at the 1993 New Forest Show, ahead of a very well known team of four horses.

Riding for the Disabled is a well established activity in which Shetlands, as will be described later, play an active part, but *Driving* for the Disabled is more recent and less well known. Special vehicles, with wheelchair access and safety straps, have been designed, and, accompanied by an able-bodied companion with an emergency set of reins, the disabled are able to enjoy pleasure drives, and also take part in special Disabled Drivers' classes at, for example, the British Driving Society's meet at Smith's Lawn in Windsor Great Park. At least one driver has included driving as her sport in gaining the Duke of Edinburgh's Silver Award.

Many people enjoy non-competitive driving. In places such as the New Forest, picnic drives are common, and some years ago the local all-Shetland group undertook an 80 mile round tour of the Forest lasting five days. Forest pubs provided accommodation for the drivers and stabling or grazing for the ponies.

In 1989, the then Vice-President of the Stud Book Society and owner of the Clothie Stud, Mrs Marie Brooker (who has competed with success in both private driving and driving trials, and, when living in Shetland, was the most northerly member of the British Driving Society), had the splendid idea of taking a group of six youngsters on an ambitious and wholly enjoyable long distance drive. From the Brooker home just outside Aberdeen, they planned to take five ponies, four vehicles, Land Rovers, trailers and a large Bedford TK lorry up to Shetland, and drive through the islands – including the northernmost point of Unst and Sumburgh in Mainland in the south. It seemed appropriate to advertise the following year's Stud Book Society's Centenary by taking a group of ponies back to the land of their birth.

It was a colossal undertaking, and preparations included arranging stables for the ponies each night – and stables are few and far between in Shetland, where the ponies all live out. Ponies, Land Rovers and trailers, plus the children and the support team, all had to undertake the 16 hour sea voyage by P & O ferry from Aberdeen to Lerwick, and bookings had to be made for the inter-island ferries. The lorry (christened 'The Shetland Bus') with the traps in it, was sent separately by Shetland Line.

Alice Bird with Boxlease Carona at the Shetland Performance Show 1995.

The party led by Mrs Marie Brooker that drove through Shetland in 1989.
(Left to right) Geoffrey Scott and Star of North Dale; Philippa Dobson and
Merry Minion of Netherley, Tim Bayman, Yvonne Nicol and Clothie Orion,
Fiona Bain, Marie Brooker and Clothie Gluss and Clothie Gloup, Graham
Leith.

The children were aged between 12 and 15 (all of whom had learned to drive with Marie Brooker, and had taken at least their British Driving Society Test l). The party camped on Yell, before crossing to Unst for the start of the great drive. There was so little traffic and the ponies were so fit and keen that they arrived back at their base in Yell far sooner than expected, and spent the evening looking at Mr Tommy Robertson's Knowe Stud, and the senior stallion, Olympus of Mousa.

The next highlight was visiting the lovely island of Fetlar, where the grey stallion, Star of North Dale, had been born 20 years earlier. The following day was to be the longest drive, through the island of Yell.

The 23 mile route included a number of diversions through Mid Yell, West Sandwick and Ulsta, at the request of a number of elderly residents who wanted to see them. Poignantly, the old people commented on what a joy it was to hear the sound of the ponies' hooves once again, as it stirred memories of when many ponies wandered freely along the roads.

Back on Mainland, the peace and almost total lack of traffic on the excellent roads so noticeable in Unst and Yell was shattered by the big lorries thundering backwards and forwards to the oil terminal at Sullum Voe – but the ponies took it all in their strides. The drive ended at Sumburgh, where Myrna Flaws of the Grutness Stud had strung out bunting and flags to welcome them. In the seven days they had covered 110 miles through the islands, made half a dozen ferry crossings, and collected a splendid sum of money for the Centenary Pageant to be staged at the celebration show the following year. Not least, it gave those children and adults who had never been to Shetland a valuable insight into the conditions under which the breed developed down the ages. Above all, perhaps, they all, including the ponies, had the most enormous fun.

In the more competitive world of ridden Shetlands, the most encouraging feature of the last 15 or so years has been the recognition by judges and the wider pony world of Shetlands as genuine performance ponies that can compete on equal terms with other breeds. Shetland enthusiasts have always appreciated the talents of the breed, but some judges have been not just prejudiced, but ignorant of their abilities.

On the whole, the breed has been accepted in the driving disciplines more than anywhere else, but even in those, it has not been plain sailing. On one occasion, a top driven Shetland was excluded, on the judge's orders, from a championship for which it had qualified. In the world of mixed Mountain and Moorland ridden and in-hand showing there have been disgraceful instances of judges enquiring, 'How on earth do I judge a Shetland?' and even voicing their opinion that 'Shetlands shouldn't be allowed in the ring with other breeds,' or, unbelievably, 'Shetlands are not suitable as Lead Rein and First Ridden ponies.' At one recent show, when a Shetland did a spectacular clear round over a big working hunter pony course, the judge was heard to remark, 'I didn't know Shetlands could jump.'

Probably the first pony to show that Shetlands could compete against other breeds was Dougal Dick's Boffin of Transy, in the late 1970s. Boffin had, of course, been extremely well schooled, and was ridden by Dougal's daughter, Sarah. At the Ponies of Britain Summer Show in England Boffin had shown up some of the more flighty riding ponies in the Child's First Pony class by standing like a rock when the riders were asked to dismount and mount – an exercise that left many of the more 'fashionable' (and expensive) ponies in some disarray. From their initial placing at the bottom of the line, they finished a creditable fourth. But the best was yet to come! Rather optimistically (or so it was thought) they had entered the Mountain and Moorland Handy Hunter class, in which they had to jump a very big course, out of ground that was like glue. The second fence was 3 feet high, with a spread of nearly 4 feet, and most of the Exmoors, Dartmoors and Welsh were eliminated at it. In came Sarah and Boffin. They popped the first, took the dreaded second without a moment's hesitation, and went on to record the only clear round to win the class. The widely held opinion was that Sarah, Boffin and Dougal had done more for the good name of Shetlands in just 24 hours than others had done in years!

His breeder agreed that Boffin was 'one is a million', and he described how, when ridden by Sarah, they had lost their way on a cross-country course, so tucked in behind a horse. Without a pause, Boffin cleared a 5-bar gate standing at 3 ft 6 inches. He was absolutely safe; if he knew he could clear a fence, he would jump it, but if he knew he couldn't, he wouldn't try. Boffin also won at dressage, Pony Club Open One Day Events, Working Hunter Pony and ridden classes, in the hands of both Sarah and her elder sister, Carolyn.

Within a year or so of this epic success, and with the growing interest in driven and ridden Shetlands, there was talk about the introduction of a Performance Award Scheme. This was keenly supported by the then President of the Society, Maurice Cox, but opposed, initially, by a number of council members, who saw the ponies solely in terms of in-hand showing. However, at a London meeting of the Society, a group of members – Mrs Rachel Bown, Mrs Pat Leivers (later Mrs Renwick), Mrs Dianna Staveley and Mrs Jane Gough – made a formal suggestion that such a scheme be run by the Society. The suggestion was finally accepted by the council, and enthusiastically supported by Mrs Marie Brooker, who succeeded Major Cox as President.

It was stipulated that the scheme, open to registered ponies, must not involve any cost or work for the council or secretary, other than the production of rosettes. Mrs Leivers agreed to run the ridden section of the scheme, and Mrs Gough the driven. Mrs Gough was succeeded four years later by Mrs Gardiner. The ridden section then formed its own working party of interested owners, including Mrs Rosemarie Webb, Mrs Rachel Bown, Mrs Vivien Hampton, Mrs Helen Thomson, and (later) Mrs Anna Stevens from Wales.

At the beginning, the scheme awarded points for places gained in a small selection of performance classes, for ponies competing in both all-Shetland and open events. The range of classes has increased enormously over the years, and the Driven Scheme is now run separately. The scheme caters for children up to the age of 14 for the ridden events, and 17 for the in-hand. Points are gained by competing and being placed in a range of performance events from gymkhana, through lead rein, first ridden, hunting, dressage, veterans, working hunter, Pony Club, picnic rides and so on. There are sections for riders of varying ages and experience. It has been, and is, a wonderful experience for the children, and has unquestionably publicised the versatility of the ponies.

The Performance Award Scheme took over, in effect, from the Nan French Memorial Trophy, donated by Mr and Mrs Swannack in 1974 in memory of Miss Nan French, who had been a keen breeder and exhibitor of ridden and driven ponies for many years. The Trophy is now awarded to the overall winning pony in the Performance Award Scheme.

It did, however, have its origins in Shetland in the 1960s, when Mr Jim Smith of Berry came back from visiting some of the ponies he had exported to Norway. He brought with him a film, which was shown to the Pony Breeders' of Shetland Association, of the ponies taking part in ridden and harness classes and in sulky racing. The outcome of this was that Mrs Brooker and Mr Bertie Nicolson of Brindister initiated the first Horse and Pony Event in Shetland, to encourage the riding and the driving of the ponies. It was a great success, as well as being thoroughly enjoyable, and shortly after that, Mrs Brooker and Mrs Helen Thomson of Broothom Ponies (in Dunrossness in Shetland) took two children (Helen's daughters, Heather and Rhonas) and two ponies (Boy Blue of North Dale and Clothie Eswick) down to compete in England. Asked who was going on the trip, Mrs Thomson replied, 'Two children, two ponies, two dogs and two silly old women!' From this initial venture, the journey south has become a marvellous annual event, with Mrs Thomson taking a party of island children and ponies down during the summer holidays to compete in all kinds of events, including the Grand National qualifiers.

It was only a short step from the performance scheme to having a Shetland Performance Show, and the first was held in 1991. It has now become a very popular and successful annual fixture, taking place over two days instead of the original one. In 1996, the Performance Show is to be international, with ponies coming to Britain from various European countries.

Individual ponies have had outstanding success in a variety of ridden events. In 1983, Bincombe Pearl, ridden by Fleur Buchanan, was reserve champion in the National Pony Society's premier ridden championship, held at London's Olympia. This success was repeated in 1986 by Mrs Vivien Hampton's Bard of Transy, ridden by March Rogers (see picture pn page 134). For this championship, ponies of all Mountain and Moorland breeds compete in a series of qualifying rounds throughout Britain. One pony qualifies from each of its own breed qualifiers, and the remainder from qualifiers open to all breeds – a total of 32 finalists.

In the National Pony Society's Working Hunter Pony championship, now held at the Horse of the Year Show at Wembley, in London, the Ulverscroft Stud's Brindle Miranda won the 12.2 hands and under section in 1995. This was a remarkable performance; Shetlands are at a disadvantage in this championship, as they have to jump courses designed for ponies up to 12.2 hands. A pony from the same stable, Claylands Calypso, ridden by Parr Barratt, scored a notable 'first' at the National Pony Society's annual show at Malvern in Worcestershire 1994, when he won the Supreme Mountain and Moorland Ridden Championship of the show – against competition from all the native breeds.

In 1986, Miss Jackie Rawlings' 40½ inch (103 cm) 7-year-old chestnut mare, Boxleaze Carona, ridden by 13-year-old Cordelia Ayers, qualified in the Bath Riding Club's Junior Prix Caprilli team for the National Riding Clubs' championship. As far as is known, Carona is the only Shetland ever to have qualified in this event, which is open to all breeds and types. Carona gained top marks at the Zone final, and in the national final was placed 3rd in her arena. Carona has also been successful in the inter-Pony Club dressage team, Ride and Tie, gymkhana and jumping.

Bard of Transy is but one of a number of Shetlands who have shown their versatility over many years. Bought by Mrs Hampton at Reading in 1974 as a 6-month-old foal, Bard came out under saddle as a 4-year-old, ridden by Lindsey Robinson. His subsequent career exemplifies the problems faced by the breed in mixed Mountain and Moorland classes in the late 70s and early 80s. He started winning in Shetland ridden classes, and he was one of the first to make a serious attempt at mixed Mountain and Moorland classes. In these, he would always be down the line, with 6th place his best effort. It was made harder to accept when judges would sometimes say, 'Your pony went beautifully, I was really pleased with him' – but they lacked the courage to place him in the top three.

The situation began to improve when judges starting riding the exhibits in championships at Ponies of Britain shows and at East Anglia, and he won a number of reserve championships. Finally, at East Anglia Show in 1986, Mrs Margaret Furness made him champion Mountain and Moorland after riding him. It was a great year for Bard and for the breed. Ridden by March Rogers, he qualified for Olympia, and after a superb show, he was named reserve champion – only the second Shetland to be so recognised. The following year, he qualified once again and came fourth, having recovered from a near-fatal illness.

Bard also competed in Working Hunter Pony classes, and won his section in both the National Pony Society and the Ponies of Britain championships, over courses up to 2 foot 9 inches – very testing for a pony standing just 39 inches (99 cm). Few who saw it will forget Bard at the first NPS Working Hunter championship, clearly in two minds

Mrs Vivien Hampton's Bard of Transy, ridden by March Rogers.

about how to tackle a fence which consisted of a single pole with virtually no filling under it. He could have gone either over *or* under it,
and luckily he chose the former! This great little pony now lives in
semi-retirement, but at the age of 22, he stills enjoys a show outing
from time to time.

Bard had a great rival in Clothie Eswick, ridden by Heather Thomson.
In ridden classes Bard would be at the top one day, and 'Essie' the
next, and so on. 'Essie' also raced in the Grand National, and represented the breed in the NPS ridden championship.

The now-famous Shetland Pony Grand National, with the finals held
at a number of performances of the annual Olympia Show Jumping
championships in London, has certainly endeared the ponies to a huge
TV-viewing public. The Grand National was introduced to Olympia
by the show's director, the late Raymond Brooks-Ward. The build-up
to the races at the show is exciting, and much like a 'proper' Grand
National. The ponies are led into the parade ring in the approved manner, and are introduced to the audience. There is a 'tote', and ponies
are 'backed' or sponsored by a number of well known companies. The
jockeys, dressed correctly in racing silks and crash helmets, come in,
mount, and go to the start, before being sent on their way, encouraged
by a race-reading commentator. The race is real, the pace is frantic,
and falls can occur. It is a 'regular' at the show, and certainly one of the
most popular attractions.

In the early days of the Grand National, ponies and riders were chosen from among Performance Award competitors, but it has been such
a success that now a series of qualifying rounds is held at various shows
throughout Britain. Riders and ponies must have belonged to the Performance Award Scheme for at least a year. This is to ensure a safe
standard of riding, as racing on a Shetland demands a very high degree of skill. On one occasion, some of the sons and daughters of famous
event and show-jumping riders found out just how skilled, when they
tried their hands at it. The organisers, unimpressed by the riding abilities of some of the prospective jockeys, chose only the most reliable of
ponies that they knew would stop at the end of the race! Even so, a
number of the novice jockeys discovered that staying on was not as
easy as it looked, and regarded Shetlands and their riders with rather
more respect as a result!

The Grand National is now organised by Pat Renwick and the original Performance Award Scheme group. Not only are there qualifying
rounds, but demonstration races are held at various shows and fairs
throughout the summer. All, including the finals, are run in aid of a
named charity, for which tens of thousands of pounds have been raised

The Shetland Grand National.

over the years. Initially the Sue Ryder Homes benefited, then, for many years, the world-famous Great Ormond Street Hospital for Sick Children, and now the charity is CLIC – the Cancer and Leukaemia in Childhood Trust.

Almost since its inception, the Grand National Team at Olympia has had a mascot – either a very tiny pony, or one that has an outstanding personality. One such was 'Doodle' (more correctly known as Robin's Brae Winsome) belonging to Mrs Helen Thomson. Each year the mascot, accompanied by some of the young racing riders, goes up in the lift at Olympia, to the private boxes on the balcony overlooking the arena, where it visits the very special children, many of them blind, disabled, or terminally ill, who attend some of the performances. The children get *such* pleasure from touching and patting the little pony. Every pony seems to have that 'sixth sense' that tells it that these children are special, and the pony behaves accordingly.

In 1992 CLIC also benefited, to the tune of about £8,000, from a remarkable ride undertaken in Scotland by ponies owned or bred by Pat Renwick's Ulverscroft Stud. The aim of this, the 'Twin Peaks Ride' was for the seven ponies and riders, plus their attendants, to ride up to the top of Cairngorm, the 4,084 foot peak, near Aviemore, and after their descent, to ride, in stages, the 100 miles across Scotland, by way of

Feshiebridge, Kingussie, Newtonmore, Laggan, over the Corrieyairack Pass to Fort Augustus at the southern end of Loch Ness, and then along the tow path of the Caledonian Canal to Fort William – a distance of about 100 miles. From there, the group tackled the ride to the 4,406 foot summit of Ben Nevis. As for the drive through Shetland, the organisation for the ride was formidable.

The mounted group ranged from a 4-year-old to a 14-year-old. The two youngest riders were led throughout the ride – a pointer, as was remarked at the time, to some judges who say that Shetlands are not suitable Leading Rein ponies!

The ascent of Cairngorm was accomplished without incident, as was the following day's ride to Newtonmore, and the next via Glentruim and Laggan to Garva Bridge, which spans the Spey River. The latter ride was marvellous, as there were long stretches of grassy verge where the ponies could go on a bit without the worry of traffic.

The fourth day was one that none who took part are likely to forget. It entailed crossing the 2,500 foot Corrieyairack Pass, by means of one of General Wade's Military roads – a stone road that had been built in the early 18th century to facilitate the movement of troops through the Highlands. The ponies and riders had a wonderful day, travelling over rugged moorland, amid some of the most magnificent scenery Scotland has to offer.

The ponies, riders and walkers, meantime, now incredibly fit, had forged enthusiastically ahead, and were soon out of sight. But even they slowed down when we came to tackle the section which climbed to the summit of the pass. This consisted of a series of 13 very tight hairpin bends or traverses, on a surface that, while still liberally strewn with rocks from the original road, was basically very slippery peaty soil.

The summit was eventually achieved; the weather, which had been horrible, changed, and the remainder of the ride down into Fort Augustus was completed in sunshine and relative ease. After a rest day, the group set off up the steep, rugged track towards the 4,000 foot plus summit of Britain's highest mountain, Ben Nevis. Sadly, this brave expedition ended in tragedy, when, about 600 feet from the summit, one of the walkers with the group suffered a fatal heart attack. He would have been the last person to want to detract from the magnificent achievement of ponies and riders in conquering Cairngorm, riding 100 miles across Scotland and all but reaching the summit of 'the Ben'.

The ridden group did not make it to the summit of Ben Nevis, but in 1988, Sam McArthur, from Nairn, had led his 10-year-old chestnut pony, Cyril, to the top. Cyril was fitted with a special pair of rubber shoes,

The Twin Peaks ride – heading towards the Corrieyairack Pass.

and Mr McArthur also took a pair of aluminium ramps to help Cyril across the roughest of the boulder fields on the higher ground.

Many a keen rider to hounds has been introduced to hunting on the back of a Shetland pony. Anyone who imagines that the little pony will be content to potter along quietly on a lead rein and watch proceedings from a distance seriously underestimates the breed! It will do so if asked, of course, but once the young rider is competent, a

Shetland is quite capable of keeping up with all by the very fastest field, by going over, under, or even through, the various fences, hedges and ditches on the average run. There are countless stories of small, determined Shetlands and equally small, determined riders, emerging, more or less on hands and knees, from under a thick bullfinch hedge – too high to jump, but not too thick to crawl through. There have been occasions when a Shetland pony has given a lead to a reluctant horse over a trappy place – humiliating for the horse, perhaps, but, oh, how satisfying for the pony and rider.

9

THE CHANGING SCENE

The almost total change in the role of Shetlands that has taken place during this century has been accompanied by a drastic decline in numbers of ponies in the islands, a huge increase in ponies worldwide, and an appreciation by at least some members of the Stud Book Society and its Council that their role, too, has changed and extended.

The council itself has changed considerably. It began with a membership of twelve, including the president and the honorary secretary. All, except the president, were resident in Shetland or in Scotland. The first president, the Marquis of Londonderry, served for 2 years, and his successors until 1938 were in office for a year. Mr J. E. Kerr served from 1938 until 1955, followed by Mrs Cox until 1959. Since then the presidents have held office for a fixed term of 2 years. The council now consists of 21 members (plus the immediate past president), each of whom serves for a 3 year term. This may be followed by a further 3 years, after which the member must stand down for a year before seeking re-election. Council members are now resident in all parts of the United Kingdom, including Northern Ireland. There is a full-time professional secretary with supporting office staff. The society, whose offices are now in Perth, has become a limited company, and is also a registered charity.

The scope of the work undertaken by the council on behalf of the society has widened enormously since its formation, and continues to do so, as every aspect of the pony world becomes more formalised and regulated.

One of the most important steps taken by the council to safeguard the standard, and a viable and acceptable population of ponies in the islands, was the Premium Stallion scheme, and, later, the Filly Premium Scheme – both of which are in existence today.

Maintenance of a population of our native breeds in their natural habitats is of vital importance for several reasons. Firstly, they are a unique part of the British natural heritage, and have been a feature of the Mountain and Moorland landscapes for many thousands of years. Secondly, as was explained earlier, they are the products of their environments, and it is important that a viable population be retained in that habitat, and subject to it – in contrast to the often rather artificial conditions under which the majority of the breeds now live. The Shetlands, possibly because of the degree of purity of the breed, are arguably less affected *physically* by living away from their own habitat than most of our other native breeds. These tend to lose some of their hardiness, their long bones, i.e. the leg bones, tend to lengthen, thus altering the ratio of body depth to length of leg (which should be 1:1). They certainly lose, and are often encouraged to lose, correct movement of all the joints which enables them to cover rough ground safely – and this *is* happening to some Shetlands.

What they also tend to lose is some of their native instincts – which have been such a vital part of their ability to survive. For instance, a Shetland breeder in the English Midlands, who has both home-bred and island-bred ponies, commented that the island-bred animals will instinctively jump a ditch safely, whereas some of the home-bred ponies are likely to clamber down into it, and possibly become trapped; the island-bred stallions still retain their instinct to 'herd' their mares during the stud season – an instinct that has been lost in some of the home-bred ones.

The importance of these instincts in the native pony is illustrated by two stories of Mrs Brooker's stallion, Star of North Dale, who took part in the Centenary drive through Shetland. He lived much of his life turned out on a hill in Mainland Shetland with his mares. One day, when Mrs Brooker went to check the ponies, she saw that Star was badly cut and torn underneath, so she asked him to jump into the back of her Land Rover, took him down, and attended to his wounds. It was not until some time later that she learned how he was injured. A crofter had seen that a new-born foal had rolled under the fence away from its dam. Star apparently noticed this, because he jumped the fence, *and actually pushed the foal back into the field to be with its dam* before jumping back, and catching himself on the wire in so doing. More predictably, perhaps, Star always knew when it was going to snow, and herded his mares down from the hill to shelter – even on one occasion actually getting out of his field by the croft to do so. These survival instincts have played such an important part in making our native breeds what they are, and, arguably, can only survive in their native habitats.

It might be said that the Stallion Scheme had its roots in the first decade of this century, when there was a great increase in demand for ponies from the USA and Canada, with over 1,300 being shipped across the Atlantic. In 1907, ponies bound for America were fetching good prices – the poorest quality 2- and 3-year-old fillies sold for £15, and stallions for up to £50. This trade, together with the continued need for pit ponies, had a predictable effect on ponies in the islands.

For some years, a stallion scheme had been operated in Shetland by the Congested Districts Board, a body set up in 1897 to help areas of the Highlands and Islands where the population was too large to support itself. In 1912, the Board handed the stallion scheme (of which very little is known) over to the newly created Board of Agriculture for Scotland (B.O.A.S.).

The B.O.A.S. evidently appreciated that, if ponies were once more to contribute significantly to the crofting economy, action was needed to re-establish a better type. Under the scheme, the board gave grants to owners of nine stallions to make them available to crofters' mares. Initially it was a somewhat haphazard affair, with no overall standard being set, or registration in the Stud Book required. That was remedied in 1915, and 580 mares were covered by 22 stallions in that year. The crofters paid a 2 shilling and 6 pence (30 pence) fee. Some of the stallions were tethered, so crofters had to take their mares to be served, but others were travelled. The stallion owners were paid an annual premium of £7.10s. for each stallion. The scheme as such appeared to be working satisfactorily, and in 1925, 23 stallions served 690 mares. Seven years later, however, it was abandoned for reasons that have become all too familiar over the years – cuts in Treasury expenditure. The tragedy was that although the scheme worked, it coincided almost exactly with the worst slump to hit the breed – both in the islands and in mainland Britain, so its impact was, arguably, less than it should have been under more favourable circumstances.

The years of World War 1 saw an abrupt cessation of exports to America, although there was still some demand for pit ponies. As this was only for colts and stallions of 3 to 4 years, the crofters had to keep them for several years, until they were bought by dealers at near giveaway prices. There was no thought of registering them; it was just not worthwhile. To add to the problems, the sale of ponies for pleasure became virtually a thing of the past.

The situation did not change greatly after World War 1, although exports to America picked up a little. Previously prosperous and well known island breeders went out of the pony business. Before long, the Depression of the 30s took a further toll, and many other studs ceased breeding. European countries imposed tariffs on ponies imported from Britain; in 1932 this amounted to £7.10s. a head for Shetlands into Germany, and between 210 and 630 francs, depending on age, into France.

To add insult to injury, foreign ponies – from Russia and Iceland – were imported into Britain to work in the mines. The cumulative effects were devastating. Ponies in the islands for which there was no sale were shot. Prices in mainland Britain were at an all-time low. At the dispersal of the Earlshall Stud, top quality ponies went for an average of just £6.14s.1d., with Dollar Boy, at a mere 33 guineas, sharing top price with the 4-year-old mare, Elderflower II of Earlshall. The general decline was reflected in the Stud Book, from just under 800 registrations in 1914, to a mere 147 in 1935.

Fortunately for the breed, a number of studs in mainland Britain soldiered on between the two world wars, and, in spite of restrictions on the use of land (among other things), also survived through World War II. The standards in the islands remained deplorable; because requirements for the coal mines had changed somewhat, with the demand being for the taller, leggy type, standing up to 42 or even 43 inches (109 cm), the crofters used tall, leggy stallions in the immediate post-World War II years.

In the 1950s, however, the export trade to North America began to revive, and soon the demand was such that ponies of all shapes, sizes and colours were shipped across the Atlantic. Greys, chestnuts and duns were in particular demand. Freight costs from Glasgow to Montreal were just £23, and hundreds of ponies left the islands – further denuding them of quality animals.

This time, thankfully, help was at hand, and it was a case of 'Cometh the hour, cometh the man' – or, more accurately on this occasion, 'Cometh the men and woman'! The men were Mr James Dean, Livestock Officer for the northern region of the D.O.A.S., his immediate superior, Mr Bean, and Major Maurice Cox. The woman, and the dynamic driving force behind the subsequent battle to improve the Island stock, was Mrs Betty Cox.

Mr Dean, as Livestock Inspector, expressed concern at the situation, and as a result the D.O.A.S. resumed the practice (which had been suspended in 1932) of sending some better class stallions from the north of Scotland to be used on the crofters' mares. The Stud-Book Society Council was not, at that time, very interested in what was happening in Shetland, but Mrs Cox had just become Vice President. She certainly *was* interested, and properly concerned.

In the spring of 1948 James Dean invited the Coxes to accompany him on a tour of the islands, during which he was to assess the effect of the stallions on the breed, and also to inspect and mark any mares put forward by the crofters. The inspection scheme had been approved by the council, who agreed that suitable mares not exceeding 42 inches

(107 cm), in foal to one of the stallions placed by the Department, be accepted as Inspected Stock. These mares were marked by an ear tag. (This was not, apparently, the first time that ponies had been marked by ear tags: in 1838, a practical joker spread the story that a ship of war, with a number of men and bloodhounds on board, had arrived in Bressay Sound for the purpose of seizing all unmarked ponies in Shetland for government service. For three days, so the story went, every crofter in the island took to the hills to catch up his ponies and ear mark them!)

During the tour, the Coxes were less than impressed with the ponies they saw, apart from some better quality ones on Unst and at Walls. Many had dreadful long, coffin-shaped heads, weak quarters and cow hocks. They agreed that really good quality stallions of about 37-38½ inches (94-98 cm) were required, with plenty of bone and good limbs. Of special value to them, and, subsequently to the breed as a whole, were the genuine and lasting friendships the Coxes made with so many of the island breeders.

Back in Scotland, Mrs Cox again tried to persuade the council that the society should become involved in the stallion scheme, but the prevailing attitude was that 'it would be a complete waste of money, that there were no ponies left in the islands worth bothering about, and that no one up there would bother to do anything about improving them'. That most of the council, including the President, had never been to Shetland was, to say the least, unfortunate. Mrs Cox *did* manage to persuade the council to invite James Dean to attend a meeting to explain the difficulties, and put forward the Department's suggestions for placing more stallions on some of the scattalds. Unfortunately, his explanations were cut short somewhat peremptorily, and he was advised that the council was not interested.

Betty Cox, however, was a dedicated and very determined lady, and, despite this rebuff, she, James Dean, and the newly appointed secretary of the society, Mr Tom Myles, worked out a detailed Premium Stallion Scheme, and also discussed the possibility of giving premiums to promising fillies if kept for breeding (a scheme that was eventually implemented in 1983). In 1955, the then President, Mr J. E. Kerr of Harviestoun, retired; Mrs Cox took over as President, with Mr William Mungall of Transy as Vice President. With the support of Mr Mungall, the Stallion Scheme for the islands was approved, although not without some residual opposition.

Under the scheme, which was put into operation for the 1956 season, thirteen registered pedigreed stallions were to be selected by the Stud-Book Society, and approved by the Department, who would pay premiums to the owners. Account was taken, as far as was possible, of the size, colour, etc, of the stallion required by the crofters with rights on each scattald. Because of lack of good stallions in Shetland, most of the Premium animals had to be transported by ship from the south, and were then turned out on selected scattalds, to run with the mares. Stallion Custodians were appointed to oversee each scattald. The Scheme was much helped by The Crofter's Act of 1955, which established the Crofters' Commission; this had power to regulate the running of the Common Grazings (i.e. the scattalds). From time immemorial, crofters had had the right to run any mare or stallion, registered or otherwise, on the scattalds; had this practice continued, the Premium Scheme could not have operated. However, under the Act, it was agreed that only registered pedigreed Shetland stallions could be turned out.

The list of the first Premium stallions in the scheme gives some idea of the high standard of animal selected (although 13 were selected, only 12 were turned out). They were: Viking of Houlland, a 40 inch (101 cm) black by Berlad of Transy out of Amelia of Dunira; Sovereign of Marshwood, a 39 inch (99 cm) skewbald by Rustic Sprite of Standen out of Jessica of Marshwood; Littlestoke Neptune 11, a 38 inch (96 cm) grey, by Littlestoke Jack Frost out of Littlestoke Nepeta; Robin, a 38 inch (96 cm) chestnut by Cuckoo out of Rising Star; Spaniard of Marshwood, a 39½ inch (100 cm) black by Rustic Sprite of Standen out of Jessica of Marshwood; Sprinkle of Marshwood, a 40 inch (101 cm) black by Supreme of Marshwood out of Heldrista of Transy; Trigger of Marshwood, a 38 inch (96 cm) black by Sophimore of Transy out of Rossette of Marshwood; Blue Bonnet of Mundurno, a 40½ inch (103 cm) grey by Silver Prince of Mundurno out of Blue Bell of Mundurno; Norseman, a 39 inch (99 cm) piebald by Berlad of Transy out of Ireta of Longhaugh; Nimbus, a 39 inch (99 cm) piebald by Mundurno Banker out of Golden Girl of Mundurno; Wells Prince, a 37½ inch (95 cm) black by Harviestoun Prince out of Harviestoun Troya: Benvorlich, a 37 inch (94 cm) piebald by Wells Commander out of Kingsford May Queen; and Brian Second of Longhaugh, a 39 inch (99 cm) black by Harviestoun Brian out of Sadie of Fothringham.

Although Maurice Cox in his book wrote that, 'From the start this scheme has been thoroughly satisfactory, and the vast majority of crofters were co-operative…', his close involvement and that of his wife precluded him from mentioning that it was largely due to the immense amount of work undertaken by them, and by James Dean, that this was the case.

The Coxes visited Shetland for up to 6 weeks every year, smoothing out potential difficulties. They lived in a caravan – one of the first to be seen in Shetland, and in this they could park near the scattalds, and study the ponies. Such was the knowledge they acquired, not just of the ponies, but of the breeders and crofters, that they were able to suggest suitable stallions according to the type of mares they had seen for themselves on the various scattalds, and in their discussions with the owners. The Stallion Scheme is still in operation, has proved an enormous success, and the standard of the ponies in Shetland has improved out of recognition. It has meant the continuation of breeding of the ponies in their native habitat, under natural conditions. There are now, however, because of changing circumstances, far fewer scattalds on which stallions are turned out.

The work did not end with the allocation of Premium stallions. Any crofter who had rights on a scattald, and whose mare foaled to a Premium stallion, could have that mare inspected for registration. Initially this very daunting task was undertaken by the Coxes, who travelled the length and breadth of the islands. In those days, the roads were rough, and instead of the convenient roll-on roll-off vehicular ferries of today, inter-island travel was by means of the inter-island ship, the *Earl of Zetland*, onto which vehicles (and ponies) were loaded by means of slings.

Most of the mare inspections took place either in early spring or in the autumn, i.e. before they were turned out on the hill or when they came 'in-by' again. The weather in Shetland at those times of the year can be fierce. Stables are virtually non-existent, and sheds not always available, so the inspections were often carried out in the open, in the wind, the sleet or the snow. The Coxes travelled miles, both on sea and land, inspecting mares, many of whom had hardly been handled, and were as wild as hawks. On one visit to Fetlar, they were confronted with 25 to 30 ponies, some of them Highland crosses, that had been herded into a small school yard. Somehow or other, those that were of Shetland type had to be cornered, measured, and their mouths inspected. Some young men tried to catch the ponies, and the Coxes were forced to press themselves against the walls of the yard as the herd of animals rocketed round, their tethering ropes with stakes attached behaving like unguided missiles to be avoided by whatever means possible.

As the scheme progressed, there were, inevitably, some problems, and Betty Cox used to joke that when mares failed to foal, she was held personally responsible! On one scattald, complaints were received well into the season, that the stallion was useless, he never served the mares, and was falling off in condition. It was too late to replace him, but he was removed and sold. Imagine the surprise when a full crop of quality foals appeared in the following spring! The stallion obviously

The sale ring at Lerwick. Mrs Betty Cox is on the right.

had served the mares quickly and without fuss, and left them – and this accounted for his loss of condition. The breeder who bought him at a bargain basement price was delighted, and used him successfully for years. The importance of the Stallion Scheme was such that it actually led to the breaking (if only temporarily) of the Seamen's strike in 1966. Four stallions for the scheme were waiting to be shipped up to Shetland, but were held up by the strike. It was explained to the Glasgow strike committee that if the stallions were prevented from travelling, they would miss the breeding season, and that an important part of the Shetland pony market might be lost to the Welsh. Agreeing that the ponies should be allowed to sail, the Glasgow strikers' organiser is reported to have said, 'I am allowing the stallions to go to protect a home market. I understand the Welsh are trying to get in on this market, and if the stallions do not get to the islands in time we could lose it.'

The financing of the Stallion Scheme was eventually taken over by the Stud Book Society, and the premiums are now paid out of a much-appreciated grant from the Horse Race Betting Levy Board, distributed by the National Pony Society. It is administered by The Pony Breeders of Shetland Association.

This association was founded in the early 1970s, with Betty and Maurice Cox very much involved. Every spring, offers are invited from breeders to supply stallions to go out on the scattalds. There are now only 5 scattalds on which the stallions run, nearly all in Unst, in contrast to the dozen or so when the scheme first started. These days, nearly all Premium stallions come from within the islands, in contrast to the situation in the early years, when they were brought up from the south. The stallions are all inspected by the association because, even though they are all fully registered and licensed, they may have had a bad winter, or some other temporary problem. Once accepted, they are turned out on the scattalds about mid-May to run with the mares until the end of July or the middle of August – the comparatively short season ensuring that there are no very early or very late foals. Mrs Flaws, the secretary of the association, has an interesting chart, showing the stallions that have been on all the scattalds from the very start of the scheme right down to the present day. It shows how the number of scattalds requiring ponies has varied over the years, rising to a maximum of 18, and gradually reducing to the present 5.

While the Stallion Scheme has been established for many years, a more recent introduction, also funded by the society through the Horse Race Betting Levy Board, is the Filly Premium Scheme, started in 1983. This, too, is administered by the Pony Breeders of Shetland. The committee inspects 3-year-old fillies, and awards premiums to those they consider suitable, provided the owners guarantee to retain them for three years. In that time, it is hoped that they will breed good foals, and in the long term, improve the overall quality of the stock in the islands. There is general agreement that the scheme is fulfilling its aims very satisfactorily.

As soon as the Stallion Scheme became established, and foals of greatly improved quality began to arrive, it was clear that a more satisfactory outlet for selling them was necessary. Most crofters sold direct to the local dealers for what they could get, and soon began to remark that it was hardly worth the trouble of going in for improved breeding if the prices were not going to reflect the rising standards of their stock.

Mrs Cox and Tom Myles visited Shetland Marts Limited in Lerwick, and arranged that in October 1958 an auction sale of foals would be held at Baltasound in Unst, under the auspices of the society. Maurice Cox's description of the journey from Lerwick to Baltasound underlines the fact that the pony breeders and buyers in those days needed to be every bit as hardy as the ponies. 'Most of the buyers left Lerwick about 6 am in sheets of rain, travelling by bus on what was known there as the "Overland" route. This entails a bus ride of about an hour, then half an hour in a ferry boat, back into another bus for an hour's run, in those years over an untarred road with what can only be politely called an indifferent surface, once more into a boat for a twenty-minute crossing to Unst, and then a bus for a further twenty minutes to Baltasound.' Added to this was the fact that the sale was held outdoors, still in sheeting rain, on a piece of ground above the bay. Spectators and buyers sat round on benches, their knees forming the ring.

The top price at that first sale was a remarkable 116 guineas for a pedigreed yearling filly from Mr Bruce's stud at Mousa, and 92 guineas for a yearling filly owned by Mr Henry Henderson. The latter was just about to celebrate his 89th birthday, and had been a persistent opponent of the Stallion Scheme; he had entered a few foals with a degree of reluctance! This first sale was a phenomenal success, and began a tradition that has continued to this day.

A few years ago, comparative luxury arrived in the form of a Nissen hut type building to house an indoor ring, with a range of pens outside. It is draughty, and when the wind blows (which is often!) it is extremely noisy – but at least it is dry. It does not impress everyone. In 1994, a party of breeders came up by bus from Leicestershire to attend the sales and tour the islands. On arriving at the sale, the bus driver was heard say, 'All this way from Leicestershire to sit in a tin shed … they must be mad!'

The success of the Baltasound Sale was such that it was quickly followed by one at Lerwick. A few years later another sale was instituted at Aberdeen, and later still, one at Reading in Berkshire. Nineteen ninety one saw the introduction of a sale of Registered Shetlands at Telford Agricultural Centre in Cheshire, and in 1993, a mixed Mountain and Moorland sale was held at Penrith in Cumbria in which Shetlands participated with the approval of the society. This latter sale shows every sign of becoming an annual event. All these sales are held under the auspices of the Stud Book Society. From 1985, following concern at the standard of some of the foals being offered, the society decided that all foals should in future be inspected for conformation and movement by an inspection panel of senior judges, with a veterinary surgeon present in case of dispute. Any foal failing the inspection has its registration withdrawn and is removed from the official sale.

Each sale is preceded by show classes for the young stock to be sold. These days, judges for the island sales are often invited up from mainland Britain. At Baltasound, in particular, this can be an experience they are unlikely to forget! The sale ring, in which the ponies are judged, is extremely small, and there is no space at all to run the entries out to

The problem of judging foals in the sale ring at Lerwick.

see their action. The judge thus has to adjudicate in the ring, amid a
sea of pushing, whinnying, excited, and largely unhandled foals. Some
have been halter broken, or, as appeared in a recent catalogue 'Halter
broken, briefly'. As one judge explained, 'It's so crowded you can usually only see one end of each foal; I was thankful for a helpful steward
who, when I was about to place one foal top, quietly asked me if I'd
seen its back end. I hadn't; it was appalling, and I quickly changed my
placings!' One of the 'spectator sports' is watching the range of ex-
pressions on the faces of first-time judges, which usually passes rapidly
from disbelief, through outright panic, to a kind of glazed puzzlement!

In the early days of the sales, the ponies were shipped from
Baltasound to Lerwick aboard the *Earl of Zetland*. At Lerwick, they were
unloaded onto the pier before being re-loaded into the *St Clair* for the
crossing to Aberdeen. There have been a few unscheduled incidents.
The Scotsman of October 20th, 1927, described under the headline 'Left
Before Ship', how 26 ponies awaiting shipment broke through a bar-
rier, raced across the pier, and plunged into Lerwick harbour. Confusion
reigned for some little time but they all eventually came ashore by
means of a slipway, and after veterinary checks were loaded to undertake their journey in a more conventional manner. The Shetland Pony
Stud Book Society magazine of 1975 recorded how a foal jumped off
the pier into the water and set off swimming strongly at a good five

The Shetland breed standard

Height: Registered stock must not exceed 40 inches (102 cm) at three years or under, nor 42 inches (107 cm) at four years or over. Ponies are measured from the withers to the ground, by measuring stick, and a level stance, preferably concrete, should be used.

Colour: Shetland ponies may be any colour known in horses except spotted.

Coat: The coat changes according to the season of the year; a double coat in winter with guard hairs which shed rain and keep the pony's skin completely dry in the worst weather. By contrast, the summer coat is short and should carry a beautiful, silky sheen. At all times the mane and tail hair should be long, straight and profuse, and the feathering of the fetlocks straight and silky.

Head: The head should be small, carried well, and in proportion. Ears should be small, and erect, wide set, but pointing well forward. Forehead should be broad, with bold, dark, intelligent eyes. Blue eyes are not acceptable. Muzzle must be broad, wide with nostrils wide open. Teeth and jaw must be correct.

Forelegs: Should be well placed, with sufficient good, flat bone. Strong forearm. Short, balanced cannon bone. Springy pasterns.

Hindlegs: The thighs should be strong and muscular, with well shaped strong hocks, neither hooky nor too straight. When viewed from behind, the hindlegs should not be too widely apart, nor should the hocks be turned in.

Feet: Tough, round, well shaped – not short, narrow, contracted or thin.

Action: Straight, free action using every joint, tracking-up well.

General: A most salient and essential feature of the Shetland pony is its general air of vitality (presence), stamina and robustness.

knots towards the island of Bressay. The purchaser, seeing his sixty guineas' worth of filly disappearing across the harbour, commandeered six small boats, and the foal was eventually lassooed and brought back in the Bressay ferry.

Nowadays, all the Baltasound ponies are transported to Lerwick by road, and as the Lerwick sale is on the following day, the two batches of foals travel together in the ferry to Aberdeen. On the pier in Lerwick they are all carefully loaded, with frequent veterinary checks, into large open trailers, which are then towed into the hold of the ferry. Hay and water is provided en route, and most ponies travel well. The ferry company will not allow them to sail if severe weather is forecast.

In Britain, the Shetland Pony Stud-Book Society has been the backbone of the breed since it was founded in 1890. It has nearly always been forward looking, and it has adapted to suit the changing conditions in the pony world. The Stud Book has been opened at various times for the inclusion of inspected mares, and was opened again recently for inspected geldings. (There has been a separate section for fully pedigreed and registered geldings since 1970.) This was done because it was felt that there was a number of good geldings of obvious Shetland breeding which had not, for whatever reason, been registered as foals, although, quite often, either their sire or dam was known. These ponies are useful as performance animals, and, as in the past, they were registered as Inspected Stock (IS).

As is apparent, the society has, throughout its existence, sought to improve the standard of the ponies, and with this in mind, it inaugurated a Stallion Inspection Scheme in 1973. This was suggested by Maurice Cox in 1969. He felt that the mandatory Stallion Licensing conducted by the Ministry of Agriculture was not wholly satisfactory. At first, the inspections applied to England and Wales only, but they were extended to cover the whole of the United Kingdom in 1974. The scheme set the pattern for a number of other native breed societies.

Now known as the Stallion Assessment Scheme, passing it is compulsory before a stallion licence can be issued. There are two assessment 'seasons' – in the spring and the autumn – although out of season assessments may be available if a colt is to be exported. Any colt is eligible from the age of 2 years, but it is advised that only exceptionally mature 2-year-olds should be presented. Two- and 3-year-olds passing the assessment are required to return as 4-year-olds to be re-measured.

Each pony presented is examined by three panel assessors, who individually, not collectively, assess his action, conformation and breed characteristics, and enter their opinions on a form. The assessors may consult a veterinary surgeon before coming to a decision. If the colt passes the assessment, he is then examined by a veterinary surgeon appointed by the society. The vet. measures the pony, completes an identification chart showing all whorls and natural markings, and any permanent identification markings such as freeze-branding or microchipping. Irrespective of passing or failing, all colts must be blood-typed and identified. If the colt passes the assessors and the veterinary inspection, he is issued with a stallion licence.

A colt that has been referred by the assessors to the veterinary surgeon may be deferred by the vet. for further examination after a specific period. A colt that has failed the assessors may return once only after the first year for further assessment; if it fails the veterinary examination for any reason other than immaturity or injury which the vet. considers will come right in given time, the colt will not be eligible for further assessment. All colt owners must sign an application which states that they agree to abide by the decision of the assessors and the veterinary surgeon.

When assessing potential stallions, the assessors are guided by the official breed standard. It comes as a considerable surprise to realise that, apart from the height limit of 42 inches (107 cm) stipulated for ponies being included in the first Stud Book, there was no official breed description until the 1960s. This was revised in 1991, specifically to exclude blue eyes. These had crept into the breed within the few years preceding 1991, in the form of blue-eyed creams, which came into the breed, it is said, by way of an inspected mare, and possibly the illegal use of a Welsh Mountain pony stallion.

In contrast to most European societies, the British Stud Book Society does not inspect fillies or mares that are from registered parents.

In 1994, guidelines for showing were published.

1. Ears may be trimmed flat (no trimming inside of ear).
2. Trimming of whiskers on jawline acceptable.
3. No false hair.
4. No artificial colouring or make-up should be used.
5. No pulling of manes or tails; however, tails may be rough- trimmed to clear ground if dragging.
6. No trimming of feathers on legs.
7. Working ponies ONLY may be clipped in the interest of welfare. Under no circumstances should foals be clipped.
8. Members are asked to refrain from using whips or show canes longer than 30 inches (76 cm) overall.

Readers may wonder why some of these were necessary! The necessity arose because, in the last few years, exhibitors of certain Mountain and Moorland breeds, especially the lighter ones who also compete in Riding Pony classes, started a fashion of using various substances to enhance, and in some cases alter, the appearance of their ponies. For instance, unattractive markings could be altered, eyes made to appear larger, white ponies made dappled grey, presumably to make them look younger, and so on. Manes and tails, those typical and useful attributes of any native breed, were being pulled excessively, thus eliminating the true native appearance. In some cases, wispy manes and inadequate forelocks were being 'improved' with false hair. There have been instances of judges lifting forelocks and/or tails, only to have them come off in their hands – a somewhat un-nerving experience! At sales, not under the auspices of the society, foals were being clipped out.

The overall result of these practices was to make some native ponies look rather ridiculous, and far removed from the tough, hardy, workman-like animals they are supposed to be. This modern development does not benefit the breed, and the society has moved to curb it with commendable promptness. On the other hand, and in a completely different context, the development of the comparatively new veterinary procedures of artificial insemination and embryo transfer can be beneficial. The society has therefore set up a committee to investigate these procedures and to draw up a list of guidelines. The procedures have not yet gone beyond the experimental stages with the breed in this country, but A.I. is practised in Holland.

For such an active society with a large membership, it might be thought that an official Breed Show would have been instigated many years ago. In fact, it was not until 1982 that the first such show was held at Park Hall, Lincolnshire, and it has been staged at different venues throughout the country ever since. From the start, separate in-hand classes have been held for black ponies, coloured ponies and ponies of 34 inches (86 cm) and under. Each section has its own champion, which then competes against the other two for the Supreme Championship. Ridden and driven classes are also included.

Prior to the arrival of the official breed show, Shetlands had competed in all kinds of shows throughout Britain from at least the closing years on the 19th century. All-Shetland shows have been held for many years, including those organised by Mrs Hester Knight of the Lockinge Stud, and held at Newbury Racecourse from 1964 until 1973, followed by shows at Huntingdon Racecourse, organised by Mr Hamilton Renwick of the Birling Stud in 1974 and 1975, and the Autumn Shetland Show at Wellington Park in Berkshire.

Without doubt, the most exciting Shetland Show ever held in Britain was the 1990 Breed show, staged as part of the celebrations to mark the Centenary of the founding of the Shetland Pony Stud Book Society. It was held at the Royal Highland showground, Ingliston, Edinburgh, and was one of the highlights of 10 days of events in August that brought together Shetland breeders and enthusiasts from all over the

Overseas representatives at The Centenary Show, with British Stud-Book Society officials, 1990.

world. The Centenary Committee, headed by Mr Dougal Dick, spent three years planning and organising the celebrations. One of its most imaginative ventures was to publish a delightful book, *A Century of Shetlands,* edited by Mrs Angela Gosling of the well known Wetherden Stud, which contained reminiscences and articles giving a nostalgic, fascinating and often amusing picture of the breed in all its many facets. Mrs Gosling was, for many years, the editor of the society's excellent magazine, which was produced initially twice a year, but now annually.

The Edinburgh celebrations began with a two-day conference at Heriot Watt University. In addition to guest speakers, reports were given by representatives from the Breed Societies of Australia, the Netherlands, Finland, Sweden, France, East Germany, Japan and Denmark.

The two-day show at Ingliston attracted an astonishing 2,500 visitors, of which 300 were from overseas. In addition to the usual show classes, the second day included a spectacular pageant of Shetlands, organised by Mrs Marie Brooker, and demonstrating many of the uses to which Shetlands have been put during the last 100 years. It was a magnificent show, brilliantly ʝnised, and thoroughly enjoyed by everyone. Following the show, a party of 117 went up to Shetland to see the ponies in their native environment, and to attend the Shetland members' celebration show at Lerwick.

Looking back over the activities of the breed down the years, and at shows in particular, the contrast between present-day shows and those of the pre-World War II era is marked. There were far fewer shows than there are today, but perhaps one of the biggest differences is the means of travelling the ponies. Today, ponies all travel from home to show-ground in motorised vehicles, ranging from single towed trailers to huge and luxurious horse-boxes, once described as resembling 'a row of cottages on wheels'. Pre-war travelling up to about 15 miles was done either 'on the hoof' or in a horse-drawn float; beyond that, the ponies went by train. In unpublished writings, Maurice Cox described how it worked:

> At the really large shows, such as the Royal, the Highland and the Bath and West, until about 1935 most of the stock, ponies included, arrived and departed by rail. That is to say, they arrived at the nearest station by railway horse box and in many cases continued on to the show ground in a railway-owned horse-drawn float. At these grounds, the railway companies had huge horse float parks, or just occasionally, there was a siding actually in or adjacent to the showground. This travelling by rail was very satisfactory and the companies extremely helpful … Trouble was invariably taken to ensure the quickest journey, and the railway servants handling the stock were almost always thoroughly experienced men. Unless the railway porters actually loaded or unloaded your horse or pony and some mishap should occur to you or your animal, the Railway were not responsible, so these skilled handlers were essential.
>
> There would be no difficulty in arranging a (rail) horsebox to take a horse or two ponies say, from Bridport (Dorset) to Perth or Edinburgh, and the journey would be as fast as possible with no undue delays or changes.
>
> It was usual for the local station master to get in touch with anyone in his area who was in the habit of showing stock, to find out where one was showing at any of the big shows, so that rail transport could be arranged. Sometimes this meant the assembling of a small special train to meet a larger one at some junction, or it might mean the special routing of a single vehicle to some distant place. The Railway companies, and for a few years, British Railways, always had an office on the showground where information about services and alterations or additions to them might be made.

Even after nationalisation of the railways, it was possible to send ponies by train. 'On one occasion, we sent ponies up to the Highland Show and the Railways *did* slip up. This time, instead of arriving at about midday on a Monday, the journey finished at 2 or 3 a.m. on the Tuesday ... I did at once approach the Railways and was immediately assured that the return journey would be hastened and no delay allowed. On arrival home a few days later I enquired of Maunder (the stud groom) how he had fared ... whereupon I had a harrowing tale of how he and the lad with him had spent as much time in the air as on the seat, and that the ponies were almost exhausted keeping their balance, as the box had been put on the tail of a fast express to London!'

Single ponies were also sent in crates in the guard's van, as Maurice Cox described. 'About twenty minutes before the train was due we arrived at the station with pony and crate (we used to have three crates, strong but light, and of course, returnable). We would lead the pony to the heavy parcel weighbridge, where he or she and the crate would be weighed separately. Then we led the pony across the lines to the "down" platform, and the crate was barrowed over. Shortly before the train was due, the pony was quietly put in the crate, and when the train came in, the crate was wheeled to where, with two or three willing helpers, it was lifted in the guard's van. Some guards, I must say, did not look altogether with favour on their guest. The average weight of crate and pony was around 4 to 4.5 hundredweight and the charge was not unduly high, and we never had a case of accident or injury.'

10

TO THE FAR CORNERS
OF THE WORLD

---◆---

AUSTRALIA

Shetland ponies have been exported, first from the islands, then from all over Britain, to countries in every corner of the globe. Many thousands of ponies are bred outside the British Isles, and, indeed, in just one European country – Holland – there are now more Shetlands than there are in Britain. In total, it is calculated that there are some 75,000 Shetland ponies worldwide. Of these, about 15,000 are to be found in the United Kingdom, including approximately 600 in Shetland.

The most distant travellers from Shetland were those bought by the brothers William and Andrew Lyall of Victoria in Australia. Brief mention was made of them in Chapter 4 , and the fact that of the 2 stallions and 22 mares that set sail from Britain in 1857 aboard the *General Nowell* (or the *Norfolk*, according to which account is taken as correct!) 18 mares and the stallions arrived. That only 4 died says much for the resilience and adaptability of the breed. In these days of swift, safe and relatively comfortable air travel for ponies, it is difficult to imagine what a sea journey lasting many weeks must have been like. The conditions in the ships were far from luxurious for people, let alone for ponies. The passage took them through some of the world's roughest waters, and in the tropics the heat would have been far greater than anything they could possibly have experienced.

The landing from the ship would probably have caused them little concern, as swimming ashore behind a rowing boat is something that many would have experienced in their native islands. But, once ashore, they must have needed all their renowned hardiness to adapt to conditions that could hardly have been more different to the Shetland islands. But, being Shetlands, of course they did adapt, and with remarkable success.

Fourteen of the mares and the stallion, **Dockin**, went straight to William Lyall's farming property, **'Harewood'** in the Gippsland district of south-eastern Victoria, bordering Westernport Bay. The country was described by Patricia MacWhirter, a member of the family who now own 'Harewood', as 'largely uncleared (of bush) and probably for the greater part uninhabited, except for local wildlife and a few Aborigines'. In addition to being remote, Harewood was, in the early days, on the edge of a large swamp (later drained) that flooded regularly, and drownings were not uncommon. One stallion had to be removed from the paddock when the mares foaled to prevent him drowning the foals in the flood water. Highly venomous snakes also took their toll, and for those ponies that survived the floods and the snakes, the bush fires, often caused by the high summer temperatures, were an added hazard. Although not to be classed in quite the same 'hazard' category, the attentions of the swarms of flies and other insects must have been a considerable irritation. In spite of all that, the ponies survived, flourished and bred satisfactorily. It is said that for the next fifty years, almost all the winning ponies in the colony traced back to Dockin.

Four mares and the second stallion, King Pippin, went to Andrew Lyall's property in western Victoria. What actually happened to King Pippin is uncertain. The most dramatic tale is that he disappeared soon after arrival, supposedly killed and eaten by the local Aborigines. Records, however, suggest he was bought back by William Lyall. It could be that, as Patricia MacWhirter wrote, 'the old Australian tradition of never letting facts get in the way of a good story had an early beginning'! Whatever the truth of the matter, King Pippin left no progeny. Of the remainder of that first shipment, three, and possibly four, of the mares were sold for a total of £295 shortly after their arrival – so the Lyalls quickly recouped at least some of the £920 they had paid for the ponies.

William Lyall died in 1888, and the ponies were divided between his children. His youngest son, John, continued to breed Shetlands at Harewood, and in 1889, the stud was visited by Lord Hopetoun, then Governor of Victoria, and subsequently to become Governor-General of Australia. He was accompanied by Lady Hopetoun, who returned the following year to buy a pair of ponies to drive. The Hopetouns were no strangers to Shetlands. Lord Hopetoun was the brother of the Ladies Estella and Dorothea Hope, and Lady Hopetoun had been persuaded to keep ponies by those two indomitable enthusiasts. (The great stallion, Multum in Parvo 28 was, at one time, in her possession.)

The arrival of the Lyall's ponies was well recorded, but other Shetlands must have been imported undocumented, as by the 1870s there were several large herds in Victoria – in numbers too great for all to

Shetlands under a River Red gum tree at the Fenwick Stud in Victoria.

have been descendants of the original shipment. At least two herds in mainland Victoria consisted of over 100 animals, while on Phillip Island, in Westernport Bay, Captain Cleeland had a significant number of ponies, some of which may have traced back to Lyall ponies, but others are said to have been crossed with Timor ponies. Even in those days there was a considerable demand for the ponies as children's mounts, for harness and for circuses, and annual drafts of ponies from Phillip Island were sent to the mainland. They swam across the narrow but often turbulent strait which separates Newhaven on the island from San Remo on the mainland, in which sharks sometimes took a small or weak animal. Later, the journey was made safer by the introduction of a punt towed by a launch.

SHETLAND HEIGHTS

Once on the mainland, the ponies were driven past what was to become, arguably, the most significant Shetland pony stud in Australia. This was established by Colonel Thomas Small, who had come from New South Wales in the 1890s and settled on a farm near San Remo. It overlooked Bass Strait, the stretch of water between Victoria and Tasmania, and had a rugged southern coastline not unlike parts of Shetland. Colonel Small called his farm 'Shetland Heights' – a name that is revered in the Australian Shetland pony world to this day.

The origin of the Shetland Heights ponies is not absolutely certain, but Colonel Small is believed to have imported a shipment from Shetland before the turn of the century, and also to have bought some descendants of the Lyall ponies. What is certain is that he loved his Shetlands, and put them to good use as riding ponies for his many children.

In 1910, however, when his family had grown up, Colonel Small decided to sell the property. Following the sale of Shetland Heights, Colonel Small did not fade from the Shetland scene completely. He bought a property on French Island, which is adjacent to Phillip Island in Westernport Bay. He called his new stud 'Bressay', and this was continued after his death by his daughter, Mrs Bayford.

Fortunately for the breed in Australia, another of Colonel Small's daughters, Marion, was, when her father decided to sell Shetland Heights, acting as secretary-companion to Mrs J. Maclellan of Windsor in Melbourne. Mrs Maclellan was also a Shetland enthusiast, having kept some of the Small ponies at her home. Although the two were abroad when they learned of Colonel Small's decision to sell, Marion Small was able to persuade her employer to buy the property. The ladies then continued their holiday, but with the added incentive of buying some registered Shetlands (the previous ponies sent out were unregistered) to take back to Shetland Heights.

Thus, in 1911 the first registered ponies to arrive in Australia were two of their purchases. One was a broken coloured mare, Whitesox of Knockholt 27 IS, whose white saddle marking can be seen in coloured ponies today. Bred by Mrs Beadle in Kent, Whitesox was an inspected mare by Lightening 381, and traced back to the Hope sisters' stallion, Jill 19 (see page 53), and to Lord of the Isles 26. The other was the filly, Jadestone, by Touchstone 284 out of Jewel. Touchstone was a 38 inch (96 cm) black bred by Lord Londonderry, by Thor 83, and out of Topaz 116 by Oman 33. Further Londonderry blood was introduced the following year with the arrival of the stallion, Halcyon of Bodiam 600, a 38 inch (96 cm) black pony bred by the Ladies Estella and Dorothea Hope, and sired by Thoreau 392 (by Jack 16's son Odin) and out of Helga by Lord of the Isles 26. Halcyon was thus the foundation sire of registered Shetlands in Australia.

Arriving at the same time was the filly, Miss Floss of Blyth, who was bred by Capt. the Hon. W.R.D. Forbes of Turriff, and was by Magician 154, the sire of Lightening 381, and traced back to Laird of Noss and Odin. Miss Floss became a great family favourite, as well as a good brood mare, whose descendants could be seen at Shetland Heights many decades later. World War I put a temporary end to further imports, but in 1921 the stallion Viking of Methven 896, bred by Col. Smythe of Perthshire, arrived. This fine stallion also traced back to Londonderry, being by Selwood of Transy 619, who was by Seaweed 333 (by Oman), and out of Virgin of Methven 2774, who traces back to Odin and Prince of Thule. Yet another stallion with Londonderry blood went out in the 1920s. This was Didyme of Penniwells 1088 bred by Mrs Duffus, by Blitz 848, who was by Wynyard Flash 632, a grandson of Oman. Didyme's dam, Diddums 3094 was by Rabbi 386. A further six mares and fillies also went out from Mrs Duffus' Penniwells Stud.

Just prior to Mrs Maclellan's death in 1931, two mares and another stallion arrived. The mare Bermunda 4045 was bred by Mr R.H. Bruce in Shetland (by Thor's grandson Veracity 436 and out of Baroness of Sumburgh 3323, who traces back to Laird of Noss). The other mare was Monksgreen Heather Bell 3802) by Bell Rock of Earlshall 586/ Flemington Sunbeam 472 IS. The stallion was the 42 inch (107 cm) black, Marvel of Earlshall 1225, bred by Mr R.W.R. Mackenzie, by Helmet of Earlshall 408, a grandson of Multum in Parvo 28. Marvel's dam was Margery of Weddiker 3930, bred by Earl Lonsdale, sired by Minotaur 607, who also traced back to Multum in Parvo. Margery's dam was Marmot 2344 by Emeer 131 by Laird of Noss.

Mrs Maclellan died just before the formation of the Australian Pony Stud Book in 1931. The latter publication became the official stud book for all pony breeds in the country, and, as far as Shetlands were concerned, it accepted only those ponies that could be traced in an unbroken line to the British Stud Book. From 1934, the Royal Shows throughout Australia would only accept registered ponies.

It is ironic that the move to form the Australian Pony Stud Book was prompted by the success of a Shetland pony named Banjo, foaled in 1925, who subsequently was excluded from the Shetland section of that Stud book! **Banjo** was bred by Mr Lyall, and was subsequently shown with great success on behalf of Mrs L.A. Nicol. A black pony of outstanding conformation and temperament, he won at many country shows, and also took the 'Blue Riband' of Victorian Shetland awards, by winning the championship at the Melbourne Royal three times, standing above a number of imported (and no doubt, expensive!) ponies. Banjo certainly *was* a genuine Shetland; he was by Scot Free (by Robert) out of Kelter, but his records had been lost in a fire. Almost inevitably – the showing world being what it is – murmurings about the authenticity of his breeding began. The necessity for a stud book was suggested, and, in due course, acted upon. Banjo, with no recorded extended pedigree back to British stock, could only be entered in the general section for pony stallions.

Sadly, too, none of the imported stallions at Shetland Heights was registered in Volume 1 of the Stud Book as reference stallions. The only Shetland Heights ponies to be registered were those bought by other studs. As a result many of the very best ponies were excluded, but in 1948 the Stud book was opened briefly for the acceptance of those with authenticated pedigrees.

On the death of Mrs Maclellan, Marion Small was again the saviour of the Shetland Heights stud. Mrs Maclellan's husband had no interest in the ponies or the property, but Marion engaged the interest of Mrs Maclellan's daughter-in-law, Mrs A.C.G. Maclellan. Mrs Maclellan and her husband took over the ponies, and showed the stallion Marvel of Earlshall very successfully, winning the championship at the Royal Melbourne Show.

Fenwick

For some time, a relative of the Maclellans, Mrs A.D.D. (Dora) Maclean of the Fenwick Stud near Yan Yean in Victoria, had taken an interest in Shetland Heights. Ponies were often swapped between the two studs to use as out-crosses. The mare, Bermunda, although imported by Mrs Maclellan, went to Fenwick, and was the first Shetland mare to be registered in the Australian Stud Book, and bore the number 1S. In the 1940s, a number of Shetland Heights ponies were bought by Fenwick, and a small number of other Maclellan ponies were kept there until 1958. This included the stallion Porthos of Hanson 1506, bought from Mr K.A. Duncan of South Australia. Porthos, foaled in 1946, was by Athos of Dunira 1285 (by Bravo of Earlshall 1115 out of Eliza of Earlshall 4295) out of Glory's Fairy 4644 (by Glory of Earlshall 1159 and out of Black Fairy of Maryfield 4425). Black Fairy of Mayfield traced back to Oman through her grandsire, the Hope-bred Bumble Bee 479.

In 1958, the Hon. Mr Robert Maclellan, a grandson of Mrs J. Maclellan, took over Porthos and the small number of ponies not bought by Fenwick, and returned them to Shetland Heights. In 1970, Mr Maclellan (who is Minister of Planning in Victoria's State Parliament) bought Fenwick Fleming as a sire, but the remarkable fact is that, up until 1981, no mares had been bought into the stud for about 45 years. This, combined with skilful selection, ensured an exceptionally even line of mares. Happily, the Shetland Heights reference stallions have now been included in the Australian Pony Stud Book Society's records. The stud is still in existence, but not registering progeny.

The Fenwick stud, which has just celebrated its 70th birthday, is now the oldest stud that has been in continuous existence in Australia. It was founded with the importation of ponies from the Penniwells Stud in 1924. These were Flourish of Penniwells 3515 (by Haldor 270, a grandson of Laird of Noss, out of Floreat); her colt, Favourite of Penniwells; May Duke of Penniwells, a weanling colt; and the yearling filly, Rosary of Penniwells by Huzzoor of Penniwells 864 (also by Haldor), and out of Rhynd Rossie 2525 (by Steinar 283).

Later that year, 6 more ponies were imported, from the Douglases at Auchlochan, from Earlshall and from Transy. They were the mares Flashlight of Auchlochan 3849 (Phoebus of Auchlochan 777 out of Fidelity 2145), Faithful of Auchlochan (Blackbird of Auchlochan 688 by Thor/Fidelity), Flame of Auchlochan 4730 (Warrior of Auchlochan 1111/Flashlight of Auchlochan 3849), Briar Rose of Earlshall 4072 (Bessbrook of Earlshall 397/Brenda of Earlshall 3391), Rosalind of Earlshall 4157 (Boanergis of Earlshall 689/Rowenna of Earlshall 4157) and the stallion Pat of Transy 776 (Silverton of Transy 519/Princess Patricia 2559). During the late 20s and early 30s, a further 8 ponies were imported, including the stallion, Dibblitz of Penniwells 1087, a 39 inch (99 cm) black stallion, who was a very good pony and a beautiful mover, and generally regarded as the best bred by Mrs Duffus. He was by Blitz 848 (by Wynyard Flash 632) and out of Diddy 2193 (a grand-daughter of Odin), bred by Mr F.N.M. Gourlay. The grey stallion White Olaf of Manar 1281 (bred by Alex. Malcolm, by Olaf of Middlefield 1266, a son of Snowstorm of Auchlochan 623), and out of Nola of Manar 4470 by Light Boy of Earlshall 927, was imported in 1933, with another grey, Vert of Earlshall 1380 (by Darnel of Earlshall 1190 by Gluss Norseman 759, and out of Vaila Emma 3634).

Since World War II, ponies from Harviestoun have influenced the stud, with purchases from Britain and from other Australian studs. Harviestoun Soutrie (by Balgair 1403 out of Satia of Transy 4449) arrived in 1947, and in 1952, the stallion Harviestoun Pat 1416 (Dollar Boy 1242/Harviestoun Pixie 4727) was bought from his importer, and has made a great impression on the breed, principally on account of the mares he sired, but also as the sire of the great stallion, Yarra Lea Glitter. In 1955 Harviestoun Pedro 1442 was bought from Mr Duncan of the Hanson Stud in South Australia.

The Fenwick stud is now run by the founder's daughter in law, Mrs Heather Maclean, and grand-daughter, Miss Vicki Maclean. There are at present over 40 mares and 9 stallions at Fenwick, combining both old and new bloodlines, with many tracing back to the early Fenwick imports. Mrs Dora Maclean's love of coloured ponies is continued by her successors, and, in addition to the blacks, the present stock includes

Dibblitz of Penniwells (left) *and Maydew of Penniwells* (right).

piebalds, skewbalds, various shades of dun, palominos, and greys. One grey stallion and 7 of the 8 grey mares trace back to the original grey stallions, White Olaf of Manar and Vert of Earlshall. Since the beginning of the 1980s the Macleans have been endeavouring to bring back some of the earlier lines lost to the stud, as well as introducing new bloodlines with recent imports such as Rodney of Marshwood 4162 (Rosetaupe of Transy 2017/Crinkle of Marshwood 8458), Wells Vintage 2783 (Wells Superb 1721/Wells Vasha 5480), Fasque Fire Crest 2165 (Wells Supervisor 1890/Wells Finality 6097) and the filly, Expectation of Wetherden 2117 (Highfield Leander 2450/Ermine of Wetherden 6012).

At Fenwick, the aim is to breed true-to-type ponies with good temperaments, which can do well in breed classes *and* in performance events. For example, the current resident skewbald stallion, Fenwick Whistle, has succeeded in Shetland breed classes, in led Pinto and led Open pony classes, and under saddle has done well against all comers, and been placed in dressage against Hacks and Galloways. He goes well in harness, jumps, and, as Vicki Maclean says, 'gives pony rides to just about anyone no matter how big or small'.

The importance of Fenwick to the breed in Australia is considerable, as ponies with bloodlines from the stud appear in the pedigrees of the majority of ponies being bred today. Where Harewood, Shetland Heights and Fenwick led the way, other studs followed, and the story of the spread of the breed from Victoria throughout the rest of

Australia is full of interest. Possibly the most remarkable feature is the way in which the breeders have managed, in a huge country with climates ranging from tropical rainforest in the north of Queensland to the frosts of southern Victoria and Tasmania in the south, to retain the true Shetland type. The breeders are rightly proud of this uniformity, and claim, with some justification, that their ponies would not be out of place in their original habitat in the Shetland islands. British judges visiting Australia are invariably delighted with the standard of the majority of the ponies they see. Dougal Dick, of Transy fame, who judged huge classes at the Royal Melbourne show in 1984 (50th anniversary year), was very impressed with what he saw. He said he had been led to believe they might be long and leggy, but that was not the case at all. He commented that they were excellent, of good quality, and they moved well. His only criticism was that they tended to have rather narrow feet. Skilful breeding from the original quality lines imported from Britain is the key to this success, and it is fascinating to follow the establishment of the various studs and see how the same ponies' names appear again and again.

Following Shetland Heights and Fenwick, another well known Victorian stud was **Rob Roy**, founded by W.E. and C.A. Clinton, whose imported Bell Metal of Mundurno (by Mars of Earlshall 1292, a great-grandson of both Multum in Parvo and Oman, out of Myra of Parkhill 4577, who goes back to Odin) was registered as No. 1 in the stallion section of the Stud Book. They also imported Comet of Bodiam, Gem of Manar and Harviestoun Haldor. The mares came from Shetland Heights and from Penniwells, and the stud developed a definite type which formed the basis of a number of other studs. Rob Roy no longer exists.

Another prominent stud formed between the wars was the late Mrs H. Bartram's **View Bank**. Mrs Bartram leased Blackthorn of Penniwells 1142 in 1944. Blackthorn had been imported by Mrs Bayford for her Bressay Stud in 1927. He was bred, not by Mrs Duffus, as might be expected (in those days, it was often the buyer of the pony who attached the prefix, and not the breeder, as is the custom now), but by William Roy, and was a great-grandson of Laird of Noss. Described as one of the most beautiful ponies ever brought into Australia, Blackthorn is considered to be the source of the good heads seen on many of the ponies today. He appears, as will be seen, in the pedigree of a number of outstanding ponies, including the great Barrymoor Marquis. In 1948, Mrs Bartram's nephew imported four ponies from Mrs Atkinson of Felbridge, including the colt, Avening Fagas (Avening Jupiter 1410, a great-great grandson of the South Park stallion Helium 452, and out of

Avening Fudge 4853, a great great grand-daughter of Helium), who stood at View Bank throughout the 1950s.

A stud that has played an important role was **Fairway**, owned by Miss Margaret Bell, and founded on Shetland Heights and Fenwick ponies. In the 1940s, her ponies could be seen in a paddock surrounded by houses in Melbourne's most exclusive suburb! Miss Bell later married George Lewis, and they began to breed Shetlands seriously, but retaining the original foundation stock. They had a beautiful property near Coldstream, outside Melbourne, with architect-designed stables, and they built up the Fairway Stud there from 1955, winning many championships at the Melbourne Royal show over the years. They imported Harviestoun Sattoc 1803 (Harviestoun Puck 1518/ Harviestoun Shean 5133) after a visit to Scotland in 1962. Both Mr and Mrs Lewis have died, but the influence of their stud continues.

Of the studs formed after World War II, one of the most significant was **Yarra Lea**, founded by Mr R.G. Bills. His foundation stock was given to him by Gertrude Small (another daughter of Colonel Small of Shetland Heights). Yarra Lea was to prove influential in the breed, not least through the previously mentioned son of Harviestoun Pat, Yarra Lea Glitter, a 38 inch (96 cm) black pony out of Yarra Lea Spangle, who traced back to Halcyon of Bodiam and to Viking of Methven 896. Yarra Lea is another stud that is no longer in existence.

Yarra Lea Glitter stood at Mr W. Buckleigh's **Green Valley Stud** at Upper Beaconsfield (Victoria), which was founded on the familiar Shetland Heights and Fenwick lines, as well as those of Yarra Lea. The stud is now run by his widow, Mrs J. Buckleigh at Dalyston, near Wonthaggi in south eastern Victoria. Glitter had many successes in the show ring, but it is as a great sire that he is especially remembered, with his influence extending beyond his native Victoria. Four of his sons in particular, sired while Glitter was standing at Green Valley, have made their mark. These were Green Valley Sonny, Green Valley Teddy, Green Valley Frosty and Green Valley Aris.

Green Valley Sonny sired Green Valley Garry, who went up to Mr Sonny Dumke's **Riverlea** Stud in Queensland, which combined Green Valley and Yarra Lea bloodlines; another Sonny colt proved an extremely successful sire for Mr and Mrs Lloyd Hill's Mulwaree stud in New South Wales – this well known stud now being run by the Hill's daughter, Mrs Valmai Hunt and her husband, Eric.

A number of Green Valley ponies were bought by Mr and Mrs Read of the **Wandarra** Stud, near Drouin. These included a daughter of Sonny, Green Valley Tiny Tips, who was champion mare at the Victorian Shetland show. After spending a number of years as a mount for

Wells Rising Star, imported by George and Chrissie Barrett of Shady Glen Stud.

the Reads' son, she was put to Harviestoun Sattoc, and produced Wandarra Tip Toes, who was champion and grand champion at the Melbourne Royal in 1976. In the same year, the stud leased Arrogance of Netherley 3571 (by Gay Gordon of Netherley 1653 out of Ava of Netherley 5434), who had been champion stallion at the Melbourne Royal in 1975, when leased by an Arabian stud owner from his importer, Mr Chris Howe of Mooroopna. Bred by Miss Aileen Ritchie of the Netherley stud in Aberdeenshire, Arrogance sired many champions and supreme champions for his owners and for other studs. Most of the Wandarra foundation mares go back to the stallions Harviestoun Pat, Harviestoun Sattoc or Blackthorn of Penniwells, and the mares to Fenwick, Green Valley and Fairway. More recently, a Wells Imperial 2379 (Wells Three Star 1598 / Avonleigh Missy) mare was bought by the stud, and more Wells blood was introduced by sending mares to Wells Rising Star 4002 (Topper of Berry 1802/Wells Vanity 5935). The grey Green Valley Frosty went to Mr and Mrs L. Taylor's Merlyn Stud, and, although not a young pony at the time, he won the Royal Melbourne Championship for them, as well as siring a number of good ponies. The stud later bought Yarra Lea Glitter's great grandson, Spring Park Triumph.

Green Valley Aris was the sire of Carinya Duke, the foundation sire of the **Avonleigh** Stud, founded in 1965 by Barrie and Heather Cameron at Carrum Downs in Victoria. Duke's dam was Carinya Bonnie, who also goes back to Yarra Lea Glitter. One of the early Avonleigh mares was Rob Roy Bess by Harviestoun Haldor (Bergastor of Transy 1360/ Harviestoun Bess 4595). More recently, the Cameron's daughter Louise had a grey mare, Barrymoor Pearl (bred by Mrs Heather Ronald), by Kimba Captain out of Barrymoor Jewel, who traces back to Glitter. Pearl's daughter, the piebald Avonleigh Paula, won the Victorian Stud Pony Show Supreme championship in 1995.

COLMAUR

Probably Duke's best-known and successful son is **Barrymoor Marquis**, foaled in 1972. Bred by Mrs Heather Ronald, he was sold by her to Colin and Maureen Goldsmith as a 7-month-old weanling. Marquis, together with two filly foals from Green Valley, was the foundation stock of the Goldsmiths' now famous Colmaur Stud at Upper Beaconsfield, Victoria. His extended pedigree is almost a history in miniature of the early Australian studs.

The photograph on page 171 shows that Marquis has grown into a lovely pony, with plenty of bone, and he stands 41 inches (104 cm). The Goldsmiths showed him extensively in every state – and in a country the size of Australia that is no small undertaking, and included a three and a half day drive to Perth in Western Australia, crossing the famous Nullabor Plain in the process. Marquis retired from showing in 1992, but his record is extraordinary. He won 600 titles, including 80 supreme championships, 384 championships, and 136 reserve championships. He was also part of the stud's team of ponies that won a commemorative gold medallion in each State where the Stud Shows were held as part of the Stud Book Golden Jubilee Celebrations in 1981.

Marquis is, however, so much more than just an outstanding show animal. He is a greatly loved family pet, known to the Goldsmiths and to the Australian showing world as 'Love'! Colin Goldsmith was widely known as 'the chap who led Marquis'. Travelling with him in the truck (horse-box) could be trying. Family and pony lived in the truck, and Marquis – always a great character – behaved more like a dog than a pony in at least one respect: he required to be 'let out' during the night, as he declined to stand in his own droppings. He made his requirement known by tapping on the floor with a hoof – a habit that not even the most devoted owners could find endearing!

This great pony is also a successful sire, but, as his owner has said, 'To breed another Marquis is an impossibility' particularly as he is the last of his line – his dam Barrymoor Edwina died giving birth to her third and last foal which also died. However, the Goldsmiths decided they would try to get as close as possible, so (shades of the early breeders in Britain) they put Marquis to one of his daughters. The result has been two of the most beautiful foals (a colt the first year and a filly the second) they have ever bred, with no inherent faults.

BARRYMOOR

Mrs Heather Ronald's Barrymoor Stud at Koo-Man-Goo-Nong near Pakenham in Victoria was founded in 1951. Mrs Ronald had been breeding Shetlands since the 1930s; her first Shetland was bred to 'Banjo' (see page 174). The resulting foals were beautiful, but were never registered, and they could only be shown at country shows.

The foundation mares were bought as fillies at Mrs Bartram's View Bank dispersal sale. They were View Bank Darkie and View Bank Trifle. In 1952, the grey, Darkie, foaled to Rob Roy Monty, on loan from Mr Buckleigh's Green Valley Stud. Rob Roy was bred by the Clinton's, by Bell Metal of Mundurno out of Rob Roy Possum (by Blackthorn of Penniwells). The foal was a black colt, Barrymoor Debonair, and later he sired Barrymoor Tulip, foaled in 1955, out of the other foundation mare, Trifle. Tulip did very well indeed in the show ring, winning many championships in hand and under saddle.

View Bank Darkie was the dam of the stud's next stallion, Barrymoor Black Diamond, who was by the famous Yarra Lea Glitter. Black Diamond left outstanding progeny.

At the 1963 Fenwick stud reduction sale, Mrs Ronald bought the top-priced filly, Fenwick Miladi Jane, and the yearling filly, Natalie. Miladi Jane was put to Harviestoun Sattoc, and the resulting filly, Barrymoor Roberta, in due course went to Yarra Lea Rosgair, by the great imported sire, Balgair. Roberta produced a filly, Barrymoor Rosita, which Mrs Ronald considers the best mare she has bred. Rosita gained the Junior Championship at the Victoria Stud Pony Show as a 3-year-old on her show ring debut. Her proud breeder describes her as 'a pony full of personality' and she won her last championship when she was nearly 20.

Fenwick Miladi Jane next went to Barrymoor Black Diamond. Experience with hyperlipaemia decided Mrs Ronald not to send mares away to stud with foals (as travel stress can sometimes bring on the condition). The filly foal from this mating was Barrymoor Edwina, who later went to Carinya Duke, and produced the magnificent Barrymoor Marquis (see opposite). Breeding a daughter of Rosita to Marquis re-

Barrymoor Marquis, bred by Mɪs Heather Ronald and owned by Colin and Maureen Goldsmith of the Colmaur Stud in Victoria.

sulted in an outstanding colt, Barrymoor Viscount, who swept the board when shown as a 2- and 3-year old.

In 1977, new blood was introduced into the stud by importing the yearling colt, Emblem of Wetherden (Highfield Leander 2450/Elation of Wetherden 9466), from the Gosling's Wetherden stud in Suffolk. He had good movement, an attractive head, and the depth which is lacking in some Australian ponies. His foals out of Barrymoor Rosita are excellent, and it is one of these, Barrymoor Eastern Star, who now heads the stud. Mrs Ronald has all but retired from breeding Shetlands, but still retains her interest, and has been Patron of the Victorian branch of the Australian Pony Stud Book Society. Her son, Jason, has his **Brolga Stud**. One of his foundation mares was Fenwick Natalie, and one of his stallions, the piebald Devlin Park Comanche, is a grandson of one of the Logiealmond ponies, Logiealmond Pinto Lad. Comanche is now over 20, but is still siring beautiful ponies, and animals with the Brolga prefix are found in most Australian states. Mrs Ronald and her son both send mares to Fairway Ashley, a son of Harviestoun Sattoc.

Mrs Betty Myer's **Pentland** Stud at Ballarat is one of the largest in Victoria and yet another to be based on Fenwick and Shetland Heights bloodlines. Mrs Myers originally planned to breed grey Shetlands, and her first purchase, in 1952, was White Petal, a grey daughter of the Fenwick Stud's White Olaf of Manar out of Snowflake. Mrs Myers does not show her ponies, but she holds an annual sale of weanlings, and animals from the stud have been sold all over Australia.

The breed had its Australian foundations in Victoria, but in due course, studs were started in other states. South Australia was early in the field, when the Duncan family of **Gum Tree South**, Farrell Flat, imported five ponies from Britain. These included four mares and the Peter Manson-bred stallion, Cross Jack of Maryfield 1117 by Beau Brummel 846 who was by the Hope-bred Bumble Bee 479 (by Oman 33 and out of Savona 3112 [by Erling 448, a grandson of Odin]). The mares were Laamara 4427, bred by R.H. Bruce, by Bandmaster 965, a grandson of Erling, Blackmaid of Maryfield, Blackbird of Maryfield 4424 (by Coram 810, a son of Transy Superior 577), and Black Fairy of Maryfield 4425 (also by Beau Brummel and out of Sweet Fairy 3571 by Chacma 290 by Thor). Black Fairy was the grand-dam of Porthos of Hanson.

Most of the studs founded after Gum Tree bought ponies in, mainly from Victoria and some from New South Wales. The **Newbold** stud of Pat and Don Barkley of Gawler River, founded in the 1970s, bought some ponies from Gum Tree, and from Mulwaree in New South Wales, as well as importing the mare Mermaid of Annwood (Merlin of

Mrs Heather Ronald's Barrymoor Rosita.

Luckdon 2039/Dusky Maiden of Southley 7782), bred by Mrs O'Brien at her Annwood Stud in Sussex, and the stallion Wells Kismet, who was later sold on to New South Wales.

In 1977, Rosemary and John Hill founded their **Laurelwood** stud on the hills outside Adelaide, and bought Thorpeville Idol, a 40 inch (101 cm) black pony, as their foundation stallion. He has been been a wonderful sire, being placed in the Stud Book Society's South Australian Sire Ratings many times, as well as winning numerous championship in hand, under saddle and in harness. Two of Idol's sons, Laurelwood Gatsby and Laurelwood Dynasty, are shown in harness, put to a piano box buggy, and driven by John Hill with his wife as passenger. Gatsby is out of Koolangatha Emma, whose sire was Fireblaze of Marshwood (Fireball of Marshwood 1650 & 1688/Blatant of Marshwood) who was exported as a colt.

The Hills, now based at Macclesfield, have ponies with heights ranging from 32 to 40 inches (101 cm) of the multi-purpose variety, not too heavy but not leggy, that can go equally well under saddle and in harness. They have a number of miniature Shetlands, including the now retired 32 inch (81 cm) piebald Blue Meadow Fury, 28 years old, and bred in New South Wales.

Other well known South Australian studs include Yvonne Johnsson's

Kerulen, founded on Willowgreen lines – Willowgreen being a New South Wales stud based on Green Valley ponies. A relatively new stud is that of the Lambert's **Lambrae**, with the now retired foundation stallion, Shady Glen Minstrel (Wells Rising Star 4000/ Shady Glen Marguerite).

The first Shetlands to be registered in New South Wales were owned by Sir Archibald Howie of the **Navua** Stud, Grose Wold, who, in 1934 bought 'Banjo', and six mares, including Rosary of Penniwells, Harlexton Moth, Pigeon, Fenwick Black Beauty and Myrtle.

A prominent post-war stud in NSW is **Mulwaree**, named after the Aboriginal tribe which used to live in the area, and gave its name to the Mulwaree River that flows through Goulbourn. The founders were Mr and Mrs Lloyd Hill, who bought the grey stallion Riverside Flora's Fancy, by Fenwick Tommie, and two mares of Riverside and View Bank bloodlines, including the grey View Bank Dorothy May – who set a very useful trend, producing a filly foal every year from 1954 to 1959, a trend continued (although not equalled!) by two of her daughters, the black Mulwaree Fairy and the grey, Mulwaree Lilac, who produced 8 fillies between them from 1960 to 1965, all by the new stud stallion, Green Valley Barry.

Mr Hill and his wife died within 6 months of each other in 1969, and the stud has since been managed by their daughter Valmai and her husband Eric Hunt. In 1966, they bought a new stallion, Yamboon Park Muffin, whose sire and dam were both out of Fenwick mares who were grand-daughters of Marvel of Earlshall 1225. He was used particularly on Green Valley Barry's daughter – Barry himself being out of a Fenwick mare who was also a grand-daughter of Marvel of Earlshall. Muffin was followed in 1974 by Fenwick Seaton, who provided another infusion of Marvel's blood, as his sire, Fenwick Claude was a grandson (on both sides) of Shetland Heights Gingernut, a son of Marvel, and out of a mare who was a grand-daughter of Shetland Heights Marbell by Marvel.

Eric Hunt is a keen and successful whip, and has an additional skill – that of building his own vehicles, including the four buggies and sulkies, all drawn by Mulwaree ponies, used at his daughter's wedding.

The stud has been outstandingly successful in the show ring, both in hand and under saddle, and Mulwaree ponies have been exported to New Zealand, New Caledonia and the New Hebrides.

The **Shady Glen** Stud, at Robertson in NSW, was founded in 1960 by George and Chrissie Barrett. Their foundation mares came from the Pidgeville Glen Stud, and were mostly by Harviestoun Pat; their first

The Maben Pony Stud's Shady Glen Lorna.

stallion, bought a few years later, was Green Valley Sputnik. At the same time, they bought the mare, Loch Lomond Misty, who was a very successful performance pony before becoming a brood mare. Her son, Shady Glen Skye, by Green Valley Sputnik, was supreme champion at the Sydney Royal. In 1975, the Barretts bought Wells Rising Star 4002 (Topper of Berry 1802/Wells Vanity 5935), during a visit to Scotland, and his progeny have been a great success in Australia, New Zealand and Malaysia. The Barratts are the only Shetland exhibitors to have won the Most Successful Exhibitors Award (over all other horses and ponies) at the Sydney Royal in successive years.

The arrival of the first registered Shetlands in Queensland was spectacular, to say the least! Mrs Ruth Hamon, who then lived on a cattle property in central Queensland, bought three ponies from the Fenwick Stud. The ponies' new owners rode the 20 miles to their nearest railway station to collect and drive them home. Shetlands had never been seen in those parts before, and when they were unloaded from the railway truck, a sulky horse, which had been driven into the township for supplies, took one look at them and bolted. That was not the end of the trouble they provoked, as, when they arrived at their new home, there was absolute havoc among the stock horses, who also took off at first sight of them.

The three ponies, which were the foundation of Mrs Hamon's **Clifton** stud, were the grey and white stallion Phantom, bred by the Small family, by White Olaf of Manar, and the two mares, Kyora Jewel and Fenwick Aussie Dibblitz. A descendant of Phantom's, Clifton Khyberie, was described by Maurice Cox as the best Shetland he had seen in Australia (Khyberie was then at Mrs Myer's Pentland Stud in Victoria). The ponies were not shown while the stud was at Clifton, but were ridden by the children, and even helped in mustering the stock during the war years when help was very difficult to obtain.

When Mrs Hamon moved to her present home just south of Brisbane, she imported Harviestoun Haco 1476, champion at the Royal Highland, and chosen by the late Reggie Summerhayes. Haco was by Balgair 1403, and out of the Royal of England champion, Helsa of Transy, a grand-daughter of Seaweed. From her present home, Mrs Hamon showed with great success at the Brisbane Royal Show. She judged the Shetlands at the Royal Highland in 1987.

Among the thirty or so Shetland studs now established in Queensland is George and Lorna Vyner's **Rainbow Park Stud** north of Brisbane. Their first pony was Meandara Julius (known as 'Scotch'), followed a few months later by 2 mares and a foal from the Kempse Stud and the same from the Laguna Stud. In 1978 they bought a Shady Glen colt, and later, some Wells Rising Star mares and a stallion. Their most successful stallion has been Shady Glen Majestic (by Wells Rising Star out of Loch Lomond Misty), who was Supreme Shetland at the Queensland Stud show 5 times, Supreme Shetland twice at the Brisbane Royal and at the Sydney Royal, and Champion Harness Shetland at Sydney Royal three times. Further Wells blood was brought into the stud in 1982, when the Vyners bought Wells Remarkable 3211 (Wells Vintage 2783/Wells Perfecta 9713) after seeing him take the Shetland championship at the Royal Highland show, and in 1984, they bought Wells Valetta.

The breed has had a somewhat chequered career in Western Australia until relatively recently. The earliest imports appear to have been by a Colonel Le Souef, probably in the first decades of this century. He was said to have brought in some very good ponies from Scotland, including a stallion called Alec, and several black mares. An Abbot buggy was imported from the USA, and Colonel Le Souef is remembered driving this vehicle with four black Shetlands at the South Perth Zoo, of which he had become curator. No record of these ponies appears to exist, but in 1926, a herd of pure-bred ponies was seen running on a cattle station in the far north of Western Australia, and these were said to be descendants of the Le Souef imports. Unfortunately, a number of these were crossed with Timor ponies, as, apparently, were some of the other early imports.

Apart from four Fenwick ponies brought over from Victoria by Mr Stuart Harkness in the 1950s, it was not until the 1970s that serious breeding began, and then only on a comparatively small scale. Mrs L. Leece's **Trickle Creek** Stud was founded in 1974, with another four ponies from Fenwick, and when the stud was dispersed in 1986, two of the mares, Fenwick Amara and Fenwick Clarine, went to the Redfield and the Rockfield Studs respectively. Also founded at about the same time was Mrs R.F. Dear's Shady Tree Stud, with a stallion and mares from the Pentland Stud. These ponies were sold, and became the foundation stock of the Bow Bells Stud, owned by L.F. & D.S. Griffith. When the Griffiths retired, the prefix and some of the ponies were taken over by Mrs Pam Herrick. The Cavalier Stud, still in existence, was started by Judy and Jim Park, with ponies from the Fairway Stud by Fairway Jonothan. Mares with Green Valley and Pentland prefixes were added, and another stallion, Mulwaree Danny Boy. The stud became Western Australia's largest, but in the late 1980s, a reduction sale was held.

Waruga Hill Stud, owned by Rhonda and Roger Warren-Langford, was set up in 1978 at Mundrabilla. The bloodlines are principally Pentland, but with three mares coming from the Kempse stud in Queensland. Mundrabilla is on the Eyre Highway, near the coast of the Great Australian Bight, and on the southern fringes of the Nullabor Plain, not far from the South Australian border. It is not an environment in which Shetlands might be expected to thrive – but they did! An account of the ponies, written by Roger Warren-Langford in 1985, for *Ten-Two News* (the Australian Shetland Pony Magazine) illustrates once more just how adaptable Shetlands can be! It also gives some idea of the vastness of the Western Australian outback. 'At present there are approximately seventy ponies running on the plains, around thirty-eight registered Shetlands, some Shetlands I wasn't happy with and did not register, and the others are a Shetland/Welsh cross that I will sell as children's ponies.

'The ponies have completely unlimited range, as there are no fences at all north of the Hampton Range in our area, and so their range is limited only by water availability.

'I do not run them all together, as this ruins the certainty of knowing who is the sire of the foals. They are run in different mobs, miles apart. I turn only one stallion out at a time and keep strict account of the dates and mares they may be running with.

'It will be rewarding to organise eventually at Gidgegannup [the home to which they moved], and be able to set out a breeding programme for the year, without all the problems that crop up out here, such as the continual driving over many miles to check on the ponies' welfare against the normal invasion of fox-shooters in winter; dingoes all the time; inconsiderate tourists, and lack of good water supplies, necessitating at times to have it carted in, until it rains once again. Last year, we had no stock water for three months, so you can imagine the problems of carting 2,000 gallon loads in from outside the area.'

In 1981, Pat and Des Pope, who also breed Welsh and Australian ponies, added Shetlands to their **Redfield** Stud at Wubin, some 125 miles north-east of Perth. Their original fillies came from John and Sue Bell's Dunbarton stud. Mares have come from a number of Victorian Studs, including Barrymoor, Brolga, Green Valley and Fairway, while the stallions used include the blacks, Linden Park Peter, Green Valley Felix, Bryalea Bye-bye and the chestnut, Redacres Robby.

In recent years, the 41 inch (104 cm) Green Valley Felix has been one of the two great influences on the breed in Western Australia. Bought by the Popes as an immature 2-year-old, he has a superb length of rein, outstanding movement and great quality. Like so many of the Green Valley ponies, he is line bred to Yarra Lea Glitter, and Glitter's sire, Harviestoun Pat. He was bred for performance; his sire, Green Valley Jonothan, is noted for his movement, and his dam, Spring Park Flicka, won many ridden classes in Melbourne and Sydney. It was intended that he should appear in driven classes, but he fretted when taken from his mares, so was retired from showing. He won major awards in his limited show career, but it is as a stallion that he has excelled. In 1993 and 1994, he has topped the sire ratings in the Western Australian branch of the A.P.S.B. – a competition that is restricted to selected shows, and the points gained are for progeny in led, harness and ridden classes. The award is for all breeds, but Felix's achievement is the more remarkable as Shetlands, unlike other breeds, are only permitted to gain points within their own breed. Felix is not at public stud, and he has only a few mares each year; his progeny is predominantly female, and they have won many championships.

Barrymoor Dougal (Fairway Ashley/Barrymoor Rosita) was brought to Redfield to be bred to Green Valley Felix mares. He is a 39 inch (99 cm) black, and was Supreme Champion at all the major shows in Western Australia before retiring to stud. He then made a come-back in

1992 to win at the Perth Royal, but was beaten into second place at the A.P.S.B. show by his daughter, Redfield Mystique (out of Redfield Mistletoe), for the Supreme championship. Mystique is a grand-daughter of Green Valley Felix.

Of the outstanding mares, Fairway Trixie (Fairway Jonothan/Fairway Mirabel), bred in Victoria, and owned by the Cavalier Stud in Western Australia, was prominent in the show ring in the late 1970s. She was the first winner of the Harkness Trophy (presented in memory of Mr Stuart Harkness), the Supreme Championship at the Perth Royal. In the 1980s, another mare, Barrymoor Pawnee (Delvin Park Comanche/Barrymoor Jewel), won the Harkness three times, a feat not yet achieved by any other pony. Pawnee won many other top awards before being retired to stud. But she, too, made a show-ring comeback, but as a harness pony, then as a leading rein and a first ridden. She was very successful in these fields, before being retired once more. In 1994 and 1995 some new stallions have made their appearances. The piebald Janal Janus (Shady Glen Mystro/Green Valley Jarran), now owned by the Redfield Stud, came from Victoria with an impressive show record, and won the Supreme at the Perth Royal in 1994. He is a grandson of Wells Rising Star. Another newcomer is Redfield Kingston, a black 38½ inch (98 cm), one of the last sons of Arrogance of Netherley, and out of Kimba Karley. In 1995, his first year in senior classes, he won the Harkness Trophy.

A young stallion whose progeny are beginning to make their mark is Shady Glen Jerrard, brought to Western Australia by the Apollo Stud. Because of the distance from Perth, he has not been shown extensively, but he was successful in youngstock classes in New South Wales before coming to Western Australia. Jerrard is by Wells Rising Star.

There is no doubt that Shetlands are now firmly established in Western Australia, and the owners and breeders have formed a very active Shetland Enthusiasts' group, with the head of Barrymoor Dougal as their emblem. They run children's instruction days, harness instruction days and many information and educational field days.

The administration of all pony breeds is undertaken by the Australian Pony Stud Book Society, which is controlled by a Federal Council consisting of three delegates from each state, meeting twice a year. There are elected Branch Committees in the states of Victoria (which also represents Tasmania), New South Wales, Queensland, Western Australia and South Australia.

Under A.P.S.B. rules all adult registered stallions must be passed by a veterinary surgeon as being free from congenital eye defects, ringbone, curb, bog spavin, congenital stringhalt, defective genital organs, wobbler syndrome, cleft palate, osteo chrondditis dessican, sidebone, bone spavin, umbilical or scrotal hernia, cryptorchidism or monorchidism, locking stifle, albinism, parrot mouth (overshot by more than 5.0 mm – may be re-presented at 4 years of age). All ponies born after August 1st, 1968, must be branded within 12 months of foaling or when sold, whichever is the sooner.

Of the 4,000 members of the Stud Book Society in Australia, 1,800 or 45% are Shetland members.

NEW ZEALAND

Shetlands ponies appear to have arrived in New Zealand in the last quarter of the 19th century – although whether the first ones came from Britain or from Australia is not clear. According to *Ponies in New Zealand*, published by the The Pony Breeders' Society of New Zealand in 1982, Shetlands were the basic pony bred in New Zealand from about 1890. Many of these were descendants of ponies imported some time after 1880 by Paul Hunter, a third generation New Zealander, to his 27,000 acre family farm on the east coast of the North Island. He bred a large herd, which spread all over the Hawkes Bay area. At first, the ponies were very much working animals, ridden by the children, who played a significant part in the farm work of some areas. They really came into their own at sheep mustering time. Their job was to ride

'The Zilco 10' team of Shetlands, with Lucy Giles driving. Three of the team are part-breds.

along the sheep tracks into the dense scrub where the horse could not go, and round up the stragglers which had taken refuge there.

The ponies were also used as safe and reliable means of transport to school, until buses took over after World War II. One pony is said to have taken children to school for more than twenty years. Many of these ponies came from the Barber family, from Foxton, also in the North Island. They began breeding Shetlands in the early years of this century with foundation stock bought in 1900 from Mr Goulter near Marlborough (N.Z.) Later, a stallion was imported from Australia to improve the stock. The Barber ponies gained a great reputation throughout New Zealand, and there is one delightful (and wholly believable!) story about a family who arrived at the Barber farm and bought a young unbroken pony. They took it home in the back of a Baby Austin, and, it is said, by the time they arrived, the pony was broken in!

The first pony to go to New Zealand was said to be in 1909, but no details of it can be found. In 1910, however, Charles Goulter, from Hawkesbury in the North Island, and his brother, while in Britain, visited several studs, and bought a black stallion, Viceroy, and an in-foal mare, Maid of Merle (no details can be found of these two ponies); also Minum 2508, foaled in 1906, by Havelock 241 out of My Lady 1355. Viceroy became a typical family pony, and when ridden bareback by the Goulter children, he perfected the art (as have other Shetlands before and since) of sweeping them off by darting under a mulberry tree.

Another early export to New Zealand was in 1911, when the black

38 inch (96 cm) stallion, Mike 301, bred by the Rev. C.E. Barnes of Saffron Waldon, was sent out by Mrs (later Lady) Hobart, to R. Mackenzie of Dunedin. Mike's sire was Handfu' 224 by Jack 118 (not Jack 16 of Londonderry fame), and his dam was Mischief 1167, who was by Alfred 49 (by Prince of Thule) out of Maggie 647 by Prince of Thule. The next, in 1921, was the stallion Duckworth of Earlshall 859, a black 38 inch (96 cm) pony, but to whom it was sent is not recorded. This pony was truly classically bred. He was by Bismarck of Watford 441, out of Duchess of York 1522. Bismarck was a son of Frederick 223 by Oman, and Duchess of York was by Odin, and out of Die 524 by Lord of the Isles. Unfortunately, no further details of these two ponies are known.

Sadly, after World War II, the popularity of the Shetland declined. No more were required as school ponies, and the formation of the Pony Club brought about an increase in demand for larger ponies (a situation with which some owners in Britain are all too familiar, even today!). There was thus a very long gap before more ponies were imported into New Zealand, and these came from Australia. In 1942, the stallion, Fenwick Starlight (White Olaf of Manar/Fenwick Nightlight), went to Mrs R.J. Thompson, of Masterton, and in 1969, two mares and a stallion, also bred by the Fenwick Stud, were imported by Graham Preston, of the Beach Hill Stud. They were Beach Hill Tim, Beach Hill Joy and Beach Hill Wendy. In those days, it was difficult to register New Zealand-owned stock in Australia, and there was no breeders' society in New Zealand; consequently, the progeny of those early imports were not registered.

The New Zealand Shetland Pony Breeders' Society was formed in 1979. The first stud to be registered was the Katushka, which had been formed in 1975 by Royce and Gaye Richards. This was later dissolved, and Gaye (now Price) has the small **Broompark** Stud. The Wynyard Stud was next on the scene, but it, too, was dissolved, and is now the **Llewellyn** Stud, owned by Paul and Lesley Lewis. The foundation stock for the two original studs were imported from Australia, including the Cox-bred Fireblaze of Marshwood (Fireball of Marshwood 1686/Blatant of Marshwood 7958).

These two studs were on their own for some years, and at the local three day Canterbury Agricultural and Pastoral Show, they were the only exhibitors, and entered as many ponies as they could handle! After a slow start, the renewed interest in the breed increased dramatically, and there are now over 2,200 ponies on the register. There are numerous small studs throughout New Zealand – mostly in the South Island around the Christchurch area. Over the last five years or so, there has been an increasing trend for city people to move to 'lifestyle blocks' within commuting distance. These blocks are between about two and twenty acres, and this could account for some of the growing demand for the ponies.

Shetlands are used primarily for in-hand showing and in harness. There is a keen demand for geldings to drive, and the New Zealand Driving Society's South Island Combined Driving Championship, open to all breeds, has been won on at least two occasions by Shetlands. A Shetland has also won the Supreme Champion of all Breeds at the prestigious Canterbury Horse and Pony Breeders' in hand show. There are no ridden classes for Shetlands, but they compete in the one class held at most Agricultural and Pastoral shows, for ponies under 10.2 hands, suitable as children's riding ponies.

One of the leading lights in the driving world is Mrs Lucy Giles (see picture on page 181), who drives the only team of Shetlands in the country. Mrs Giles drives teams of 4, 6, 8 or 10 ponies to entertain the spectators at shows, as well as a pair or a team of 4 in combined driving. The majority of drivers have a single pony.

In the New Zealand Stud Book, there is a register for Adult Stock, and until recently, foals remained on a Foal Recording record until eligible for Adult Registration at between 2 and 4 years. Now they have adopted the Australian system in which filly foals and gelded foals receive full registration and a number; colt foals remain Foal Recorded until they are between 2 and 4, when they may apply for Stallion Registration. The gelding of colts is encouraged by imposing a high Stallion Registration Fee, ($NZ150) so that only quality animals will be bred from. This compares with $20 for a mare and $5 for a gelding. There is always a demand for females, as the number of studs is still quite small, and most of the newer studs retain their fillies for breeding.

EUROPE

Europe – and more specifically, **Holland** – was almost certainly the first country to which Shetlands ponies were exported. Records already referred to in previous chapters show that the ponies have been in Holland for at least two hundred years. Although not officially recorded, the Dutch speak of ponies bought in by fishermen as early as 1680.

The real surge in the use of Shetlands came between the two world wars, when the Dutch government banned the use of dogs for pulling small loads on the farms, and the smallholders looked around for a substitute. They found it in the Shetland pony, which proved to be cheaper to feed than a dog, and, furthermore, the dog harness and the small carts were easily adapted for use by the ponies. Each farm had two or three mares, and these mares would be taken to a nearby stallion. More ponies, however, were needed, and many Shetlands were imported from the islands – mostly non-registered – but a number of pedigreed animals were included. The first licensed stallion in Holland was the 9-year-old Rettendon Squire, who came from the Shetland Islands, and was licensed by the Dutch government official in Rotterdam. He was owned by John S. Wurfbain of Rijswikj.

The Dutch Shetland Pony Stud Book Society was founded in 1937 by G.C.C. Pels Rijcken, A.F.W., Baron van Brakell, C.B. Alshe, Th. Sanders and P.J.M. van den Berg It is the oldest stud book society in Holland. Obviously the society's activities virtually ceased during the war years. During the war, a number of the ponies, possibly the best, were removed by the German Army, but some were hidden in woodlands or spent long periods in underground shelters to avoid capture. Among those successfully hidden were ponies belonging to Mrs Simon Thomas de Vries, who ran a British-style stud, founded on ponies bought at the dispersal of the Overacres stud in Northumberland. These were mostly black ponies, a colour against which there was great prejudice in Holland.

When Maurice and Betty Cox visited Holland not long after the end of the war, they soon realised that the majority of Dutch breeders were trying to breed Shetlands like small draught horses for work, and the results were heavy ponies lacking in quality, stuffy, thick, and often with straight shoulders, bulky necks and short fronts. None of them was black.

Fortunately, some breeders preferred the lighter, more typical type of pony, and exports from Britain, this time of registered ponies, slowly began to increase. Mrs Simon Thomas de Vries imported the fine stallion, Supreme of Marshwood 1467 (Sprinter of Marshwood 1423/ Jessamine of Marshwood 4845), and Mr van Dam van Brake imported Spotlight of Marshwood and the mare, Rosepetal of Transy 4930 (Sataro of Transy 1401/Roseminta of Transy 4772). Both the stallions had a considerable influence on the breed in the Netherlands. Stallions imported later from Britain included Firkin of Lukdon 1738 (Thunder of Marshwood 1525 out of Mystic of Netherley 5028 by Harviestoun Beau 1369) in 1967, Scurry of Marshwood in 1975, Rosson of Transy in 1976, Robin of Transy in 1978 and Stelmore of Transy 1701/1775 (Joseph of Marshwood 1561/Stelfrenda of Transy 4932). Later again, Wells Fireman was used a great deal.

In spite of these imports, it was not until the 1960s and 70s that much

Dutch ponies demonstrating their former use in horticulture.

larger numbers crossed the Channel to Holland – 405 in the 60s, a further 430 in the 70s.

The breed expanded rapidly, to the extent that at the present time there are more Shetlands in Holland than there are in the United Kingdom. The figures are quite astonishing. In 1993, the Dutch Society registered no fewer than 4,527 foals, about double the number registered in the U.K. The Dutch Society has 5,000 members; the British about 2,000. As the Dutch breeders produced their own stock, the importation of ponies from Britain decreased, while the exports from the Netherlands to many other European countries increased dramatically.

The Shetland pony world in Holland is rather different from that in the United Kingdom. There are very few, if any, large studs, and breeders tend to own just one or two ponies, and hardly any own stallions. As in most European countries, the breeding of the ponies in Holland is exceedingly closely regulated, and the activities of the Society highly organised, in contrast to the generally more 'laissez faire' approach in Britain.

The Stud Book Society headquarters is situated at Zutphen, and there is a branch of the Society in every province of the Netherlands, with its own management board, a representative of which is on the national board. The national board has a number of sub-committees, and also a veterinary adviser. Each branch of the Society organises an annual premium show for mares,

A series of inspections for all stock is undertaken. All potential stallions from the age of 3 years are inspected at the annual National Stallion

The Dutch 40-pony hitch.

show in January. This is undertaken by three judges and a veterinary adviser. In addition to the usual assessment of conformation, and examination for hereditary defects, the pedigree is examined and the premium status of the sire and dam are taken into account. So strict is the inspection that very few animals are passed for licensing; for example, in 1992, only 11 out of 100 miniature stallions were passed, 7 out of 44 small stallions, and 22 out of 143 large size. All stallions presented for the first time are now blood-typed. Graded Premiums are awarded at this show.

Licensing is on a yearly basis initially, and, depending on subsequent progeny inspections, this may be extended to three years, or it may be withdrawn permanently. All foals from licensed stallions and registered mares are registered in the foal-book, and all foals are inspected before weaning. If necessary, the foal is blood-typed.

Full registration of mares is usually done at the age of 3 years. If a mare measures over 41 inches (104 cm) at 3, she must be measured again at 4; the maximum size accepted is 42 inches (107 cm).

Following the introduction of more black ponies just before and since World War II, the larger blacks were very much in demand. More recently, however, the miniatures (34 inches/86 cm.) and under, and either black or chestnut, are the most popular. This is causing concern among some observers, because of the relatively few bloodlines in this height range. Among the lines used are Parlington Pimpernel and Vorden Buddlea.

The ponies are used mostly for in-hand showing, but driving is popular, and, for the 55th anniversary of the founding of the breed society, Mr G. ten Pas drove a spectacular team of 40 ponies – a feat which earned recognition in the *Guinness Book of Records*.

There are some ridden Shetlands, but this is declining in terms of competitions. There is, however, a Shetland Grand National team, which gives demonstrations at big shows such as Jumping Amsterdam. In the summer of 1995, a team of 12 ponies and children from Holland took part in the British Shetland Performance Show at the Three Counties Showground at Malvern, Worcestershire, and then travelled on to the Great Yorkshire Show, where they competed against the British riders in a Grand National demonstration. This group enjoyed themselves enormously, and were apparently astonished at the range of performance classes available for the Shetlands. Perhaps this could be the inspiration for more performance classes in Holland in the future?

Recorded exports to **France** began in a very small way in the 1920s, with just 12 ponies. There was then a total cessation of exports from Britain until the 1960s, when 502 ponies crossed the Channel, making France the largest importer of Shetlands in the world at that time, even outstripping Holland with 405. After that the numbers not surprisingly dropped, with 93 in the 1970s, and just 27 in the 1980s.

Among French enthusiasts who started their studs in the 1960s was Comte Louis de Pas, of Bois Guilbert in Normandy. In 1960, he found he could not buy two small ponies in France for his children to ride, so he imported a stallion and 9 mares from Holland. Being an astute business man, he quickly realised that there was a demand for ponies, so he travelled to Scotland, and bought a further 21 mares and another stallion. By 1966 he had built up the largest stud in France, with 120 ponies. These were fetching prices of between £110 and £185 – a good sum in those days. In 1968 the Comte bought a further 70 ponies at the Lerwick sale in Shetland, to help satisfy the greatly increased demand for breeding and riding animals. He paid the then record prices for Lerwick of 570 guineas for a filly foal and 400 guineas for a colt foal, both bred by Maurice and Betty Cox at their Gletness Stud on Shetland.

The situation in **Germany** is somewhat confused, especially since the re-unification of East and West. In the former West Germany, each province had its own Shetland Breed Society, but there was no overall authority. (This has now been remedied, to conform with the European Community regulations.) The breed has diverged in terms of colour and sometimes of height, with the introduction of spotted and

Appaloosa-marked animals which are not, of course, acceptable for entry into the British Stud Book. There are also animals referred to as 'sports ponies', which bear a very close resemblance to the American Shetland, and which, on grounds of conformation and type at least, do not conform with the British standard. There are, on the other hand, ponies which give the appearance of being true Shetlands, but with the obvious introduction of outside blood into the breed as a whole, the difficulties are obvious, and have not been resolved so far.

Shetlands have been in some of the Scandinavian countries since the beginning of this century, but recorded breeding on any scale dates only from after World War II. In **Sweden**, the foundation stock of the post-war breed came from well established British and Dutch lines, and, from 1957, was registered by the Swedish Pony Society, founded in 1954. Interest in the ponies increased markedly during the 1960s, and in 1967, on the initiative of Count Call Johnan 'Joja' Lewenhaupt, the Swedish Shetland Pony Society was formed. It now has 1,250 members. The society began to register ponies in 1968, although the ultimate responsibility for the stud book remains with the Swedish Pony Society.

One of the first breeders was Mrs Maud Engberg of the Rossönäs stud, who imported three in-foal Harviestoun mares, and the stallion Bay Leaf of Felbridge 1641/1885 (Emillius of Earlshall 1121/Sweet Home of Sansaw 4570 by Sunbeam of Maryfield 1254) in 1948. In the 1950s, Carin Vikefeldt imported 6 mares from Scotland, and in 1953 added Kirkbride Beau 1479 (Balgair 1403/Bergia of Transy 4608). Other early breeders included the Hakenäs stud (now known as the Patrons Stud). Mrs Asta Ohllson and her son Bengt own the Hammarshus and the Furunäs studs respectively, the Björnslunds stud is owned by Rolf Ggyllin, the Wärnanäs by Ann Charlotte Svinhufvud, Margareta Wingärdh's Näset stud and Gunborg Hofsten's Kilagärden.

Among the early registrations were, in addition to Bay Leaf of Felbridge and Kirkbride Beau, Roosînäs Erik, a stallion which had been imported in utero in Harviestoun Edie 5385 (Balgair 1403/ Elderflow 2nd of Earlshall 4604) by Bergastor of Transy 1360 (Pole Star 884/Bergia of Transy 4608), Harviestoun Habbie 1497 (Balgair 1403/Heleminta of Transy 4819), Marquis of Netherley, Harviestoun Celt 1619 (Harviestoun Emblen 1517/Harviestoun Susan 4930), Dragonfly of Marshwood 1685 (Supremacy of Marshwood 1612/Ashbank Firefly 4861), Harviestoun Ringan 1689 (Beachdair of Harviestoun 1427/Harviestoun Rene 4974), Kirkbride Golden Boy 1839 (Sport of Marshwood 1485/Kirkbride Coster Girl 5286) and Feather of Marshwood (Firebird 1440/Heather of Marshwood). The first mares registered were Harviestoun Edie 5385 and Harviestoun Sandra 5243

(Beachdair of Harviestoun 1427/Stelmone of Transy 4668) and these were followed by others with the Marshwood, Kirkbride, Deeracres, Felbridge, Netherley and Transy prefixes.

There is an annual stallion inspection in March, and mare inspections at a number of venues during the summer. Each year, about 1,250 ponies are registered, 1,900 mares are covered, and 200 mares and 10 stallions are accepted into the Stud Book.

The true versatility of the breed is much appreciated in Sweden, where the ponies are used for showing, riding, trotting competitions, racing, driving and a little show jumping – but, above all, as Kristina Blad, who manages the Swedish stud book, says, a Shetland pony is 'a very good friend and partner'.

Norway and the Shetland Islands have always been close historically, and, as has been recorded, there has been speculation about the relationships between the ponies of the two countries. It is thus not surprising that Norway has a very active group of Shetland breeders – the only cause for comment being that the ponies were not imported into Norway until the 1950s.

Norwegian breeders register their ponies with the Norwegian Pony Breeding Society, founded in 1970. The first Shetlands were imported

The Swedish stallion Allgunnens Micko RS259, owned by Asa Tider.

from Britain by Lars Lende of Stavanger at the end of the 1950s and the beginning of the 1960s, but, because there was no breed society at that time, many of these ponies were not registered in Norway, and little is known about them, although a few of their descendants appear in the breeding of the present-day Norwegian Shetlands. Two of the the imported stallions were registered as Nos 1 and 2 in the Stud Book in 1970, when sold to Mr Per Helgen. These were Vane of Berry 1766 (Wells Rainbow 1550/Violet of Berry 5151) and Rustic Odin of North Wells 1700 (Piccolo of North Wells 1545/Rosette of Marshwood 4848).

Mr Per Helgen imported a considerable number of ponies in the late 60s and early 70s, including the old stallion, Merry Boy of Berry 1626 (Airborne 1426/Golden Girl of Mundurno 4913). In 1967, ponies bought by Mr Helgen made up the first complete plane-load of ponies – 33 in all – to be exported from Shetland to Oslo. They had been bought by Mr Helgen at the islands sales, and before leaving from the airport at Sumburgh, they were looked after by Eva and Jim Smith at their Berry Stud. When the Dakota landed in Oslo, the ponies were greeted by hundreds of people.

Mr Helgen bought more ponies in 1975 and 1980, but unfortunately he did not register them all in the stud book. Ponies were also imported from Holland during the 1970s, but a number of these, too, were not registered, and during the 1980s some came in from Denmark and Sweden, and in the 90s, further imports from Britain. It is interesting (although hardly surprising in view of the origin of the early imports) that many of the stallions are island bred – 60 having been licensed since 1970. These include, in addition to those already mentioned, Spark of Murrion, Robin of Bardister, Calypso of Berry, Chucklenuts of Hoswick, Dirk of Clivocast and Ungi of Setterhall – all influential in the breed in Norway. During the last five years, the most prolific stallions have been Darwin (Sweden), Bayard (Sweden), Klaus af Ravnstrup (Denmark), Lauge Bomlund(Denmark), Sollflaks, Rockoness (Sweden), Paradiset's Bjarke (Denmark), Filip fra Helgen and Lockinge Mervyn (Britain).

Most Norwegian breeders now register their ponies with the Pony Society (108 were registered in 1995), but there are still a significant number of unregistered animals. The society now wants to close the stud book, so it has obtained permission to inspect unregistered mares and those without papers at official shows. If they pass on type and conformation, they will be admitted to the stud book, and their foals may be registered, provided they are by a licensed stallion. The book is to be closed after December 1996.

Under Norwegian law, horse/pony breeding is strictly controlled, and a foal may not be licensed unless by a licensed stallion. A colt may be licensed for the first time as a 3-year-old – the licence being valid for a year or more. The licensing takes place at official stallion shows held at three different venues in the spring, and consists of a veterinary inspection, judging of conformation and action, and a special performance test. The latter often includes driving, in which action, technique and temperament are judged, and they can also be ridden at walk, trot and gallop. Every November, a special committee decides which stallions may be shown again for further licensing. Stallions of 5 years and over may be awarded premiums.

Official shows are also held for mares during the summer and autumn, where they are judged for breeding purposes. Mares without foal at foot may undergo a performance test before they are eligible for a premium for breeding purposes.

All ponies entering the official shows must be registered with the pony society, and they are recorded for the stud book; when they are licensed or are awarded another degree or premium, they are admitted to the special stud book for breeding purposes. The judges really have to work hard at the official shows! They must fill in a detailed form for each pony, awarding it points from 1 to 10 in each of three mandatory sections. Part A is for the general appearance – type, conformation, limbs, movement at walk and trot, and overall impression; Part B is for performance, either from competitions or from the test held at the show; Part C is for temperament, which is judged by the competition judge, the performance judge and a veterinary surgeon. In addition, the judges may make verbal comments on the above, also on Part D (durability/hardiness), E (progeny), F (veterinary) and G (measurement of height [two different methods of measuring], chest, and length and circumference of front cannon bones); H (premium grade).

The Shetlands in Norway are used as children's ponies, and in riding schools for teaching the smallest children to ride. Although there are not many competitions for them, some take part in jumping and in racing. Interest in driving the ponies in trotting competitions has increased recently.

When Shetlands first arrived in **Denmark** is uncertain, but the first recorded exports from Britain were in the 1930s, when 5 are recorded in the British Stud Book. In 1959 a number of imported stallions are mentioned as being of importance to the breed; these were Harviestoun Ptarmigan 1559 (Bergastor of Transy 1360/Harviestoun Pansy 5021), Harviestoun Bombshell 1655 (Harviestoun Puck 1518/Harviestoun Bersa 4824), Hurtwood Rannoch 1723 (Rushlight of Felbridge 1433/

Redwing of Felbridge 5068), Kirkbride Gleaming 1774 (by Littlestoke Fairy Lantern 1623, a grandson of Electric Light 650, and out of Kirkbride Glamour 5020) and Sultan of Woodhall.

Exports from Britain increased during the 1960s, with a total of 236 ponies, but have declined steadily as home-bred stock has increased, with 85 in the 1970s, and 29 in the 1980s. In recent years, stallions from Methven, Waulkmill and Transy have been imported.

The Danish Society was formed in 1959/60, with the first stallion selection taking place in 1959. The society now has about 250 members. As in other European countries, the mares and stallions must pass an inspection before admission to the Stud Book, and this enables their offspring to be registered. The younger stallions are licensed for 1 year, and at 4 years they must pass a performance test (lungeing, riding or driving). If lungeing is chosen, the pony is lunged to a set sequence, which includes jumping over small poles. The stallions may then be classified in three grades. Once classified, they are licensed for life. Mares are classified in the same way from the age of 3. There are about 120 licensed stallions, with approximately 20 new licences being issued each year. About 350 foals are registered annually.

The Danes show their ponies in hand at the very few shows available, which include agricultural shows and the assessment show. British judges, who are often invited to ensure that the standard is maintained, have been impressed by the ponies in Denmark, and with their continuing improvement. The quality is good, and they have true pony heads. The action, which used to be suspect, especially behind, is improving year by year. The ponies are mostly shown by young people, who run them out very freely.

At present, chestnut is the favourite colour, and heights between 34½ inches (88 cm) and about 38 inches (96 cm) are the most popular, with few ponies over 39 inches (100 cm). There is a growing interest in miniatures, and recently a 28 inch (71 cm) stallion has been driven.

In the all-breed shows, Shetlands are by no means overlooked, winning Best Mare with foal at foot championships and Best Collection of related ponies. In 1993 an October show for foals was introduced, and the success of that has prompted the society to arrange three different venues for it in future. The ponies are also used for driving, and in 1993 the first driving trial open only to Shetlands and Dartmoors was held, with dressage, cross-country and obstacle driving. This was so successful that it seems likely to become a permanent fixture.

The Danes are clearly very enthusiastic about their ponies, and they have a saying that could well be a motto for the breed worldwide, 'You never grow out of a Shetland Pony'!

Finland is yet another European country with imports of Shetlands in the first years of this century, but with no record of what they were. The British Stud Book has entries of two exported to Finland in the 1920s, and one or two in the 1930s. The earliest entry in the Finnish Stud Book was the stallion, Rosenway, imported from Sweden, who was accepted after inspection, but, after 1986 was no longer used. Rosenway was by Rouge Dragon of Deeracres (who was by Avening Caramel Cream, and out of Miss Muffet of Deeracres, an inspected mare), and out of Isabell (Bay Leaf of Felbridge 1641/1885/Susanna).

Most of the early mares in the Stud Book came from Britain and Sweden, and trace back to Deeracres, Transy, Harviestoun, Wells, and especially to Marshwood. Among the Swedish-bred mares were Kickan, a grand-daughter of both Spotlight of Marshwood and Spook of Marshwood 1632; Kärlingehulte Klarinette, tracing back to Kirkbride Golden Boy 1839; Blenda, a grand-daughter of Rosald of Transy 1699; Zita, a grand-daughter of Trim of Marshwood; Dimona, going back to Gay Gordon of Netherly 1653; Arinette, another Rouge Dragon of Deeracres descendant, and with Wells Firemen in her pedigree; Frida, another Spotlight of Marshwood grand-daughter; Dekorina, with Trim of Marshwood, Harviestoun Ringan 1689, Rosette of Marshwood 4848, and Harviestoun Sybil in her pedigree; Urneberga Vitesse, a daughter of Rosafir of Transy, and a grand-daughter of Percy of Netherley 1877 out of Merry Muffin of Netherley 5717; Sussie, tracing back to Bergastor of Transy, Harviestoun Habbie, and Sonyad of Transy; Dusessi, by Trim of Marshwood; Dockan, by Tramp of Marshwood; Rosian, another daughter of Trim of Marshwood; Regina, another descendant of Spotlight of Marshwood, and out of Rosina by Trim of Marshwood.

The majority of the present-day ponies are of Swedish or Dutch origin, but some are from Britain. The stallions, in particular, come from Sweden, and many are the sons of Firth Bracken. Bracken's first son to be imported into Finland – Ivrig has already produced 4 sons which have been accepted into the Stud Book: a record unsurpassed by any other horse or pony in the country.

At present, there are about 600 mares and 30 stallions in the Stud Book. About 200 foals are born each year (the largest number of any pony breed in the country). There are, however, over 2,000 Shetlands in Finland, because, although all ponies are registered, not all are accepted into the Stud Book. The inspections are carried out by officials of the Suommen Hippos, the national 'umbrella' society for all horse/pony breeds, and consists of a veterinary check (stallions must be X-rayed), and an in-hand show, which, if passed, must be followed by either a ridden or a driven test. Mares may be accepted into the Stud

Book at 4 years, and the grades they are awarded then are for life. Stallions may be given a one year licence to serve mares at 3, at which time they are given a I, II, or III rating (again for life) – but those gaining IIIs must be re-presented at 4 years, before being allowed to serve mares, or, if unsuitable, being rejected altogether. All stallions are checked every 5 years, or more often if there is any doubt about their progeny. All ponies are now blood-typed. Currently, no mare or stallion in another country's stud book is automatically accepted into the Finnish book without inspection. This, of course, would change if Finland joins the EC.

The Finnish Shetland Pony Society, formed in 1989, now has about 250 members; it is organised along the same lines as the British Stud Book Society.

In the early days in Finland, little attention was paid to bloodlines, but that is changing; advice is gratefully received from visiting British judges. Because there are few studs with 10 or more ponies, line breeding is not practised thus far; most breeders own just 1 or 2 mares and take them to the nearest stallion. As the breed expands, this, too, will begin to change.

Initially Shetlands were bought chiefly as children's pets, but now they are being used much more as real performance ponies. They are taking part in driving, in jumping and in gymkhana competitions, driven in trotting races, and Mrs Teri Kovacs, vice-president of the Pony Society, has been holding dressage camps during the last few summers. This was greeted with some amusement at first, but now people are queueing up to join! At the official shows, of which there are few, most of the classes are for in-hand ponies, but when Dougal Dick judged at their Society's 5th anniversary show in 1994 (in which 90 ponies were entered), a small ridden class was held.

The Pre World War II Shetland population in **Poland** was, except for a very few, virtually wiped out by the communists. Post war, the first, and so far the only stud breeding Shetlands exclusively was the Imno, owned by Jerzy Dmochowski and Alicja Zawadowicz. Following the purchase of some Dutch ponies, they imported Waulkmill McPhee in 1992, bred by Mrs Provan, the first stallion in Poland who had been fully licensed in Britain, as well as Roselily of Transy, 16986, Melland Milady 16971, Kensons Melisande 14921 and Kensons Flora 14920. Most of the stud's youngstock is now registered in the British Stud Book.

Exports of Shetlands to the **United States** in 1885 and 1887 have already been referred to, and, according to the Stud Book, a further 108 went in 1890-1899. The 'golden era' of exports to the USA was undoubtedly the first decade of this century, when just under 1,400 ponies crossed the Atlantic, including 54 destined for Canada. Of these, 638 went direct from Shetland. In Canada, they were widely used for the children who lived in the vast wheatlands to ride to school, where they could be hitched to the fence during the day, almost regardless of the temperature.

The trade diminished, but did not cease altogether during World War I, and in the years 1910-1919, 576 went to America and 265 to Canada. In addition, a number of unregistered ponies were said to have arrived in America. Throughout the 1920s and 30s, exports all but ceased again until after World War II, with the notable exception of a colt foal that was sent to one Shirley Temple, 20th Century Fox Studios, California, in 1937! The 1950s saw another increase, with 350 ponies crossing the Atlantic. A British newspaper cutting from 1957 recorded that a Mr Nathan Klein from Houston, Texas, was in Britain to buy Shetlands. 'We call them "Millionaires' Dogs" over in the States', he said. 'People with ranches like them running around the place for decoration and for their children to ride'. A really shocking practice was also mentioned – Shetland ponies by post. It was reported that so many children in the States were taking up riding that the larger mail-order stores were offering the ponies for around £100.

In those days, the ponies for export all went by sea, and it was not uncommon for the exporting stud to drive the horse box to the dockside, and load the animals; there was little fuss over documentation. There is, however, one delightful story from 1957 about the precautions that had to be taken by Scottish exporters at the time of a foot and mouth outbreak in Scotland. The ponies were to be disinfected on the dock immediately beside the ship! The exporting owner duly arrived with three ponies, and was met at the dockside by the Department of Agriculture vet. The vet., after examining the papers, produced the kind of 'Flit' spray gun commonly used for spraying flies (this was, of course before the widespread use of aerosols), and proceeded to pump away with this all round the ponies' legs and feet – after which the ponies were led on board the ship. It was reported that when they were unloaded on the other side, they immediately had their legs and feet washed down with a carbolic acid solution, and the rest of their bodies were doused with detergent.

There does seem to be some doubt about the quality of ponies that were sent to the USA and Canada after the War. One observer recorded that any pony under 10.2 hands with papers was marketable, even if it was lame, wrong in the mouth, or just a bad pony. Some over-height ponies without papers were also bought. Many dozens of ponies from the islands were inspected and went out as Inspected Stock registered in the British Stud Book, and thus avoided a heavy import duty the other side of the Atlantic. In those days, any mare could be put up for inspection; she did not have to have a foal by a registered stallion, and the inspection was done by a veterinary surgeon, who was not necessarily an expert on Shetland ponies.

Since the 1920s, however, the Americans have 'improved and refined' (to use their description) the Shetlands, by crossing them with Hackneys, Welsh and a variety of other breeds. (The previous paragraph suggests that some were in need of improving, but not in the manner that was practised in the States!) American Shetlands now resemble an extremely fine-legged, shallow, narrow Hackney pony. They stand up to 46 inches (117 cm), and have a high-stepping Hackney-type action – and certainly can no longer be classified as either a true Shetland or a Mountain and Moorland breed. Naturally enough, the American Shetland is not recognised by the British Stud Book Society.

L. Frank Bedell, in his book *The Shetland Pony*, published in 1959, claimed that 90% of Shetlands in America were of the American Shetland type. He wrote, 'I believe, however, that the American Shetland is an improvement over the original type. American breeders have for many years been selecting and breeding for refinement, action, and quality in the American Shetland. American Shetland breeders will agree, I believe, that the original imported pony of 1888 is a thing of the past.' Mr Bedell's s belief was not correct, though, because for the last 15 or so years, the trade in 'original' Shetlands to the United States has flourished again. It has to be said, however, that these are mostly miniature Shetlands, which, once they arrive in America, are often classified as 'Miniature Horses', to meet that particular market in the States. A more encouraging development is the export, in 1995, from Mr and Mrs John Staveley's Eastlands Stud in the Scottish borders, of two colt foals, a son and grandson of that great performance Shetland, Lakeland Lightning. The colts have been bought with the express aim of breeding performance ponies of standard size in the States. Could this be the start of a revival of the true Shetland?

While the countries already detailed account for the bulk of the huge numbers of Shetlands to be found worldwide, a much smaller number has been sent to a remarkable list of other countries. In 1971, for instance, a grey gelding was sent by Mrs Guy Knight to the King of Nepal. This was Lockinge Cointreau, by Littlestoke White Chartreuse out of Lockinge Cynthia. Cointreau had been carefully broken to saddle, to be ridden by the Royal grand-children. Since the turn of the century, ponies have gone to India, South Africa, Brazil, Spain, Italy, Russia, Morocco, Argentina, Turkey, the West Indies, Singapore, Kenya, Malta, Saudi Arabia, Czechoslovakia, Cyprus, the United Arab Emirates, Japan, the Falkland Islands and Egypt.

11

TOWARDS THE 21ST CENTURY

---◆---

The Stud Book Society, and indeed the breed itself, has never faced a greater challenge than that posed by the introduction of the Single Market in Europe, which officially came into being in 1992. From that date, all breeds of horses and ponies in the countries of the Common Market had to comply with 'Harmonisation of the Stud Book' regulations. Under these regulations, the stud book of the British Society, as the stud book of the country of origin, was designated the 'Mother Stud Book' of the Shetland breed, and the British Society as the 'Mother' society. All other stud books and societies within the European Community are now known as Daughter Stud Books and Societies. The breed society in each country is required to be recognised by its own government authority (in the case of Britain, by the Ministry of Agriculture) and, in due course, by the European Commission.

According to European law, the Mother Society sets the breed standards and the criteria for acceptance of ponies into stud books for all other Community societies. Ponies in Europe that meet these standards and criteria must now be accepted as eligible for entry into the British Stud Book, and our ponies into European stud books. At first sight, this sounds sensible, but once the implications of these regulations were fully understood they were greeted with dismay by virtually all native pony societies in Britain. As the practical consequences became apparent, a number of the European societies also expressed reservations.

It is invidious to detail the problems that have arisen with individual countries, so the following is a more generalised account (with one exception, applicable *only* to Shetlands) of the widespread concerns expressed by the British native pony world in general, rather than the Shetland Pony Stud Book Society in particular.

As has been seen in previous chapters, ponies from Britain have been exported to Europe for many years, and, until 1992, once the ponies left these shores, British breeders, and in due course, the British breed societies, had no jurisdiction over them. Independent breed societies were established in the European countries (and sometimes in different regions of a country), each with its own constitution and regulations for every aspect of the ponies' existence. In many countries, the breed societies are under the ultimate authority of a government department, and some receive government subsidies. Naturally enough, each country believes its methods and its ponies are the best, and would prefer to see other countries conform. Since harmonisation, difficulties have arisen because of the different approach of Britain and some of the European societies, firstly to the ponies themselves, and, secondly, to various aspects of their breeding and management.

The different approach stems from the basic fact that in Britain, the Mountain and Moorland breeds, including the Shetlands, are regarded as a valuable and unique part of our national heritage. The breed societies, in addition to performing the duties normally associated with any horse or pony breed society, are also dedicated to preserving the purity of the breeds and the unique native characteristics that have developed over thousands of years, and which are their principal assets. Not least, most also have the additional responsibility of overseeing the breeds in their native environments.

It is not realistic to expect other countries to have the same proprietorial approach to our ponies, and some, therefore, have felt (and still do feel) free to breed in certain features to suit their tastes and requirements. While there are many excellent native ponies in Europe, there are others that are so far from the true type as to be scarcely recognisable.

There is clear evidence of the introduction of outside blood, and although this has happened, sometimes legally, sometimes not, in many of the British breeds from time to time, it is has not been acceptable in other breeds for a considerable period of time, and it has never applied to Shetlands. As previously mentioned, there are spotted 'Shetlands' in parts of Germany – which are not accepted by the British Society, and that is clearly due to outside blood.

In several countries, and in several breeds, in addition to breeding the 'original' types, which conform more or less to British breed standards, breeders are producing a 'sports' type. The conformation of the latter is, in the case of the Shetlands, far more like the American Shetland – light of bone, shallow-bodied, and sometimes over height. They lack the very features of strength for size, hardiness, weight-carrying ability and durability that make true Shetlands such fine all-round performance animals. It is *just* possible, but extremely unlikely, that these ponies have been bred from pure bloodlines.

Colts at the Ulverscroft Stud play-fighting.

In spite of the above examples, the breeding and management of the ponies in Europe now is, in general, much more rigorously controlled than in the United Kingdom. As described in Chapter 10 many more inspections are undertaken, and while the advantages of this are obvious, the disadvantages are perhaps not so apparent.

There is a danger, if the inspections are undertaken by too small a panel of inspectors (as happens in some countries), that they may tend to pass the same type of pony. This, in time, will almost inevitably lead to a diminution of bloodlines, and to problems associated with in-breeding. If those inspectors are also judges, the danger is increased. In Britain, although the stallion inspectors are also judges, the judges' panels for most breeds are relatively large, as is the number of shows, so the effect is diluted. The problem is, arguably, exacerbated by the accepted practice in a number of European countries of the judges having access to show catalogues before judging their classes. That is not permitted in Britain, on the grounds that each exhibit should be judged 'as seen and on the day', without reference to its breeding, owner or exhibitor. Although this is far from being a perfect system, it does not restrict the choice of bloodlines.

A common concern for British breed societies is that comparatively few judges in Europe have seen native ponies in their natural environments, so they lack the real understanding of *why* native ponies should possess certain features. They must, therefore, have a tendency to judge from a different perspective. This is a problem with some British judges, who really have no excuse; how much more serious it must be in Europe, where judges do not have easy access to any of the Mountain and Moorland habitats of Britain.

In the long term, there is felt to be a danger that, for whatever reasons, and in spite of the breed standard, some of the European ponies will be changed, subtlely, to conform to various requirements. This is already happening. As trade barriers come down, more breeders from the continent will come to Britain looking for new bloodlines; they will look for ponies of the type being bred in their own country. There is little doubt that some breeders in Britain will breed for that market, and our ponies – which should be the true-to-type foundation stock, will also be modified. Similarly, if a breeder in Britain requires a bloodline that is easily found in Europe, they can import that pony, provided it is in the Daughter Stud Book, irrespective of what it looks like.

The feelings of concern are by no means only on the British side. Some European countries feel that there is too little control over the breeding of ponies here, and that we produce too many bad animals. Bad ponies are certainly produced here, but the British authorities are by no means convinced that strict inspection *along European lines* is necessarily the way to improve them. A specifically British problem is the apparent lack of understanding by the Brussels bureaucrats of the existence and importance of the semi-feral herds of native ponies. The implementation of all the new regulations has cost the breed societies a great deal of money, and has resulted in various fees to breeders being raised. In addition, the requirement for all registered ponies to have passports, although though not yet finalised, seems set to impose even further costs.

The consequences of all this are potentially very damaging. The semi-feral ponies (and the ponies in Shetland, although not truly semi-feral in the same way as, for instance, the New Forest ponies, may be regarded as such in this context) are nearly all sold at auction, virtually unhandled, and often bring low prices. The position is already arising where some of the breeders of these ponies consider that the costs, and the increasing amount of paper work involved, are becoming so great that it is no longer worth registering their ponies – which could lead to a decline in breeding. For native breeds, that is disastrous. Not only will it lead to a loss of important bloodlines, and loss of the true native ponies with their unique characteristics, but an important part of Britain's native heritage could disappear. Furthermore, a native breed that does not have ponies in its natural habitat is scarcely worthy of the name. The Shetland Pony Stud Book Society has set up an International Committee to deal with these problems, and in so doing has probably been more successful than any other native breed in forming useful and understanding relationships with the various Daughter Societies. Nonetheless, the overall feeling is that we in Britain could, unless great care is taken, lose control of our own breeds.

While concern is rightly expressed about the difficulties with Europe, what is the situation in Britain? Mention has already been made of the prejudice and ignorance that still remain among some judges in mixed native pony classes. The fine performances of so many of the ponies are, however, gradually overcoming these, and the popularity and appreciation of the breed has probably never been greater. Shetland in-hand and ridden classes are well supported, and the Performance Scheme has done much to improve the standards of riding, schooling and presentation.

In addition to the Performance and the Driving schemes, there are a number of thriving Shetland enthusiasts' groups throughout Britain – ιne South West, the Midlands, the Southern, the Northern Ireland, the Central Scotland and the Northern Scotland. These groups do a great deal of good work, not just on the social side, but in holding shows, demonstrations, seminars, lectures and fund-raising activities within their areas. There are, as in any breed, a few problems. Anyone who sees in-hand breed classes cannot help but notice that certain weaknesses of conformation and action remain. Hindlegs tend to be a breed weakness (a weakness, it must be said, shared with some other native breeds). They are sometimes too straight, with ill-defined hocks, and poor second thighs. Movement is also suspect, although this varies. As a very general rule, the further north in the country, the better the movement, and the ponies in the islands are almost universally good. Reference has already been made to one aspect of incorrect movement and the lack of use of all joints (see page 141) Another very noticeable fault, which naturally shows itself most clearly in in-hand classes, is a lack of tracking up – and 'tracking up well'(where, at the walk, the hind foot steps into or beyond the print left by the forefoot on the same side) is required in the breed standard. This is sometimes the fault of the handler who does not allow the pony to move freely. It is frequently because the pony is too fat, and *cannot* move freely. Excessive weight in breed (in hand) classes is the rule rather than the exception. (As a matter of interest, Maurice Cox complained about the same thing more than thirty years ago.) Far too many are so fat that they waddle round the ring, and the fat wobbles when touched. How their conformation can be judged is something of a mystery. There has to be something wrong when exhibitors of fit performance ponies are told they 'are not in show condition, and need more flesh' when they appear in in-hand classes. These fat ponies could certainly not be ridden with any degree of success (or comfort for either pony or rider).

There is is an interesting contrast between show-ring ponies and the ponies in the islands. In the autumn, those in the islands are also fat, after a summer spent storing food reserves for the winter. That fat, however, feels totally different to the wobbly fat of the show-ring pony; it is solid and hard, and is acquired while the pony walks miles and miles in the course of grazing every day.

Without question, the feature that is troubling many within the Shetland breed most is the number of small or miniature ponies – those of 34 inches (86 cm) and under – that are now being bred. As has been argued on many occasions, very small ponies have always been part of the breed, and some were registered in the first Stud Book, proving that they were found in the islands. The vital difference is that, until the last decade or so, they were very much in the minority – 5% at the most. Now, registration of miniatures in Britain is running at well over 50% of the total.

Does that matter? The answer, surely, must be in the affirmative. The key to the problem lies in a comment made by the owner of a miniature colt as it was presented for stallion inspection. 'I do hope it passes, otherwise, what can I do with it?' A gelding of standard size can be used for riding or driving – but the uses for the miniatures are strictly limited. As far back as 1913, Douglas wrote, 'It must be kept in mind that ponies of sizes of less than 34 inches (86 cm) are of little use for practical purposes ... Anything which tends to make the pony merely an oddity and a toy, and to take it out of the category of useful or usable horses, is fatal to the prospect of the breed and should be resisted by breeders and judges.'

Writing half a century later, Maurice Cox had this to say.

> It seems to me that there is too much sensational enthusiasm in the breeding of these very small ponies, for the only possible use for these little ones is that of ornamental attraction. They can be used in harness but are really too small – except for some very special and rare pursuits – and the market for them could very soon be satiated. Efforts to breed them smaller and even smaller are disturbing; this is an alarming trend which I understand has followers in countries other than our own. What I consider to be a very great danger is the breeding of thoroughly bad little ones; it must be put on record that there are quite a number of miserable little weeds, short of bone, with poor heads, badly made and with weak action. These should be of no value to anyone, but unfortu-

This picture, taken in October, shows how ponies in Shetland build up fat reserves during the summer to help them through the winter. The fat is very firm to the touch.

nately both for the breed and for themselves they are reproducing their own kind. On the other hand, there are some splendid examples of excellent conformation and action amongst these wee ones and many have an even better temperament than some of the larger, more ordinarily sized ponies.

What would Maurice Cox have thought of the present situation? Everything he described is still happening, only on an infinitely greater scale. There are indeed some lovely miniatures produced by careful breeders at well established studs. At the other end of the scale, there have been, and still are, some ponies which, tragically, however charming their temperaments, can only be described as physical monstrosities.

That this has happened can only be ascribed to 'market forces'. The demand came first from the United States, and then from Holland. In the United States, 'miniature horses' became fashionable in the show ring – and the smaller the better, no matter, it seems, what they look like. Chestnuts and broken colours are preferred. The changing colour preferences, irrespective of size, have been a feature of the breed for many, many years. While black has been regarded as the 'traditional' colour, there have been broken coloured ponies for centuries; the blacks and darker colours were, for obvious reasons, preferred for the coal mines, but not so very long ago the show-ring fashion was for chestnuts. Now, broken colours are in fashion. It is not perhaps of great significance on its own, but the demand is often for small ponies of broken colour, regardless of conformation, and that is a worry.

Ponies leave Britain as Shetlands, and arrive in the States as miniature horses, and some very high prices have been paid. By 1987, the prices had rocketed, and at Reading Sales, a number of fillies went for £1,000, and one went for over £5,000. In 1988, Mrs Adorian sold a yearling colt, Toyhorse Treacle, for a reported $20,000. The bandwagon was really rolling, and breeders, some with little or no experience of breeding Shetlands, let alone miniature Shetlands, jumped on. The result was, in many instances, catastrophic. Miniature animals of any kind are never easy to breed, and miniature Shetlands are no exception. It seems clear that efforts to reduce the sizes from the larger ponies were often made too quickly, and in some cases, possibly by some fairly dubious methods, which, because the gene for smallness was not involved, could have resulted in a return to a larger size in the next generation. Deformities appeared, chiefly in the legs (with consequent restriction of proper action).

Many of the breeders in Shetland have also been breeding the smaller ponies – not always the very tiny ones, but very few are producing the standard ones. The saving grace of the island-bred animals is that, small though many of them are, they nearly all have good limbs and good action. This is almost certainly due to the fact that not only are they kept under natural conditions where they have to travel miles every day in the course of grazing, but they are descended from generations of ponies which have lived under those conditions, and could not have survived if their movement had been restricted by poor limbs.

It cannot be good for any breed of equines for over 50% to be of such

Shetlands are ideal leading rein ponies. Mrs Rosemarie Webb's Riccalton Thunder, ridden by Rachel Nettle, and led by Lindsay Weightman.

One of Mrs Myrna Flaws' Grutness foals showing that island-bred ponies are natural jumpers.

a size and conformation that they cannot be ridden or driven in any serious context.

This explosion of miniatures would not be of such concern if it had not been accompanied, during the last few years, by a decline in the breeding and the quality of the traditional standard sized ponies, especially the blacks. These ponies have been the backbone of the breed for centuries, but it is at present becoming increasingly difficult to find good ones.

The Shetland breed has, over the centuries, survived a series of changes, good and bad. At times its very survival has been in jeopardy – but it has always bounced back. There is so much that is good in the breed at the end of the 20th century; it is to be hoped that those things that are bad will be eliminated before permanent harm is done.

12

SHETLANDS ARE FUN

It was no surprise to Shetland enthusiasts that the cartoonist Thelwell used the breed for his wonderful cartoons. Shetlands absolutely *ooze* character, with their unique mixture of humour and wickedness, and their delight in joining in everything that is going on. Over the years, they have provided such pleasure and fun for so many people, it seems only right to give a little taste of this.

The pony world has become so highly competitive these days that there seems to be little time left for relaxation at shows. In the 60s, however, costume classes, in which adults as well as children played an enthusiastic role, were quite a feature. In *A Century of Shetlands* Mrs Angela Gosling described how, having unexpectedly won the Costume Class at the Ponies of Britain show in 1962 as a group of crofters, the same group of friends decided to enter as 'The Parade Ring at Ascot' the following year. A mock parade ring was erected, a numbers board put up, and the members of the group dressed up as well known racing personalities of the time. Dougal Dick was the Aga Khan, Annabel Gosling was Madame Volterra (a well known owner), Robert Gosling was the famous racing tipster Ras Prince Monolulu, and the race-goers included Maurice and Betty Cox, and breed society secretary, Tom Myles and his family – everyone perfectly turned out, with the men in toppers, and the women in high heels and tight skirts. The jockeys were Robin Gosling (all 6 feet of him), 6-year-old Clare Myles and Barbara Wilson (halfway between). The race card of runners contained some imaginative and witty entries, such a 'Indigestion (by Fruit out of Season), Miss Representation (by Quotation out of Context), Illegitimate (by Mistake out of Wedlock), Slip Back (by Learner out of Gear) and We've Run (by Now out of Ideas)'. The ponies, of course, were there, and when the mounting bell rang 'The Aga Khan' said to his 'jockey' Robin Gosling, 'You can get on that mare, she'll be alright' – so the 6 foot jockey put his long legs on either side of False Teeth (by Time out of Place) and was led round the ring. 'The Aga Khan' watching this with interest, turned to Mrs Gosling and said, 'Shetlands *are* fantastic; that pony's never had anyone on her back before.'

The following year, the group decided to present 'Bringing the Bluestones from Preseli to Stonehenge' – a really major undertaking. The ponies were required to drag the stones. These were made of expanded polystyrene, and, to quote Angela Gosling, 'someone thought of Stone Age graffiti, and we painted slogans like BAN THE WHEEL and OG FOR CHIEF DRUID. We made harness from canvas webbing, slaves' tunics from hessian and curtains, Druidical robes from old sheets, and a classy harp in three ply, painted gold. The virgins were, of course, also in white, with oak leaf garlands round their heads, and the slave driver had a rudimentary hunting crop.

'Here again, we were asking a lot of the ponies. The huge stones made an ominous rustling noise on the grass, and were apt to take off if the wind blew in the wrong direction. However, two slaves per stone, one for the pony and one at the back, kept the stones on the ground and the ponies quickly stopped looking round in startled surprise, and treated the whole thing as just the humans being mad as usual.

'While waiting to go into the ring, one of the slaves felt an urgent desire to take the weight off his feet. When we realised what was in his mind, we let out a despairing cry of "Don't", but he had reached the point of no return, and one stone went in too mis-shapen to be raised to its dignified height.

Ponies of Britain Summer Show 1963. Shetland owners/breeders winning the Fancy Dress class with 'The Parade Ring at Ascot'.

'This time, of course, boots and high heels had been laid aside, and everyone went barefoot. The cries of the virgins mingled with the picturesque language of the slaves as the ponies trod on their toes yet again.'

Mrs Gosling paid tribute to the ponies: 'the glory really went to the ponies. It must be remembered that they were all top-class show ponies, all in the peak of show condition, none of them were, or ever have been, childrens' pets. No rehearsals took place till the evening of the day before, when the show classes were over. Then, in the gathering dusk we took them behind the pony lines and gave them an idea of what we wanted from them. They were unmoved by it all. They were unmoved by the long wait to go into the ring and by anything untoward that might happen. With ears forward and an eye on everything that was going on, I really think they enjoyed it as much as we did.'

Individual ponies, of course, are great personalities. Take, for example, the stallion, Lakeland Lightning, owned (if that's the correct word) by the Staveley family at their Eastlands Stud. Lightning was a superb driving pony, competing in private driving, scurry classes and in trials, driven by John Staveley, with wife Dianna as navigator.

Lightning had his likes and dislikes among the whips that he met in competition, and his *bête noire* was a very well known lady competitor. This lady was deaf, and shouted, which he didn't like, but she was also not above a bit of gamesmanship in the ring, and used to 'buzz' Lightning, by driving to within a couple of feet of him. At one show, the Staveleys had entered a team, and just as they were due in the ring, one of the ponies went lame. Within the space of a very few minutes, the four had become a unicorn, with Lightning as leader; the only problem was that John had never driven a unicorn. They had trouble entering the ring, and managed to get the wheels stuck firmly round and uproot a sapling that the Queen had planted as part of her Silver Jubilee celebrations. A distinctly unceremonious 're-plant' was accomplished, and they entered the ring. As they did so, Lightning realised that, being leader in a unicorn, he was on his own out in front, and no-one could get at him.

He immediately spotted his *bête noire* with her pony and trap heading towards him like, as Dianna Staveley described, 'a tanker steaming down the Channel'. This time, Lightning, not being under any kind of control, was ready. As they went past, he leaned over and bit the rival pony very hard on the bottom, causing it to shoot off like a bullet, straight past the judge, who had to take avoiding action, and finally dumped his driver on the ground. Lightning, highly satisfied, won the class.

Lightning also had his dislikes among his team mates. He was al-

The Staveley family's team of Shetlands, with Lakeland Lightning as off-side leader and Silver Jubilee as near side.

ways a leader, as he would face anything, and he did not approve of a new chestnut stallion that was leading with him. This uncouth newcomer was a bit lively, and bucked and kicked. So Lightning bided his time, until they were supposed to be going past a water hazard. Instead of going past it properly, Lightning lunged with his shoulder, and quite deliberately tipped his fellow-leader over the wall and into the water.

Needless to say, Lightning was very much a part of the family, and became extremely possessive. When the Staveleys' daughter, Anna, took a bad fall out hunting, Lightning would not let anyone go near her; she was his rider, and no-one was allowed to touch her. Fortunately, she was not badly hurt, and eventually re-mounted and continued. In a similar vein, when the Staveleys' son, Philip, was very young, he had a birthday party; as boys will be boys, a scuffle broke out. Lightning, always present, waded straight in, and dragged all the contestants away, except Philip and his opponent, by grabbing hold of their jackets.

Lightning is now a remarkable 29 years old, and still full of fire and spirit. He has just 'taken on' a field of point-to-pointers. He noticed that someone had left the catch of a gate undone, and that he could get into the field and kill these silly Thoroughbreds. He went, at full gallop, and chased them round until he just couldn't move another inch. The Thoroughbreds were completely upset, and were fighting like stallions, up on their hind legs, and as they went up, Lightning shot underneath them. The old boy had a wonderful time, but, as his owner said, 'He *was* tired after that!'

Shetlands have, of course, no conception of size; they take on anything. Mrs Pat Renwick has, at her Ulverscroft Stud, a little black island-bred stallion, called Handfu', who is all of 28½ inches (72 cm)

The Ulverscroft Stud's 'boss' stallion, the 28½ inch Handfu' of Berry – on his very best behaviour!

Mrs Renwick runs her stallions together out of season, and, as they tend to be up to height, or nearly so, she was hesitant about putting the little chap in with them. However, she decided to try, and kept an eye on them for a time, just in case. In went Handfu', and up pranced the big boss stallion, all fire and aggression and striking front feet. Little Handfu' looked up at him, from under a bush of forelock, and appeared to say, 'Well, of course, if that's how you feel, you're the boss. I'll keep out of your way.' And he wandered quietly off – until, that is, he came level with the boss stallion's hind legs. Then, in a flash, he darted in, clamped his jaws round the big stallion's leg, gave a quick heave – and the big fellow found himself in an undignified heap on the ground. Handfu' is now the No. 1, and he asserts his authority in no uncertain terms when carrots are spread out from the back of a tractor during the winter. He is the first – and if anyone else approaches, he chases them away. He works his way down the line of carrots – nearly always standing with his back to the rest of the herd, who creep up very cautiously, hoping to grab a quick carrot without being seen – but ready to take off again the moment Handfu' looks as if he might turn on them.

Shetlands are certainly no respecters of gates, as Mrs Marie Brooker observed, when, looking out from an upstairs window, she saw the gate between two fields suddenly rising up in the air. Knowing that the gate separated two fields in each of which was a stallion, she raced down to, as she thought, prevent a fight. There, lying on the ground, was the heavy iron gate. One stallion had put his head through a hole in the netting, heaved the gate off its hinges, tossed it aside, and joined the other stallion. Contrary to expectations, after some preliminary sparring, the two settled down to become the best of friends.

If there is anything that a Shetland pony dislikes, it is being left out of whatever is going on. Some years ago, in the temporary stabling that was provided at many of the major shows, the manger was bolted to the wall – far too high for Shetlands to reach. Their owners unbolted them and put them on the floor. One well known pony, Gay Gordon of Netherley, always 'cleaned up' his feed quickly, then tipped the manger over and stood on it in the front of the stable so that he could see out.

Gay Gordon's behaviour was not always exemplary, and he was inclined to sink his teeth into people when he was really corned up and fit. At some of the shows in the north-east of Scotland, where the ponies had to be tied to rails in rudimentary pens, Gay Gordon was always barricaded in with partitions from the trailer to discourage visitors. At one show, it was realised that, instead of creating his customary furore, he was standing stock still. Investigation revealed that a tod-

Helen Thomson (left) with daughter Rhonas and Doodle at Olympia.

dler had managed to creep into the pen and was sitting in front of him, stroking a fore-leg. This, it was concluded, showed that although he regarded adults as fair game, there was no real vice in him.

The Grand National mascot, Doodle (Robin's Brae Winsome), whose personality made her such a favourite with Olympia crowds, is a mare of many parts. In addition to appearing with the racing ponies, and taking part in the fancy dress class and the finale, she was invited to make an appearance, accompanied by owner Helen Thomson of Broothom Ponies, and 13-year-old Fiona McDonald, on the maiden voyage of the *St Sunnivar*, the roll-on-roll-off ferry that plies between Aberdeen and Lerwick. This she did with her customary aplomb. She was taken up from the vehicle deck in the lift to the bar, into which she made a suitably impressive entrance, neighing her greeting to the assembled crowd, who clapped enthusiastically. She was then ridden round the lounge by Fiona McDonald, and after about half an hour's general jollity, Doodle returned to her stabling in the lorry – known to the Shetland Pony Performance Group as 'The Shetland Flier'.

At home in Shetland, Doodle, at the age of 21, acted as 'Auntie' to two orphan foals – at the same time. A mare had died, and the foal – a

Abigail Hampton and Donnachaidh Pinocchio.

skewbald like Doodle – came into Helen Thomson's yard. Immediately Doodle, who had produced two foals herself in her younger days, started 'talking' to it, so the pair were turned out together. The foal followed Doodle all over the place, and she accepted it very happily. By unfortunate chance, another mare died; its foal was turned out in the field with an old mare, who, it was hoped, would adopt it. The old mare kicked out at it and drove it off. Doodle was in the same field with her orphan foal, and, when she heard the commotion, her head went up, and she went straight across to the old mare, gave her a couple of hefty kicks, and trotted off with both foals. She looked after them for the rest of the summer, bringing them up properly, and chastising them when they misbehaved.

That Shetlands can be mischievous is well known, but that they can take the greatest care of very small children is one of their most endearing characteristics. The Hampton family's stallion Donnachaidh Pinnochio was a prime example. The Hampton's daughter, Abigail, was promised that she could break Pinnochio to saddle when she was seven. Very early on the morning of her seventh birthday, Abigail appeared in her mother's bedroom, complete with hard hat, saddle and bridle, and announced, 'I'm seven, and I'm going to break in Pinnochio'

– and off she ran, down the road to the pony's field. Her anxious mother leapt out of bed, dragged on some clothes, and rushed to the gate – to be confronted with a triumphant Abigail, happily riding Pinnochio. 'I've broken him in,' she said, ' I just put the bridle and saddle on and rode him.'

13
OWNING A SHETLAND

◆

This chapter is not intended to be a detailed account of the management of Shetlands. There are a number of full length books giving advice on how to look after ponies, and the Shetland Pony Stud Book Society, Pedigree House, 6 King's Place, Perth, PH2 8AD, has produced an excellent booklet entitled *The Shetland Pony – Care and Management* that is far more comprehensive than anything it is possible to include here. Nevertheless, a few observations on topics that are particularly relevant to the breed may be a help to the prospective owner, particularly one who has not owned a Shetland before.

Shetlands, in common with the other native breeds, are generally easier and more economical to keep than other ponies and horses. As has been shown in earlier chapters, Shetlands have survived in the demanding conditions of the islands by adapting to their environment in every possible way – and those adaptations, such as the ability to keep warm, to live and actually to thrive on poor, rough grazing, to find shelter where little exists – is their natural way of life. Although it may seem hard, ponies bred away from or removed from those surroundings still thrive best when kept under conditions that approximate as nearly as possible to those that are natural to them. Thus a happy, healthy Sheland is one that has plenty of space in which to graze, is not kept stabled and rugged up, and is not fed on the protein-rich diet given to other, less hardy breeds.

Clearly, not all prospective owners can offer their pony unlimited acreage in which to graze – so what are the minimum requirements? While the pony will be happiest on rough hill grazing, a field is adequate, and ideally it should be large enough for the pony to be able to graze freely over a good area and thus help keep it exercised and fit. The minimum space required per pony is usually said to be half an acre – but it must be remembered that an animal cannot be kept on the same half acre year in, year out, as the pasture will become horse sick. Thus a larger area is required, or alternative grazing must be found for the pony while the original land is rested. Wherever the

Lakeland Lightning and Anna Staveley 'walking' a foxhound puppy.

pony is kept, a constant supply of fresh, clean water is mandatory.

Provided the field has some form of natural shelter, such as trees, hedges or walls, where the pony can obtain some protection from bad weather and from the flies in summer, it is not essential to have an artificial shelter, although an open-fronted field shelter can be a useful place in which to feed hay during the winter. Access to a stable (not necessarily in the field) is advisable, in case of illness or other emergency.

The type of pasture is important. No native pony should be put into a field full of lush grass. The digestive system of the native breeds is adapted to deal with the coarse, rough herbage found on the mountains and moorlands; and while this should not be taken to mean that a field full of weeds is adequate, an excess of lush grass or highly concentrated food of any type can and does lead to laminitis (founder). It is often said of the ponies that they live 'on fresh air' – and in addition to the risk of laminitis, overfeeding leads to excessive fatness all too easily. This is bad for ponies at any age; in youngstock it puts a serious strain on the limbs; in mares it can lead to difficulties in getting in foal, or, if in foal, to problems in the actual foaling; in all ponies it restricts free movement.

If the field is small, special care must be taken to see that the pasture is kept sweet and clean. Droppings should be removed regularly, and preferably daily. The pasture should be properly managed, and if the area is large enough, sectioned off, for example, with electric fencing, thus allowing the ponies to graze fresh areas in rotation.

The choice of a suitable pony is obviously of the greatest importance. Whether the pony is to be used for riding or driving, for breeding, or for showing in-hand, the first-time buyer would be well advised to visit as many studs as possible, to attend shows, especially the breed shows, and ask for advice. Shetland owners are, in general, very willing to help a prospective owner who is not familiar with the breed. It is vitally important not to rush into buying the first pony that becomes available. If the pony is to be the first pony for a small child, it is often considered better to buy an older animal that has been well broken in and is used to young children. Indeed there are ponies in the breed that have been passed on from family to family, teaching several generations of children to ride. Some people like the idea of buying a young pony so that 'child and pony can learn together', but unless the home is a very knowledgeable one, this can lead to all kinds of problems and disappointments. Breaking in and bringing on a young pony is not for the inexperienced.

As well as considering the vitally important matter of the temperament of the pony, you should also bear in mind the conformation: consult the breed standard on page 151. Whatever pony is finally chosen, it should be treated in exactly the same way as a full size hunter or other horse would be. People often make the mistake of thinking that because a Shetland is small, it is not really a horse, and need not be treated as one. It is – and, like any other horse, it must be correctly schooled and disciplined. As a breed, Shetlands have wonderful temperaments; they are easy to handle and very willing to please, but, like all natives, they are very bright, and if they think they can get away with disobedience, they will often do so – just like a spoilt child! In times past, Shetlands were sometimes regarded as stubborn, bad-tempered little ponies. Fortunately, these days the sight of a small child trying to manage a disobedient, strong-willed Shetland is seen less and less frequently. It is quite unnecessary, and is almost invariably the result of ignorant handling in the early stages of the pony's education. A correctly diciplined pony is a happy pony, which genuinely enjoys doing what is asked of it.

Schooling a pony can be one of the most interesting, enjoyable and rewarding aspects of ownership. It should be remembered, however, that native ponies become bored much more quickly than other breeds with prolonged repetitive work. Several short schooling sessions are much more productive than one long one, and if some of the schooling can be incorporated into a hack out, so much the better.

Having bought the pony, the question of exactly how to feed it arises. As already explained, great care needs to be taken not to overfeed, and the quantity and the type of food is going to vary according to the age of the pony, its size, the amount of work it is doing and the grazing available. Most ponies require some supplementary feeding of hay during the winter, while youngstock and in-foal mares in the final 3 to 4 months of pregnancy need additional, but small, hard feed. There are, these days, plenty of proprietary brands of feed from which a choice may be made depending on the differing requirements.

Many owners wish to show their ponies either in-hand or in performance classes, and the regime of living out can present some problems. A pony that lives out naturally requires more grooming and preparation for a show than a stabled animal. It is, however, perfectly possible to show a Shetland that lives out during the summer months, and many owners do so. A common practice is to stable the pony the night before a show, to allow a through grooming and general tidying up. The real problem faced by Shetlands is that their winter coats are often not fully shed until May, and they begin to grow again as early as mid-September. Judges do not seem to take this perfectly natural occurrence into account, so a way round it must be found. Obviously, stabling and rugging (and the use of infra-red lamps) can do a great deal, but the disadvantages of an unnatural regime have been detailed; although it has to be said that many, many owners follow this path. A useful compromise is the use, at the appropriate times, of a New Zealand rug. Rugs of this type to fit Shetlands used to be unobtainable; the fact that this is no longer the case is a sign of changing times.

The comparatively recent and increasing programme of winter indoor shows poses more difficulties to all the native breeds. Under the Shetland Breed Society rules, the ponies may only be clipped for reasons of welfare, and this surely applies to ponies that are hunted, are driven, or are regularly appearing in ridden and other performance classes during the winter. It should *not* apply to ponies that are shown in in-hand classes during the winter, as that can scarcely be described as 'work'. Again, it is possible to compete with a pony that lives out, making full use of a New Zealand rug. It does, however, raise the question of when the pony is going to have a holiday. For reasons of welfare alone, no pony should be asked to compete throughout the year without a proper break during which it is turned out and rested. If welfare considerations are not sufficient, it is plain commonsense that an animal (particularly a bright native pony) trudging round the shows week after week is, sooner or later, going become 'ring sick' and bored, with a consequent falling off in performance – and this is is noticed by the perceptive judge.

Shetlands are very healthy animals, but, as with any other equine, they should be wormed regularly, and, as already indicated, great care should be taken to avoid laminitis. The skin condition known as sweet itch affects a small percentage of ponies, and is an allergic reaction to the bite of certain species of midge. A great deal of research is in progress into the nature of the allergic reaction: as to whether the condition tends to run in families, and, above all, of course, to finding either a cure or some medication that will alleviate the symptoms. The condition manifests itself as a localised dermatitis, which usually affects the areas around the mane and poll, and the root of the tail, but can also, in severe cases, affect the shoulders and the hindquarters. The disease, of course, occurs during the summer months when the midges are active, and the first indication is usually that the pony rubs its mane and/or tail on any available post or solid object. Inspection will show inflammation, and the presence of pustules that will eventually ooze. The irritation is so intense that the animal will rub and rub until the hair is lost. At present there are various treatments, none of which are wholly satisfactory, and the only way to prevent sweet itch is to prevent the midges from biting the pony. This can be done by standing the animal in a stable in the early morning, and from late afternoon, when the midges are at their most active. In the present state of knowledge, the usual advice is not to breed from an animal that has this condition.

Another condition to which ponies and horses are liable is hyperlipaemia, and it does seem to affect Shetlands more than other breeds. It is a comparatively new condition, first observed in Holland as recently as 1969, but now occurs in many other countries worldwide. In hyperlipaemia, abnormally high amounts of fats known as lipids are found in the blood. The true cause of the condition is not yet known, but it is thought that it can be brought on by stress, perhaps by excessive weight, by disease of the digestive tract, or even by lack of correct feeding in pregnant or suckling mares. Unfortunately, there is a relatively high mortality rate, and early diagnosis is not easy as the symptoms are rather vague, and similar to some other conditions. Loss of appetite, lethargy and a reluctance to move can be followed rapidly by weakness, diarrhoea, depression, and, within a period of 10 to 21 days, death occurs in about three out of five cases. Once the condition is suspected, a simple blood test can prove its presence or absence.

BIBLIOGRAPHY

J. Brand, *A Brief Description of Orkney, Zetland, Pightland Firth and Caithness* (1701)

T. Gifford, *Historical Description of Zetland* (1733)

D. Edmonton, *A View of the Ancient and Present State of the Zetland Isles* (1809)

Statistical Account of Shetland (1841)

R. Cowie, *Shetland and its Inhabitants*

Shetland Advertiser (various issues)

Shetland Times (various issues)

Hardy, *The Land of the Simmer Dim* (W.A. Hammond, 1913)

James R. Nicolson, *Shetland Folk Lore* (Robert Hale, 1981)

Shetland Pony Stud Books (various)

Shetland Pony Stud Book Society Magazines (various)

C. & A. Douglas, *The Shetland Pony* (1913)

Maurice C. Cox, *The Shetland Pony* (A. & C. Black,1965 ; 2nd edition 1976)

John Bright, *Pit Ponies* (Batsford, 1986)

Mrs Angela Gosling (ed), *A Century of Shetlands, 1890-1990* (Shetland Pony Stud-Book Society: for centenary year 1990)

INDEX